Curious about George

RACE
RHETORIC
& MEDIA

Davis W. Houck, General Editor

Curious about George

Curious George, Cultural Icons, Colonialism, and US Exceptionalism

Rae Lynn Schwartz-DuPre

University Press of Mississippi / Jackson

The University Press of Mississippi is the scholarly publishing agency of
the Mississippi Institutions of Higher Learning: Alcorn State University,
Delta State University, Jackson State University, Mississippi State University,
Mississippi University for Women, Mississippi Valley State University,
University of Mississippi, and University of Southern Mississippi.

www.upress.state.ms.us

The University Press of Mississippi is a member
of the Association of University Presses.

First printing 2021
∞
Library of Congress Cataloging-in-Publication Data

Names: Schwartz-DuPre, Rae Lynn, author.
Title: Curious about George: Curious George, cultural icons, colonialism,
and US exceptionalism / Rae Lynn Schwartz-DuPre.
Other titles: Race, rhetoric, and media series.
Description: Jackson: University Press of Mississippi, 2021. | Series:
Race, rhetoric, and media series | Includes bibliographical references
and index.
Identifiers: LCCN 2021031930 (print) | LCCN 2021031931 (ebook) | ISBN
978-1-4968-3733-2 (hardback) | ISBN 978-1-4968-3734-9 (trade paperback) | ISBN
978-1-4968-3735-6 (epub) | ISBN 978-1-4968-3736-3 (epub) | ISBN 978-1-
4968-3737-0
(pdf) | ISBN 978-1-4968-3738-7 (pdf)
Subjects: LCSH: Rey, Margret—Criticism and interpretation. | Rey, H. A.
(Hans Augusto), 1898-1977—Criticism and interpretation. | Curious
George (Fictitious character) | Children's literature—20th
century—History and criticism.
Classification: LCC PS3535.E924 Z87 2021 (print) | LCC PS3535.E924
(ebook) | DDC 813/.52—dc23
LC record available at https://lccn.loc.gov/2021031930
LC ebook record available at https://lccn.loc.gov/2021031931

British Library Cataloging-in-Publication Data available

For Addyson Baye & Morgan Elizabeth

Contents

Acknowledgments

This project began with my own failure to read with diligence every story that made its way into my daughters' first library. I irresponsibly accepted a "classic," and read only four pages of *Curious George* before the overt racism insisted a public response. This project demanded my attention, but I could not have completed it without the support of many people and organizations who encouraged, funded, and championed me toward publication.

I owe a great deal to the University Press of Mississippi. Their desire to promote equity and anti-racism through interdisciplinary scholarship is central to the future of a progressive publishing culture. I am delighted to have my work included in their collection.

Ellen Ruffin, curator of the de Grummond Children's Literature Collection at the University of Southern Mississippi, was a tremendous and invaluable help during my visit to the McCain Library and Archives. The care and organization she and her team have given to the H. A. & Margret Rey Papers is extraordinary. I also appreciate the help of Richard Greene at the Holocaust Center for Humanity in Seattle, Washington. While I was there to see *The Journey that Saved Curious George*, I was thankful to learn a great deal about the important educational opportunities this Holocaust Center brings to the Northwest.

I am especially appreciative for the financial research and travel assistance provided by Western Washington University. The support of my colleagues and peers in the Department of Communication Studies and the Women, Gender, and Sexuality Studies Program has been essential to move this book toward publication. I owe a great deal to Dean Paqui Paredes Méndez, who, as a strong advocate for my joint appointment, allows me time and resources to learn from both of these communities. Both my 2017 TED talk and the WGSS lecture series became important outlets for me to share ideas, and forums in which I could learn from my insightful colleagues in the WWU community. Anna Eblen was my first chair, and continues to champion my work even when I doubt it myself. Her friendship and assistance with early drafts of this project were valuable. I am thankful for the numerous fine thinkers who helped me by elaborating ideas, writing letters of recommendation, reviewing my writing, and stimulating my curiosity: Chloe Fisher, Kathryn Anderson, Michael Karlberg, Hemani Hughes, Sylvia Tag, Vicki Hsueh, Mary Erickson, Danica Kilander, Joseph L. Flores, the faculty and staff of the WWU Office of Research and Sponsored Programs, and the WWU Idea Institute.

My brilliant colleagues and friends from the University of Iowa were instrumental in the completion of this project. I will always be grateful for the early guidance I received from David Hingstman, Bruce E. Gronbeck, and Barbara Biesecker. Karen Pitcher Christiansen was the first to think through the absurd adventures of George and help construct an early essay draft. The next gift came from Kent Ono, who, in his capacity as a journal editor, insisted that my article was unfit for publication because only a book could do Curious George justice. While we never overlapped at Iowa, his scholarship has significantly impacted my understanding of colonialism, and I was honored to learn that he was behind the astute recommendations made by my blind reviewer. I have also followed the scholarship of Radha Hedge; I was lucky enough to get to know her at the Cross-Disciplinary International Conference at St. Louis University in Madrid, Spain in 2017. Since then, she has become an incredible inspiration and friend. For her guidance, I owe a great deal.

Several of the peers I met as a college debater are now brilliant scholars, and it is a privilege to continue our collaborative relationships. Thank you to Idaho State University and my friend and colleague Sarah Partlow-Lefevre for inviting me to give the keynote about Curious George at the Intermountain Gender and Sexuality Conference in 2018, and to all the people who braved a snowstorm to attend. A scholar and debate coach, J. L. Schatz is an innovative thinker, and I was so appreciative of his invitation to contribute an early Curious George essay to his book, *Parenting through Pop Culture* (2019). Casey Kelly and I attended graduate school and coached debate together at Wake Forest University many years ago, and I was ecstatic to implement the thought-provoking ideas he offered as a reviewer of this book. My dear friend Michael Mario Albrecht has also carefully read countless drafts, and his insightful recommendations were instrumental in the elevation and completion of this project. I met Helen Morgan Parmett in 1996 as a member of the Lawrence Debate Union. Under the wisdom and community-oriented mentorship of the late Alfred "Tuna" Snider, we became friends and colleagues. It was Helen who first gave me faith in this project, and it was also with Helen that an early essay about George and science was published in *Textual Practice* (2018). Her ideas are brilliant, her willingness to push my writing beyond my expectations is selfless, and her friendship is a true gift.

In 2013 I attended the Rhetoric Society of America's session for mid-level career scholars. Under the guidance of Cheryl Geisler, I was put into a writing group with two of the most talented, thoughtful, and intelligent scholars I know: Stacey Sowards and Sue Hum. I could not have written this book without them. They have read countless, usually very rough drafts, time and time again. They have pushed my thinking (and my editing) to new heights. And with each revision, I knew Sue and Stacey were cheering me on. They have lovingly seen me through personal and professional challenges and accomplishments. I wish for all academics a community of support and friendship like ours.

Kylie has provided me the space to work during a pandemic by lovingly helping my children laugh and learn. My greatest gratitude is owed to my wonderful family. My grandmother passed away just before the publication of this book, but she, and my grandfather, have always been an enormous support. My Aunt Donna and Uncle Mike have not only helped me personally and professionally; they also guided me through the technicalities of the media industry. My Uncle Steven has done more for this project than I could ever have asked. He read and edited drafts, offered ingenious ideas that elevated the quality of this book, helped me navigate reviewer revisions, and championed me in every way possible each step of the way. My mother continues to remind me of the importance of my Jewish upbringing, and it was her insistence that pushed me through Holocaust readings more painful than I could have imagined. My critique of George's whimsical Holocaust adventure is inspired by her thoughtful reminders. No one has given me more support than Justin. Not only has he agreed to be my personal spelling assistant more days than not; he selflessly loves our family and unconditionally cares for my heart. The two infants I feared would be tainted by the racism in *Curious George* are now two young women with critical minds and compassionate hearts. I am so grateful to be the mother of Morgan Elizabeth and Addyson Baye. This book, and all my love, is for you.

The author and the publisher gratefully acknowledge permission for use of the following material. Chapter two is derived, in part, from a chapter published in *Parenting through Pop Culture: Essays on Navigating Media with Children*, edited by J. L. Schatz, © 2020 and reprinted by permission of McFarland & Company, Inc., Box 611, Jefferson NC 28640. www.mcfarlandbooks.com. Chapter three is derived, in part, from an article published with Helen Morgan Parmett in *Textual Practice* in 2018, available online: http://wwww.tandfonline .com/ [DOI: 10.1080/0950236X.2016.1267038]. It is reprinted by permission of Taylor & Francis.

Curious about George

Curious about George

I sat down with my two young daughters, eager to share with them the stories of my childhood. They were too little to read and barely old enough to speak. I was too sleep-deprived and overwhelmed with newborn twins to reason. Yet, as an educator and mother I knew they would benefit from the gifts of literature. So, each night we engaged in the ritual of story time. One evening, I opened the big yellow book with cursive burnt-red lettering: *Curious George* by H. A. Rey. Paying little attention to the cover image of two enormous blue-uniformed firefighters grabbing a little monkey by his upper arms, I began to read:

> This is George.
> He lived in Africa.
> He was a good little monkey
> and always very curious.
> One day George saw a man.
> He had on a large yellow straw hat.
> The man saw George too.
> "What a nice little monkey," he thought.
> "I would like to take him home with me." (H.A. Rey 1941b)

When the man put his hat on the ground beneath the jungle palm the monkey was swinging in, the monkey got curious, jumped down, and put the yellow hat on his own head. It was so big the monkey was covered, at which point

> The man picked him up quickly
> And popped him into a bag.
> George was caught. (1941b)

3

Once in a burlap bag, George was taken to the United States on a ship and sent to a big zoo—the Man assured him he would like it. "George was sad, but he was still a little curious" (1941b).

I had officially introduced my daughters to the cute, jubilant Curious George I had loved as a child. Little did I know that this occasion would be the first of countless encounters the three of us would have with George, and that numerous years of my career would be preoccupied with this cultural icon. Their eyes followed, staring at Curious George swinging on a green jungle vine, happily eating a banana. I continued to read aloud as the girls gazed at images of The Man in the Yellow Hat hiding behind a tree while attempting to lure George with his yellow hat. The story interrupted our ritual and piqued my attention. Awake with clarity, I read on as four newborn eyes glared at the cartoon monkey wrapped in a burlap bag, ostensibly choking, mouth open, with the sack's rope snug around his neck. *Curious George* was not as I had remembered. Yet, the didactic colonial narrative was one I had encountered countless times: it was the story of African capture.

While the girls slept, I re-read Curious George with mature eyes. I intuited George's sadness as The Man in the Yellow Hat rowed the little monkey in a dinghy to a big ship, filled him with alcohol and tobacco, and informed him that he was being taken to a "big Zoo in a big city." "You will like it there," the man promised. Hoping monkeys could swim, I found myself cheering silently as George tried to escape by jumping overboard. My heart raced when he was rescued/recaptured. Once in the United States, George ate and rested. But I remained disheartened as his curiosity led him to mistakenly phone the fire department, and as he was "shut" in "prison," escaped, stole balloons, and subsequently was found by The Man in the Yellow Hat (H. A. Rey 1941b). The story took me on a wild adventure until I finally grieved as George moved "happily" into the Zoo.

Unwilling to give the book away, I tucked it into the closet and went searching for scathing scholastic dismissals of the famous book series. Months of searching yielded fewer than a handful of reviews that critically considered George (Cummins 1997; Greenstone 2005; Zornado 2001). At the time, I was working on a collection of contemporary colonial rhetoric featuring scholars who theorize how and in what ways ideologies of oppression and injustice navigate the tentacles of globalization after the formal end of most European colonialism. The connection was painfully obvious.

Chapter One

Curious George, Cultural Icons, and Colonialism

Curious George is the literary child of Margret and H. A. Rey. Since the publication of the first Curious George children's book, the mischievous monkey has risen in popularity, rather than faded into oblivion. Since 1941, this cultural icon has expanded across multiple media platforms including film, educational tools, television, theatrical musicals, countless sourcebooks, story platforms, museum exhibits, stuffed animals, apparel, toys, theme park exhibits, live performances, book replications documenting the history of the authors, interactive gaming platforms, US stamps, and myriad knockoffs and parodies. Curious George is a cultural icon embedded in the fabric of US life.

The centerpiece of the Curious George enterprise is the book that bears his name. A first edition copy of the original title is worth about three thousand dollars and is considered one of the most valuable children's books (Zielinski n.d.). The book series boasts 130 titles, has sold more than seventy-five million copies, and has been translated into twenty-six different languages (Blair 2016; Rosen 2016). George is one of only a few children's book characters to have had a physical bookstore devoted entirely to his publications (Boston.com 2012).[1]

In this book, I situate the US circulation of Curious George as a cultural icon of negative US American exceptionalism—a set of discourses maintaining that the US has a divine mission to direct the actions of people and places globally.[2] US American exceptionalism provides a useful frame for critically re-reading children's cultural icons through various lenses of postcolonial theory. Postcolonialism is relevant for contemporary scholars because the challenges of today bear traces of the past, and more recent threads of postcolonial theory offer a more complex understanding of the structures of power and domination. The history of colonialism also explains how the victims of persecution and violence have been taught, and thus often repeat, the cycle of violence. Postcolonialism, that is, can explain how Curious George can be a colonial text submerged in the racism of slavery while at the same time being celebrated as a Holocaust survivor/hero. This project highlights the productive work postcolonial scholarship offers to make sense of cultural icons like Curious George.

2016 marked the seventy-fifth birthday of Curious George. The cultural icon provides an example par excellence of how colonization functions as an insidious and pervasive discursive tool in the present. In this project, I take up four of the mediated reincarnations of George—his rise to literacy success, his emergence in film, his placement in STEM education, and his Holocaust remembrance narratives—in order to demonstrate how contemporary postcolonial theory can offer a provocative re-reading of each discourse individually. Doing so situates Curious George within a colonial genre that shares a racist history with other popular narratives such as Joseph Conrad's (1899) *Heart of Darkness*, Charlotte Brontë's (1847) *Jane Eyre*, and Harriet Beecher Stowe's (1852) *Uncle Tom's Cabin*. Furthermore, the wealth of Curious George media collectively helps to explain the ways that postcolonial theory continues to provide a vital tool for unpacking the rhetorics of colonialism that circulate within US media.

I also bring attention to the ways in which children learn colonialism through children's books, toys, shows, and film. Young children learn from an early age who is acceptable, who is not, and what ideologies bind their country. Media plays an essential role in teaching contemporary forms of colonialism. Countless children's classics remain in print and continue to enjoy great popularity. "Children's literature is one of the most important areas in which to combat prejudice" (Nel 2017, 202). Children's literary critic Philip Nel (2017) demonstrates racism in many classic novels for young people including: *Tintin in the Congo* (Hergé 1931), *Little House in the Big Woods* (Wilder 1932), *Little House on the Prairie* (Wilder 1935), *The Long Winter* (Wilder 1940), *The Story of Babar* (de Brunhoff 1934), *The Adventures of Huckleberry Finn* (Twain 1884), *The Cat in the Hat* (Seuss 1957), *Charlie and the Chocolate Factory* (Dahl 1964), and *Curious George* (H. A. Rey 1941b). While each of these books is worthy of critical examination, some have garnered a great deal more scholarly attention than others. In March 2021, Dr. Seuss Enterprises made a decision to cease the publication and sale of six popular books, including Theodor Geisel's (a.k.a. Dr. Seuss) first publication, *And to Think that I Saw It on Mulberry Street* (1937), and issued a statement acknowledging the books' racist themes (Alter and Harris 2021). Though Curious George is an example of a book that has received limited attention from critics and great applause from parents, educators, and children, the withdrawal of the Dr. Seuss books, in addition to spurring a public debate over cancel culture, heightened the attention given to this racist narrative of a white man bringing home a monkey from Africa within Curious George books (Pratt 2021).This project helps to explain how George's circulation within the rhetorics of scientific education and Holocaust remembrance shields him from critique.

This monograph not only makes an intervention in postcolonial scholarship and cultural icons but also makes a case that Curious George is a colonial text. This introductory chapter explores three areas of inquiry that unite this book: Curious George, cultural iconicity, and contemporary postcolonial theories. My focus on the public persona of Curious George does not suggest that the curious monkey has a private life; rather, it highlights the conditions of possibility for US public consumption of the narratives of Curious George. I also am not invested in the private conversations that George's authors have had regarding their intentions for George and deliberately avoid attempts to read "the meaning" or "intent" of Curious George as a cultural icon. Instead, I attend to particular media texts in which this cultural icon has moved through both time and space, in an effort to discern the ways in which the US public is positioned to understand this characterized monkey.

Curious George circulates in books, television shows, films, and museum exhibits. As in Raka Shome's consideration of media materials of Princess Diana, I take up everyday popular culture and the "seemingly banal forces through which . . . media construction eddies and swirls in the public sphere" (Shome 2014, 38). These everyday Curious George materials circulate through both time and space in ways that affirm the colonial logics of US exceptionalism. Rather than attempt to glean the authors' intentions, I focus on how Curious George directs audiences. This introduction helps to explain how George emerged and has subsequently circulated for over seventy-five years as a beloved US cultural icon with very little critical attention.

The next section of this chapter explores the history and popularity of Curious George. Chapter 2 examines the roles and functions of cultural icons. I draw on Curious George as a primary referent within a larger theoretical investment in order to map the complexities of a cultural product and as a way to understand how postcolonial theory can be used to make sense of contemporary colonizing agendas. My aim is not to provide a comprehensive survey of iconicity; instead, it is to highlight current conversations that use this terminology and consider how these terms circulate in US conversations and conventions. In so doing, I differentiate culture icons as elevated icons with the ability to shapeshift, taking on attributes of the cipher, figure, and sign. This section considers the scholarship on iconicity and then explains the distinct, referential, and significant roles that cultural icons take. In many instances, children's icons are the first and most informative way that people learn about their cultural identities. This exploration of cultural icons provides the foundation for the central questions this project asks: what about the cultural iconicity of Curious George enables him to play an ever-growing and increasingly prominent role in US culture? In what ways is Curious George used to embody popular US discourses about the Other? How is Curious George protected from popular skepticism or academic critique?

The final section of this chapter engages areas of postcolonial theory. While postcolonial theory continues to thrive in Europe and Latin America, US scholarship seemed to have turned away from postcolonial scholarship. I outline some of the most pervasive arguments advanced by primarily US-based critics of postcolonial theory not only to mark the limitations and challenges that traditional threads of US postcolonial theory have overcome, but also to lay the foundation for a postcolonial resurgence. The history of colonialism infests US literature, media, science education, and memories in ways that no longer reflect a clear line between colonized and colonizer; rather, they insidiously assail the ideologies that members of the public come to understand as natural.

Curious George: History and Popularity

George the monkey first appeared in print in Paris in 1939, in an H. A. Rey (originally Hans Augusto Reyersbach) publication titled *Cecily G. and the Nine Monkeys* (Rey 1941a). While Margret Rey co-wrote *Cecily G. and the Nine Monkeys*, she thought it would not sell with a women's name on the title, so the Reys only listed H. A. Rey as the author. The Reys wrote the book, and other children's literature,[3] while H. A. and his wife Margret (Margarete Elisabethe Waldstein) took a four-year honeymoon in Paris (M. Rey and H. A. Rey, video interview, 1966, in H. A. Rey and Margret Rey n.d. [cited hereafter as Rey Papers], Box 261, Folder 4). The story features a sad giraffe, known as Cecily G. (her original name was Raffy), whose friends had been captured and sold to the zoo. She befriends nine traveling monkeys who had lost their home to woodcutters. Cecily G. helps the monkey cross a ravine by lending her neck as a bridge. George (referred to as Fifi in this book) is the first monkey to befriend the giraffe (Marcus 2001). During their adventures, the monkeys help Cecily G. put out a house fire by climbing her back and neck. As a result, the ten animals become good friends. H. A. Rey ended the story with a song. The sheet music version of the tune is on the last page of the book. Cecily G.

figures as the treble clef and the monkeys as individual notes. Interestingly, none of the monkeys have tails in this musical composition, since they would be undetectable below the music bars. This insight is memorable because almost sixty years later, the controversy over Curious George's tail became a topic of great public interest.

Cecily G. and the Nine Monkeys was first published by Chatto & Windus in the United Kingdom (H. A. Rey 1941a), and eventually in the United States in 1989 and again in 2007 (H. A. Rey 1989 and 2007). In 2018, Swann Auction Galleries sold H. A. Rey's 1939 color pencil, charcoal, and watercolor illustration for Cecily G. and the Nine Monkeys for $17,500—the highest price paid for any of H. A. Rey's illustrations (Swann Auction Galleries 2018). Grace Hogarth, who had left the London-based publisher Chatto & Windus to take a position with Houghton Mifflin in Boston, read the Reys' work and contacted them around 1939, offering the first right of refusal on their next publication (Marcus 2001; Silvey 2001). After fleeing Nazi-occupied Paris, the Reys traveled through Spain, Portugal, and Brazil, eventually arriving in New York City in the summer of 1940. They contacted Hogarth with the original version of Curious George. She offered the Reys a rare four-book deal with a thousand-dollar advance, and suggested that they change the central character's name from Fifi to Curious George (Marcus 2001). In the seventieth anniversary edition, publisher Anita Silvey explains, "by modern standards, Ms. Hogarth moved with lightning speed" (2001, 3). In August 1941, "Curious George was published with a print run of 7,500 copies and a sale price of $2.00" was set (Silvey 2001, 1). Since its initial 1941 publication, the original Curious George has never gone out of print (Warren 2019).

Curious George, the first book in which George is the central protagonist, introduces readers to the two central characters: George the monkey (without a tail) and his captor/caretaker/pathetic father/friend figure, The Man in the Yellow Hat. Six years after the original publication, the Reys released Curious George Takes a Job (H. A. Rey, 1947). Fans of the collection point out that this is the first of many times that the Reys make a cameo in their books; on page fifteen, Margret and her dog appear near H. A. and his friend walking down Fifth Avenue. Five years later, the third book, Curious George Rides a Bike (H. A. Rey 1952), tells a tale in which George is captured again, this time by an animal circus. In their fourth publication, Curious George Gets a Medal (H. A. Rey 1957), George takes his first rocket ship ride (he would take several more in later books). Notably, George's rocket ship launched just a week before the Soviets launched the Sputnik II satellite, "which carried the first animal, a small dog named Laika, into space" (Marcus 2001, v). Two years later, the United States launched Gordo, a squirrel monkey, into space aboard Jupiter AM-13. This fourth publication is significant because George continues to appear in space suits, a point I address in depth in chapter 3. The fifth book, *Curious George Flies a Kite* (H. A. Rey 1958), marks a decisive turning point where George evolves from a bold mischief maker to a sometimes frightened and even anxious figure (Greenstone 2005). *Curious George Learns the Alphabet* (H. A. Rey 1963) was published next and makes an explicit effort to link George with children's education. Boston Children's Hospital, guided by pediatric educators, commissioned the seventh and final book in the original series, *Curious George Goes to the Hospital* (M. Rey, H. A. Rey, and Boston Children's Hospital Medical Center 1966), in order to ease children's anxieties about hospitals (Marcus 2001).

The first seven books are called the "original" or "complete adventures of Curious George." The Reys never intended to write a series, but the large quantity of fan mail encouraged them to compose more Curious George tales (M. Rey and H. A. Rey, video interview, 1966, in Rey Papers, Box 261, Folder 4). Often, the few critics who consider Curious George confine their reading to these seven books, which are the only texts authored solely by Margret and H. A. Rey. Though publishers did not think that a children's book authored by a woman would sell, Margret wrote the text for all seven books (and many more), and H. A. was responsible for the illustrations prior to his death in 1977.

Margret authored publications after 1977 with various editors as co-authors. In 1991, she told National Public Radio that she had no idea what Curious George would become, only that the Reys loved monkeys and wished to write a book about them (Blair 2016). The series retained H. A. Rey as author because future illustrators, such as Alan J. Shalleck, intentionally emulated Mr. Rey's techniques. H. A. had drawn each image using a method of preseparated art. Preseparated art was a low-cost common method of illustration used in twentieth-century children's books before advancements in printing technologies (University of Minnesota Libraries n.d.). Each color used was made on a printing plate called color separations. Then the separations were overlaid to make one printing plate. The technique was difficult for illustrators, who have to draw in black and grey but think in color. Several of the images are on permanent exhibit at the Rey Papers Collection at the de Grummond Archives at the University of Southern Mississippi.

In each of the seven original books, the adventure story had the same style, same motion, and same liveliness. The storylines adhere to a single didactic narrative: The Man in the Yellow Hat has a commitment and leaves George alone, George has an adventure—to ride a bike, to fly a kite, to get a job, to go to the hospital, etcetera—and The Man in the Yellow Hat returns (never a point of contention). "George, curious about something, gets into trouble, angering authority figures. He then inadvertently or intentionally does something heroic that allows him to be redeemed and overshadows his resistance" (Cummins 1997, 80).

By 1950, Curious George was a best seller, appearing beside Caldecott winners *Make Way for Ducklings* and Dr. Seuss's *Cat in the Hat* (Marcus 2001; McCloskey 1944; Seuss 1957). A leading literary magazine, *The Horn Book*, interviewed Houghton Mifflin's Director of Children's Books, Walter Lorraine (who held that position from 1965–1995), and he explored what drives children's love for Curious George:

> The Curious George books have enjoyed a level of popularity akin to that of Hershey's chocolate and *National Geographic*. Generation after generation has passed them down. Kids love the books, though not so much because of the exceptional nature of the artwork or of the text. It has more to do with the concept: that a little monkey, or little child if you will, always gets in trouble, and that he never means to: he is just curious. And it isn't that curiosity is a bad thing either. George's misadventures arise outside of his control. Kids are the same way. They often don't understand what the heck they did that so irritated the adults around them. So George's story is very satisfying to them. (Marcus 2012)

By 1958, Curious George had sold over 10,000 copies (Silvey 2001), and the first stuffed Curious George was produced in 1971 by Commonwealth Toys (Jones 2001). (I was gifted one at birth in 1977.).

A host of international licenses for Curious George remain operative: book and toy stores, apparel and accessory companies, collectibles, promoters of domestic room décor and housewares, entertainment media, educational markets, and video contracting ("Curious George list of licenses," Rey Papers, Box 77, Folder 6; and "Curious George List of Contracts," Rey Papers, Box 87, Folder 9). These licenses enabled manufacturers to produce hundreds of thousands of Curious George products such as: lunchboxes, clothing, Viewmaster reels, stickers, puzzles, board games, coloring books, video games, school supplies, birthday party goods, dishware, nightlights, figurines, tea sets, Christmas ornaments, locked diaries, clocks, and climbing ladders that replicate the jungle tree from which The Man in the Yellow Hat lured George before his capture. In December 2016, the Curious George Zoo Animal Application had over a million downloads, earning a spot in Apple's App Hall of Fame (Raphel 2016). Branding scholar Daniel D. Hade remarks that owning a Curious George product is not about the material as much as it is "the opportunity to continue experiencing the feelings, ideas, and virtues that go along with Curious George . . . it is merely a container, a means of accessing Curious Georgeness" (2001, 161). Hade's point is significant because it underscores how "Curious Georgeness" functions as central to the ideologies inculcated in impressionable children. "Georgeness" especially influenced the minds of consumers when Curious George first appeared in film.

Although his popularity continued to soar in books, it exploded when Curious George made it to the big screen. In 1971, Sandler Burns Marmer Productions tried to make a film about Curious George but ultimately let the option go, writing Margret Rey: "the qualities that were so endearing in your books just did not seem to translate to film" (Allan Sandler to Margret Rey, in Rey Papers, Box 110, Folder 5). In the same year, Teaching Resources Film (a division of *The New York Times*) produced a series of elementary school filmstrips replicating the Curious George books. Vice president John A. Miller explained: "filmstrip version of classroom-tested, library-approved books that have proven their value for children who are *getting ready to read*, *learning how to read*, or *learning to read better*" (letter from John Miller to Reys, in Rey Papers, Box 93, Folder 3). Each filmstrip includes a teaching guide, "prepared by an experienced teacher."

In 1979, Margret Rey granted Milktrain Productions the option to produce 104 five-minute animated Curious George episodes for television audiences (Biederman 2007). The project had financial setbacks, and by 1979 Milktrain had only produced thirty-two of the episodes. By 1982, all 104 episodes had been created and sold to the Sony Corporation, which transferred the film negatives to videotape. In 1991, Margret Rey filed suit against Sony for copyright infringement and won (Biederman 2007). In 1982, Ruby-Spears Enterprises tried to make a deal with NBC to secure a Saturday morning slot on their network. In 1986, the private production firm of Duncan & Katz worked to get Curious George on CBS's Saturday cartoon lineup, but failed because the network claimed that "George does not appeal to kids over six years of age" (letter from Katherine Duncan to Mrs. H. A. Rey, 1986, in Rey Papers, Box 92, Folder 5, p. 1).

From 1988 to 1993, *New Adventures of Curious George* (ongoing series) featured new material from Margret Rey and several co-authors, with updated storylines. The series debuted in 1988 and followed a similar narrative style, but featured George engaged in more modern tasks, such as *Curious George Makes Pancakes* (M. Rey, H. A. Rey, and Weston 1998), *Curious George Goes to a Movie* (M. Rey and H. A. Rey 1998), *Curious George: A Winter's Nap* [aka hibernates] (H. A. Rey 2010), *Curious George Visits the Dentist* (H. A. Rey 2014), and *Curious George Discovers Recycling* (H. A. Rey 2017).

The Reys were also influential philanthropists who created various organizations using Curious George as their icon. They formed the Curious George Foundation in 1989 in order to fund programs for children. They endowed the Margret & H. A. Rey Institute for Nonlinear Dynamics in Medicine, "an interdisciplinary research laboratory at the Beth Israel Deaconess Medical Center" Margret and H. A. Rey Institute n.d.). Affiliated with Harvard Medical School and the Harvard-MIT Division of Health Sciences and Technology, this institute uses George as an icon for their various projects and findings. In addition, the Margret and H. A. Rey Center and Curious Cottage honors the Reys' spirit of curiosity and discovery by increasing understanding and participation in art, science, and nature through programs for youth, adults and families ("About Us" and "What's Happening" in Margret and H. A. Rey Center n.d.).

In 2005, Louise Borden refigured George for more mature audiences. *The Journey that Saved Curious George: The True Wartime Escape of Margret and H. A. Rey* chronicles Margret and H. A. Rey's escape from Nazi Germany (Borden and Drummond 2005). The book remains a recommended resource by the United States Holocaust Memorial Museum. This Holocaust narrative has two independent traveling exhibits. The first, more exclusive exhibit was hosted by the Jewish Museum of New York and by the Contemporary Jewish Museum in San Francisco. The Nebraska Jewish Historical Society created a second exhibit that traveled in a Holocaust memorialization circuit as an educational tool from 2006–2017.

Using a grant from the Curious George foundation and raising funds on Kickstarter in 2017, filmmaker Ema Ryan Yamazaki—who grew up reading the Curious George books in Japan—created a new documentary detailing the lives of Margret and H. A. Rey: *Monkey Business: The Curious Adventures of George's Creators*. The documentary, a winner of Best Documentary at the Fargo Film Festival (2018) and the Audience Award at the Nantucket Film Festival (2017), "utilizes original hand-drawn animations in addition to interviews and archival sources from the Rey estate" (Ainley 2016, para. 2).

By the time Universal Studios acquired the trademark for Curious George in the 1990s, the icon had over fifty licenses for products in high class, or "upstairs" retail markets ("Curious George Brand Plan," p. 2, in Rey Papers, Box 117, Folder 7). Since then, Universal has rolled out products to mid-tier and mass-market retailers all over the world. Though *Curious George* books played a featured role in Paramount Pictures' Academy Award–winning film *Forrest Gump*,[4] George had to wait until 2006 for his own blockbuster. In 2006, Universal Studios released *Curious George*, starring the popular Will Ferrell as The Man in the Yellow Hat. It grossed $69.8 million, making it the seventy-fifth bestselling children's movie of all time Box Office Mojo n.d.). The movie soundtrack topped *Billboard* charts.

On the heels of the film's success, the Public Broadcasting Service (PBS) spearheaded a new Curious George television series. Since 2006, it has been one of the most popular children's programs (PBS Kids 2012 and 2013) and has won two Emmys for outstanding Children's Animated Program (2008 and 2010). The program claims that George can teach young children the importance of science, technology, engineering, and math (STEM) (Concord Evaluation Group 2012). In its thirteenth season (2020), the educational philosophy of the program is as follows:

> Science, engineering, and mathematics are disciplines representing years of accumulated knowledge. The objective of the Curious George series is to help children appreciate these disciplines and the wealth of knowledge contained in them. Appreciation and understanding begins for young children with exploration, observation, discovery, and most importantly, curiosity. Curious about the world around them, children begin to observe properties, discover how things work, and, ultimately, develop scientific thought processes. (PBS Parents 2016)

Each episode offers a lesson that correlates to science, technology, engineering, or math (STEM). These lessons include: aeronautics, buoyancy, orienteering, animal habitats, magnetism, plants and seeds, levers, prosthetic parts, bone anatomy, solar energy, and insulating methods. The program also supports web-based, interactive educational tools that reinforce STEM-based lessons.

The publicized relationship between Curious George and STEM education prompted a 2007 partnership between the Minnesota Children's Museum and Universal Studios Consumer Products Group to create "Curious George: Let's Get Curious!"—a traveling educational exhibit that introduces young children to the world of the beloved monkey and leads families on an adventure filled with fun, interactive math, science and engineering-based adventures" (Minnesota Children's Museum 2015). The exhibit has been a huge success and has traveled to over fifty children's museums over the course of nearly a decade. A year after the museum project, Universal Studies hosted two "Curious George Goes to Town" play areas at their theme parks in Orlando and Hollywood,[5] and the Minnesota Children's Museum designed an interactive 2,500-square-foot traveling exhibit that was booked through 2020, but was put on hold as a result of COVID-19.

While the television series is still a very popular program (Steinberg 2014), made-for-television movie sequels including *Curious George 2: Follow That Monkey!* (Virgien 2009) and *Curious George 3: Back to the Jungle* (Weinstein 2015) were distributed by Universal Studios Home Entertainment, released directly to DVD, and they also ran as special features on PBS. The sequel, *Curious George 4: Royal Monkey* (Murphy 2019), will be followed by a 2022 computer-animated adaptation of Curious George as a prequel to *The Royal Monkey*. Alec Baldwin will star as The Narrator and The Man in the Yellow Hat (now called Ted). In 2016, the popular streaming platform Hulu "announced that it has the exclusive subscription streaming rights to Curious George for both past and future seasons of the show" (Spangler 2016), gaining a library of over 100 episodes and TV specials that have been the top children's animated, preschool series across all TV networks. George is accessible via the commercial-free environment of Hulu Kids in both English and Spanish (Hulu 2016). Since the Hulu premiere, Curious George has been its number one show for two- to four-year-old children (Raphel 2016).

In July 2020, Peacock, America's newest streaming network (owned and operated by NBC Universal, a subsidiary of Comcast), launched. Peacock's official trailer features a montage of Curious George animation with an omnipresent narrator letting viewers know that "he's [George] back now for new adventures and fun" (Peacock 2020). The presumption is that George is returning while in actuality George has maintained popularity. What makes NBC's new network so appealing is that Peacock has the rights to make new Curious George episodes. At three a.m. on July 15, 2020 the new Curious George episodes aired with a not-so-new educational agenda. "With a focus on education," Peacock declares "the series incorporates early science and math content and draws upon George's curiosity-driven adventures to target pre-school age viewers. George's entertaining and ultimately informative experiences have proven to parents and children worldwide that there is nothing wrong with wanting to learn about the world around you!" (Schwartz 2020).

As Curious George book marketing and animation thrived, the overall fame of the monkey skyrocketed. He has appeared as a forty-foot balloon at the Macy's Thanksgiving Day Parade in New York City; the Stamford, Connecticut Thanksgiving Parade, considered the second biggest parade of balloon characters (*Artazza* 2012); and the oldest Thanksgiving Day Parade in Philadelphia (Visit Philadelphia 2019). In 2011, George appeared in his ballooned space suit for the McDonald's Thanksgiving parade in Chicago (TeddyTurkey 2012). In 2014, a stuffed version of George made the press, pictured with an Olympic silver medal during a trip to Russia, as the US ski team's informal mascot (Knight 2014).

Curious George has also starred in Theaterworks Productions' *Curious George: The Golden Meatball* (Desmon 2014). The play features a simplistic script in which George mails himself in a parcel box from New York City to Italy to win a meatball-tasting contest for a friend. The musical is produced by an educational nonprofit organization owned by Universal Studios' subsidiary group, Universal Stage Productions. Geared toward school-age children K-3, the production comes with study guides for educators to administer. Activities include balancing a tray like a waiter, making a chef hat, learning about Italy, reading a Curious George book, and theatre etiquette (Theaterworks USA 2018). In 2014, the New York

City Department of Tourism introduced Curious George as their official NYC Family Ambassador. According to the Family Ambassadors program, "George's enduring popularity, multi-generational appeal and signature sense of adventure and exploration" make him a "model ambassador" (International Entertainment News 2014). In 2016, Universal Pictures and Image Entertainment signed a contract with Andrew Adamson—the director of the first two *Shrek* movies and the *Chronicles of Narnia* franchise—to write and create a new live-action film. Curious George's fame continues to grow, outliving even his creators (Stuff 2016).

As a cultural icon for over seventy-five years, George has shifted within, around, and between discourses ranging in theme and topic. As he changes, he also remains a curious monkey poached from his jungle home. The original books have sold more than seventy-five million copies (Jones 2001; Raphel 2016) and the series' books are continually updated, with more contemporary themes such as *Curious George Discovers Germs* (Rey 2015a), *Curious George and the Summer Games* (Rey 2020a), and *Curious George Votes* (Rey 2020b).

The seventieth-anniversary edition describes Curious George as "a bright standard-bearer for universal themes of children: their large-as-life need to touch and tangle with the world and to learn by doing—even if to do so means occasionally landing in the thickets of trouble" (Marcus 2001, iv). Yet, as he changes and takes on new roles, his archetype—his monkeyness (by this I am referring to his literal monkey body) and curiosity—remain faithful characteristics of his cultural iconicity. In 2016, when Curious George turned seventy-five, the NASDAQ tower broadcast birthday messages to celebrate the occasion (Raphel 2016). *The New Yorker* reported that 75 percent of the general population in the US recognizes him[6] (Raphel 2016), and National Public Radio declared George a "global icon" (Blair 2016). Houghton Mifflin Harcourt, Curious George's long-standing publisher and copyright holder, created a bookmobile party that began in New York with two thousand spectators coming to send them off for their eight-city tour ending in Los Angeles. The publisher donated over 75,000 books along the way (Brill 2016). Houghton Mifflin Harcourt also teamed up with the American Booksellers Association to launch a reading celebration titled "Get Curious about Reading." That same year (2016), American Airlines added a Curious George in-flight channel. New York bookstores, the New York Public Library (along with other libraries), and the United Way held Curious George–themed events (Mahan 2016; Rosen 2016). The MGM Grand in Las Vegas honored Curious George with a "playful" cocktail—the St. George, a drink made of green-chili vodka, jalapeños, serranoes, habaneros, and sweet and yellow peppers (*Las Vegas Weekly* Staff 2017).

The University Libraries at the University of Southern Mississippi, home to the Reys' literary estate, challenged George fans to walk seventy-five miles between September 17 and November 12 (Smith 2016). The "Go George Go!" initiative promoted health and fitness and also celebrated Curious George's birthday. Curious George has celebrated Christmas (Hapka, Rey, and O'Keefe Young 2006), Hanukkah (Meyer and O'Keefe Young 2012) and Easter (Anderson and O'Keefe Young 2010), and in 2016 he learned about Ramadan (Mubtadi 2016; Rey and Khan 2016). While debates about Muslims occupied the political scene, *It's Ramadan, Curious George,* by Pakistani-American Muslim writer Hena Khan, topped the Amazon bestseller list on its May 2016 release (Mubtadi 2016). The Curious George store in Cambridge, Massachusetts celebrated with over a thousand fans visiting Curious George characters and indulging a Chunky Monkey–flavored ice cream cake donated by Ben & Jerry's (Toussaint 2016).

In March 2020, when the coronavirus pandemic forced schools to close worldwide, US educators turned to Curious George to aid in elementary education. "As schools suspended classes to slow the spread of COVID-19, the PBS and NPR member station, Empire KVCR, launched a partnership ... offering students, families and teachers programming aligned to California's state curriculum" where preschoolers through third graders could learn math and engineering with George between 6 and 9 a.m. (Redlands Community News 2020). PBS also used George to advertise their launch of "Camp Curiosity, a free at-home 'camp' to help meet the demand for trusted educational online resources," and Amazon promoted Curious George as part of their "Free Content to Fire TV and Fire Tablet Devices" (Barnes 2020; PBS Reno 2020). *Curious George Discovers Germs* (H. A. Reys 2015a) was promoted to help children cope with "anxious feelings" (Cavanagh 2020). Netflix advertised Curious George films to "teach your toddler all they need to know about exploring," ABC Mouse joined up with Adventure Academy and Reading IQ (home learning sites) and opened their "virtual doors to all new students for free for 30 days," to help children improve their reading skills with classics such as Curious George (Samuels 2020; Smith 2020). Nationwide, virtual story times and online museum programing featured Curious George books (Elder 2020; French 2020; Hildebrand 2020; McGarry 2020; Moyer 2020; Rice 2020). The midsummer premiere of the Peacock streaming service directed parents to entertain children by introducing them to a nostalgic teacher:

> It's lockdown and if there are kids around you, you are probably wondering how to entertain them. Well, look no further and get ready for a nostalgic trip of your own as well. "Curious George," based on one of the most beloved children's classics of all time written by Margaret and H. A. Rey, will be airing soon on Peacock, which is NBC's streaming service. You'll get to have fun with the monkey and his insatiable need for knowledge. (Palat 2020)

George's perceived link to education, in literacy and STEM, was one of the few pop icons that received a boost in the devastated economy accompanying the COVID-19 crisis, and at a time when consumer spending was low, parents could preoccupy their children with decorative Curious George–themed face masks (Levy 2020; Meador 2020). 2020 marked the best year for print books since 2010 because the pandemic turned Americans, particularly children, into readers (Williams 2021). In early 2021, publishing giant Rupert Murdoch announced he would buy Houghton Mifflin Harcourt (HMH) for $349 million (a deal that is expected to close in June 2021); all of HMH's titles "will operate as part of News Corp's HarperCollins book publishing arm" (Williams 2021). By joining the world's second largest publisher, popular series such as *The Lord of the Rings*, *Jumanji*, and *The Polar Express* will join Curious George on his new publishing adventures.

Curious George's popularity is outstanding. He endures through generations of audiences perhaps "because we can each see part of ourselves in his antics, mishaps, and solutions to comical and unexpected situations" (HMH Books 2005, para. 22). Universal Studios shares a similar sentiment; in their Brand Plan, they state that "Curious George is a classic, timeless character which has grown up with many generations and remains popular with all who have followed his adventures" ("Universal Studios: Curious George Brand Plan," p. 9, in Rey Papers, Box 117, Folder 7). However, if Curious George is to endure across generations, he must retain the principal characteristics of curiosity and monkeyness while also adapting to contemporary times. Like other countries, the US is in a constant state of reconstitution, reconstruction, and reestablishment. As such, the nation has changed a great deal since the Reys published the first Curious George book. To understand why his popularity endures requires an understanding of the ways cultural icons circulate.

Cultural Icons

Cultural icons play an important role in upholding cultural values by both expressing and influencing them. They are a type of figure whose associations and meanings change over time, and they are crucial artifacts for study because as they develop, transform, and resurface, they carry "meaning which interestingly toys with and sometimes overturns the conventions of the 'original'" (Brooker 2000, 9). Cultural icons are characterized by their physical features (in the case of Curious George, his monkey body), their attitudinal character (George's curiosity) and through repeated cultural storytelling (George likes to travel to space). Like a cipher—a recognizable product that is marketed as a consumable product (Ono and Buescher 2001)—a cultural icon is a familiar figure (or object) that can adapt to multiple narratives both simultaneously and over time. I read Curious George as a cultural icon—a specific, selective, commonly distinguishable type of icon. The scholarship devoted to cultural icons is limited, but some have considered their importance. These scholars have engaged the stable, enduring meanings attached to: Superman's commitment to justice (Brooker 2000), Barbie's materiality and presentation of the female body (Biemiller 1995), and Hello Kitty's reproduction of Japan (Yano 2013). In this book, I look to understand how cultural icons circulate through different discourses in order to discern the value of each iteration while simultaneously retaining the agency awarded to visual icons. Tracing the evolution of a cultural icon helps to illuminate how an object can represent more than itself. For example, in tracing the evolution of the Jesus fish, Todd Edmondson argues that the object serves as a faithful "badge of identification, a sign that distills core beliefs into a simple formula, a polemical weapon in the cultural battle" (2010, 65). Similarly, in their exploration of the horse icon, Edwards, Enenkel, and Graham propose that literary and visual texts shift between different discursive domains, but remain pervasive in different cultural moments (2012).

Despite the dearth of studies about cultural icons, a few scholars have interrogated the concept and characteristics of cultural iconicity, including the production, distribution, and circulation of cultural icons over time.[7] Two productive studies include Will Brooker's (2000) reading of Batman and Bernhard Lang's (2009) consideration of Joseph from the *Book of Genesis*. Read together, these two studies illuminate the ways cultural icons can adapt both temporally and spatially, even as they remain stable within their established archetypal parameters, thus guaranteeing an "overwhelming sense of comfortable security for all who followed their prescriptions" (Lang 2009, 4). Adults' nostalgia for their childhood memory of Curious George (forever a monkey with no tail and always with a curious disposition that gets him into precarious situations) secures George's innocence, increasing popularity, marketability, and archetypical recognizability as a cultural icon.

While there is a great deal of research on icons, there is little written about the ways in which cultural icons work. In his examination of the disparate texts that bear the Batman signifier at key moments in history, Brooker argues that though cultural icons are open to multiple readings, with each new adoption certain aspects of their iconic personae are foregrounded and others pushed back. A cultural icon, he clarifies,

> must remain familiar while incorporating an edge of novelty; he [Batman] must keep the loyalty of an older generation who remember their childhood through

him and secure his place in popular memory, while constantly pulling in the younger audience who constitute his primary market. He must always serve the concerns of the present day, while retaining an aura of myth. . . . This sense of myth and resonance . . . has its source not in the specifics of his changes over time, but in the opposite, in those elements which never change. (Brooker 2000, 40)

For example, most readers can identify Jesus as an icon, even if they lack religious familiarity; they recognize Disney princesses, though they may have never viewed the films; and they can describe the Afghan Girl (Schwartz-DuPre 2007 and 2010), though they may have never picked up a *National Geographic*. While the Curious George name and brand adapt over time and across space, George retains primary characteristics, such as his playful curiosity, that enable him to be both instantaneously identifiable and exemplary. Cultural icons' characteristics support their familiarity across generations, even when members of the public lack specific knowledge or relevant detail.

Though the specific theoretical investment in cultural icons remains limited, the literature examining figures, ciphers, and icons is considerably greater and offers insights into the unique power of cultural icons. Mining these related areas of scholarship can help garner knowledge about cultural icons, their novelty, their relationship to new audiences, and most importantly, the way they uphold cultural values. While most cultural icons are figures, some figures are not icons because they lack the cultural cachet. As Jasinski (2001) explains, scholars have tried to classify various types of linguistic figures into categories or tropes such as: normal, literal, conventional, connotative, arranged (for example as anaphora or alliterations), substitutive (like metaphors and metonyms), additive, or omissive. Lanham defines a figure as "any devise or pattern of language in which meaning is enhanced or changed" (1991, 179). Rhetorical figures are common in everyday media and function to shape human understandings and epistemologies. Time, love, running, and insanity are examples of figures, especially when substitution is operative. Curious George's rhetorical figuration is marked by his fluid character, archetypical brown simian body, and curious mentality. Regardless of how he changes across time, these features are never removed. Thus, while Curious George is a type of figure, his capacity to uphold cultural values over time gives him an iconic figuration. Cultural icons like George have the power of condensation symbols in that they are rich, vivid, descriptive, and evaluative qualities of potent, versatile, and effective tools that can arouse or conjure emotion to sway public opinion (Graber 1976). While cultural icons are a type of condensation symbol, their capacity to produce truths for their audiences is much stronger.

Understanding Curious George, or any cultural icon, crucially relies upon making sense of the metaphor(s) in which the icon is encased. By nature, metaphors illuminate some and obscure other elements within an artifact. In *Rhetoric and Poetics*, Aristotle explains metaphor as the transference of a name from the object to which it has a natural application (Foss 1996; Tarán and Gutas 2012). According to Aristotle, personification is the "common practice of giving metaphorical life to lifeless things" (Paxson 1994, 12).[8] For Kenneth Burke (1945), metaphor is the substitution of a word, image, or idea for another, based on an implied resemblance or analogy (a comparison of two things to explain an idea). Metaphors substitute perspective; they control perceptions by emphasizing and shading aspects of the narrative. As Michael Osborn explains, metaphors are incomplete and thus limit the naming process, "our synecdochic tendency to highlight certain features of subjects while we neglect others" (2009, 81). In this way, metaphors are critical to a reading of cultural icons because they are both filled with ideological perspectives by those that produce, own, and value them. When a text relies upon metaphor (whether or not the author so intended), it represents a double reading—one that is on the page or screen and another that refers to a past understanding. The synthesis of this double reading thus results in a new understanding. The use of metaphor is of vital importance to my understanding of cultural icons, because it helps to explain how figures obscure and highlight. I use this to present colonialism not as ordinary but as extraordinarily essential to "progressive" progress. Simply, reading metaphors enables cultural icons to reinforce, reintroduce, or reject knowledge of the colonial past and present.

Burke explains metonymy as a reduction, a substitution of the name of an attribute or an adjunct for the name of the thing. It is a metaphorical substitution based on contiguity or proximity—the ability to see one thing. In my view, this project—infused with re-presentations of enslavement as adventurous, science and technology as enlightening, and the Holocaust as whimsical—finds reading metaphor as synecdoche particularly useful to cultural icons such as Curious George because synecdoche can be a form of artistic representation in that it stands in for some other relationship of connectedness. To put it another way, visual representations invite audiences to consider one kind of thing, concept, or experience (Curious George excited while gazing at a jungle tree) in terms of another (Curious George missing the jungle in which he once lived). Metaphors need not be verbal in nature. Synecdoches spotlight certain features and leave other features in the shadow (Osborn 2009). Osborn explains that audiences should "habitually and repeatedly ask: What does this representation omit, and what are the consequences of this omission.... [This asking] is vital, because in a world of increasingly visual rhetoric, synecdoche has come to rival metaphor as a technique of depiction" (2009, 84). Although Osborn's questions of inclusion and omission are relevant in most rhetorical projects, when asked of cultural icons their double representations and historical positioning can omit and include concurrently. For instance, when Ellen W. Gorsevski reads Native American symbols and Pocahontas, she describes the heuristic value "for exploring visually rich multicultural discourses with polysemic implications" (2018, 161). Understanding cultural icons such as Pocahontas and Curious George as synecdochal metaphors enables the conditions of possibility to see these figures as more than embodying the celebrator of American multiculturalism, and instead offers a reading of them as embodying the stains of US racism and violence.

Although icons are commonplace, they lack agreed upon definitional frequency. An icon is symbolic in that it represents an idea greater than itself. Saussure contends that the theorization of language is a system of signs, or what is now termed semiotics. Historically, icons have referred to sacred religious imagery. In the late nineteenth century, Charles Sanders Peirce introduced the idea of signs or representations as iconic, indexical, and symbolic. He suggested that iconic signs resemble their objects in some way (Sturken and Cartwright 2009). Iconicity is historically a linguistic concept and refers to a harmony between semantic and syntactical utterances (Jasinski 2001). Visual and cinema scholars argue that icons represent a means of categorizing and analyzing visual motifs and styles (Hayward 2012). Marked by their simplicity, icons connote more than they denote. They are historically and culturally produced with the ability to morph in distinct temporal and spatial conditions that extend beyond their historical origins. As Sturken and Cartwright argue, icons refer "to something outside its individual components, something (or someone) that has great symbolic meaning for many people" (2009, 36). Icons represent universal concepts, emotions, and meanings. As icons circulate and are reconfigured in different discourses, they "are objects of veneration and other complex emotional responses. They are reproduced widely and placed prominently in both public and private settings, and are used to orient the individual within a context of collective identity, obligation and power" (Hariman and Lucaites 2007, 1). Though Curious George is an icon, his ability to retain his universal value (upholding an older generation's interpretation) while also taking on and adapting to multinarratives (attracting a newer general audience) gives him distinct amounts of agency. This agency is a unique quality of a cultural icon.

The agency of cultural icons exceeds the capabilities of most icons. Jenkins argues that an icon constructs a mode of seeing as symbolic realism that portrays a hypostasis—"a concrete representation of a spiritual quality" (2008, 467). The perceived reality acts as a shield for the icon, offering naturalizing features that deflect its ideological construction and also guard the icon from charges of heresy or propaganda. The safety of the audience's spiritual relationship with the icon is grounded in its assumed materiality and naturalness. Icons are culturally potent (Jenkins 2008). The object of an icon is recognizable through an arbitrary symbol. Drawing from diverse schools of thought, Jenkins explains that an icon directs critics to its circulation and compositional features. He recounts: "an icon archives the status of a divine image only when it becomes culturally accepted as a natural fusion of meaning and form through continued use" (2008, 480). Though audiences understand icons to be natural, their power comes from the accepted ideological narratives they perform.

Icons such as Captain America, Bugs Bunny, and Curious George retain archetypal features that appear natural and enable the public to recognize them. Some examples include Captain America's flag costume, his shield, and his embodiment of the American dream (Duncan and Smith 2013); Bugs Bunny's trickster depiction, his carrot, and his catchphrase "Eh, what's up, Doc?" (Looney Tunes Wiki n.d.); and Curious George's curiosity and monkeyness. In their reading of US comic book icons, Duncan and Smith (2013) explain that these cultural icons can challenge or reinforce the status quo, influence millions, and impact history. While I agree with the latter two qualifications regarding icons' influence and historical impact, it is important to note that icons can embody a group of values; many cultural icons both reinforce and challenge, often simultaneously, even if they remain relatively ubiquitous. G.I. Joe, Superman, and Curious George are all strong examples. Duncan and Smith correctly explain that icons "elicit strong reactions . . . and link different traditions and periods" (2013, xi). However, this very power enables cultural icons to position audiences to support the cultural value of the present. While cultural icons represent a specific type of icon, they share many properties with a visual icon.

Hariman and Lucaites position their understanding of icons in relation to visual rhetoric and the value of iconic images in present and future public policy. Focusing on US iconic images, they explain that naturalizing features enable icons to stand above debate and investigation. They go on to clarify that cultural icons are more than recognizable, they are in fact "experienced within the ordinary routines of everyday life" (2007, 2). While these authors are referring to iconic images in US history, I contend that iconic images share many traits with cultural icons because they circulate in US popular culture. Like Dorothea Lange's "Migrant Mother" and Joe Rosenthal's "Raising the Flag on Iwo Jima," Curious George teaches US citizens—particularly young citizens—a specific version of the past. The lessons become a means of making sense of and influencing the present and future. Icons such as Curious George possess the longevity and innocence that characterize many photojournalistic icons; they provide reflective awareness, they tap into national public memory, they re-present history, and they present little about their origins. Cultural icons share with photojournalism characteristics that Hariman and Lucaites refer to as the distinctive influence on public opinion (2007). For most US citizens, Curious George reflects specific US associations and accounts of history that service the present. These icons are seemingly ageless, articulate themselves through powerful technologies, express a dominant aspect of public identity, present a model for citizenry, and shield their seriousness through rhetorics of innocence and nostalgia. Hariman and Lucaites's study of icons provides an important understanding of icons as motivators of public opinion, especially in the national sense. While iconic photographs are located within various discursive frameworks, they lack the ability to separate from their time period and related events.

Repeated readings of Curious George's cultural values reinforce and challenge dominant ideologies. However, George and other cultural icons differ from iconic photographs because cultural icons can resurrect interpretations of the past or they can circulate while completely ignoring their past or origin story (though traces of their past may reappear). Cultural icons retain certain features, such as George's simian qualities and curious attitude; yet they can be divorced from previous iterations of their stories and contexts. Cultural icons circulate through repeated storytelling, but their stories and narratives yield polysemic responses that change over time while maintaining recognizability.

Cultural icons differentiate themselves from iconic figures and images because of the latter's inability to change and to disavow their past. George bears traces of the past while also containing the conditions of possibility to be recontextualized beyond the past. Iconic photographs also allow for the possibility of recontextualization (for example, memes), but icons are recontextualized differently, because they cannot be stripped from their historical moment of emergence.

Icons are deeply attached to meaning while ciphers, often mistaken for icons, are devoid of meaning. The cipher's very skill is its ability to present itself in an ever-present way. Like an icon, a cipher is a recognizable product of commodity culture that is marketed as a consumable. Ono and Buescher offer a reading of Pocahontas to explain the cultural power of the cipher. The cipher is a "blank slate, an empty container, an unwritten text, or an un-ornamented or unadorned figure—in short, perhaps, a free-floating signifier that ultimately is then filled with various meanings" (2001, 25). That is, the cipher does not actually contain meaning; rather, meanings are ascribed to it. Like cultural icons, ciphers can have one meaning in a certain time or space, and a completely different connotation in another. Ono and Buescher explain:

Commodities and ciphers mutually support one another in a feedback loop in which the cipher imbues the commodity with a particular kind of value, while the purchase of the commodity in the context of an entire field of related commodities further strengthens the overall desirability of products associated with the cipher. (2001, 26)

The marketability of the cipher enables it to function as a referent that can change and defend its reincarnation as a natural and common extension of its empty original. Because the cipher is an empty referent, it is constituted by the products that embody it. The cipher is always changing and moving within the market of production, making it difficult to isolate and to critically interrogate. Drawing on Ono and Buescher, Rogers reads the Native American Kokopelli as a cipher and explains that ciphers are restricted by the Euro-American cultural codes within which they are embedded. The code that guides the audience to make sense of the cipher "enables the imagery's dislocation from its historical and contemporary contexts, making it largely self-referential, unanchored by specific cultural traditions and histories" (Rogers 2007, 250). The cipher cannot exist outside the worlds of products (Ono 2009). The value of the cipher for this project is that its movement within the marketplace of products and ideas is presented as ideologically neutral. Ciphers can dislodge themselves from the narratives in which they were created and appear anew—empty referents filled up with new chronicles, plots, ideologies, and promises. "Pocahontas," Ono and Buescher explain, "existed long before Disney appropriated her for their own purposes" (2001, 25). They argue that Pocahontas is reproduced as a set of commodities purporting to offer feminist and historic Native American tales. Similarly, Curious George can be taken up to promote STEM education and Holocaust remembrance. Both cultural icons and ciphers emerge within a matrix of products (including books, films, exhibits) spanning time periods and media platforms for economic and ideological profit. Just as Pocahontas was a historical figure who was Disneyfied for economic gain, Margret and H. A. Rey produced Curious George and the economy within which he circulates. Pocahontas and Curious George share a capacity to reshape and take on new interpretations that often overwrite and/or ignore their past. The ability to shift from one set of discourses to another is an important feature of both ciphers and cultural icons.

Cultural icons share salient qualities with ciphers, namely the ability to disengage the story of origin and refigure its narrative to profit the present. Like ciphers, cultural icons retain both physical attributes and important character traits. For example, when Pocahontas is reproduced in "relationship to a single product, such as a film" (Ono and Buescher 2001, 23), she retains resemblance to a physical body and attachment to a cultural place; however, she does not necessarily retain attitudinal traits. Both cultural icons and ciphers can take on more than one ideological function simultaneously. Though Ono and Buescher suggest that the cipher can exist in the form of fictional characters such as Batman, it is likely that the products (happy meals, tennis shoes, Viewmaster reels, alarm clocks, etc.) uphold the same iconic ideological attributes as other Batman products. Similarly, cultural icons such as Curious George uphold their iconic hallmarks through simultaneously emerging narratives. While preschoolers learn science lessons from George figured in a simian body, young adults learn a rendition of the Holocaust from a whimsical narrative of two German Jews fleeing their Paris honeymoon in 1941. Adults accompanying young children and adolescents can engage both narratives while also evoking their own memories of the Holocaust through Curious George experiences from their childhood and with their own children. Curious George was created as a product; he was never a historical narrative. Yet he engages germinal US narratives—of African enslavement (in the initial 1941 book), STEM promotion (in television, films, and children's museum exhibits), and Holocaust remembrance in more recent discourses. As such, cultural icons like Curious George can be understood as a particular type of cipher, and so can reveal the ways in which ciphers function ideologically within an economy of ideas and profit. Those ciphers that retain attitudinal attributes and sell multiple, potentially unrelated narratives, to various audiences, are also cultural icons.

I suggest that Curious George presents a contemporary example of a ciphered cultural icon as a technology of popular culture. I offer a reading of a cultural icon whose marketability changes over time, upholds multiple narratives simultaneously, erases or ignores its origins, and contains archetypical features that make it universally recognized. Curious George as a cultural icon is an empty free-floating signifier like Pocahontas and also has properties that cannot be erased or changed. George retains a trace of the stain of his enslavement-based past and the current values of US exceptionalism.

Understood as a cultural icon, Curious George both maintains and erases a specific past of colonial enslavement while attending to another national narrative of the Holocaust. Conterminously, Curious George has more recently become a cultural icon for citizens invested in Holocaust remembrance. *The Journey that Saved Curious George* (Borden and Drummond 2005) exhibits, including *The Wartime Escape: Margret and H. A. Rey's Journey from France* (Dotan 2009), have attracted a great deal of national acclaim. *Monkey Business* (Yamazaki 2017), in its debut, won several film festival awards, including the Nantucket Film Festival's Audience Award (2017) and the Fargo Film Festival's Best Documentary Feature (2018).

All of these Holocaust retellings position audiences to make sense of George as an icon of Holocaust survivors. As a cultural icon of Holocaust remembrance, George can be read as the child of model US immigrants, who, immediately upon arrival, produce and contribute to the national market economy. A reading of Margaret and H. A. Rey's escape from the Holocaust explains George as a popular and protected cultural icon. In an age when the last remaining Holocaust survivors are dying and anti-Semitism is practiced increasingly and openly, positioning George within a Holocaust narrative makes him unassailable even if his original depiction mimicked a slave capture. Whether readers agree that Curious George's fiction-based story resembles enslaved Africans' accounts, once Borden and Drummond presented a nonfiction account of the Reys' escape from Nazi Paris, the Reys and George became protected, as Holocaust survivors, from the claim of racism. As Barbara Biesecker (2002) explains, the collective memory that US citizens have of World War II is one of national reunification, and one in which the memory of the "greatest generation's war" constitutes a history that US Americans celebrate. The war is embedded ideologically in US nationalism; consequently, critiquing anything associated with it remains beyond the pale.

These examples demonstrate that while some cultural icons can sometimes challenge the status quo, others (such as Curious George) resist and support existing dominant ideologies. This example also draws an important relationship between cultural icons and iconic images, which are unable to overshadow their past. George is an empty cipher, able to adapt to multiple narratives over time, and at the same time a full and stable signifier unable to distance himself from his historical roots.

Curious George transforms from a literary character into an artifact of distinct, but interrelated, discourses: film, science education, and Holocaust remembrance. The social knowledge that George communicates—children should be curious, should study STEM, and should know that the US played an instrumental role in ending the violence of the Holocaust—enables George to uphold important elements of this US ideological narrative. George's position as Holocaust hero not only frees this cultural icon from potential critique, but also functions to remind parents that their children are being hailed as the next great generation in hopes that they will reignite US dominance in science and technology as well as global leadership. In doing so, George can also silently overshadow the slave narrative (though never lose its trace) and colonial conditions of his emergence in favor of a more nuanced and culturally acceptable view of STEM education and Holocaust remembrance—a view that upholds this cultural icon as ideologically neutral.

Curious George's audiences include both young and older people, especially those involved in children' education. They are often children, parents, grandparents, teachers, and librarians—proponents of properly educating those children who might not know about 9/11, the Vietnam War, or the Great Depression. George's audience includes young children who are just beginning to experience the concepts of history, science, adventure, and obedience. Fun-loving cuddly cultural icons such as George churn US histories under the radar of seemingly nonsensical fiction, disguised by animation and protected by parental nostalgia for childhood innocence.[9]

Curious George's circulation through diverse discourses demonstrates the ways in which cultural icons can secure dominant ideologies and socialize individuals to societal norms that promote a hegemonic version of US citizenship. George's cultural iconicity can be captured through narratives of adventure and curiosity; his signature trait is his presumably natural inclination to break rules and somehow seamlessly have his disobedience transform into heroism. As such, his deployment motivates children to think beyond their assumed limits, to ask questions, and to motivate their learning through rhetorics of curiosity.

Despite the hundreds of Curious George stories, the narrative remains predictable and ritualistic; the stories observe the ritual performance of the basic tale. As Lang (2009) explains, the story is a reminder of community-shared values and traditions designed to strengthen societal cohesion, while simultaneously teaching the young. He further contends that a cultural icon is an "image of canonical status and hierarchical quality against which people measured their own moral identity" (Lang 2009, 6). Curious George's popularity during the 2020 COVID-19 pandemic demonstrates not only the extreme confidence parents bestow upon George as an educator, but also how the cultural iconicity of a cuddly curious monkey positions Curious George as a productive prototype for navigating a political moment. His innocence and sense of adventure are attractive to both younger audiences and their parents, while his iconic stability enables his translation from one cause to the next. As a model, he can at once play science teacher, Holocaust hero, model immigrant, and New York City tour guide. The reiterations of Curious George oscillate in theme between birthday parties and trips to the zoo, as well as throughout literature, television, museums, and theatrical performances. In all cases, George remains legible through irreplaceable identifiers.

Cultural icons, Eleanor Canright Chiari (2016) explains, reflect the polysemous power of icons to take on various adaptations. In many ways, cultural icons are brands that maintain their markets of identification; yet what they identify is polysemic. Each discourse positions audiences to read George differently: as an adventurous literary tool, as a cute dark infantilized STEM educator, or as a historical marker of US heroism through which audiences can engage the dark Holocaust in a digestible "feel-good" way. Stephen Brown contends that polysemy "cannot be avoided in a marketing milieu of vibrant brand communities and active consumer co-creation" (2014, 100). The ambiguity of a brand like Curious George is perhaps his greatest promise, because for each reading there is another often shadowed opportunity. Specifically, when a critique of his origin story emerges, such as the one advanced in this book, readers can pivot to become consumers of a more feel-good interpretation. For example, while other parents are preoccupied with the anxiety associated with a pandemic lockdown, some parents are reading a Curious George book, planting their preschooler down in front of a mute monkey leading an animated STEM lesson, or introducing older children to whimsical Eurocentric retellings of the Holocaust. As a fictional character without a voice, Curious George literally does not speak. Yet with the help of an omnipresent narrator, parents and educators can help children ascribe meanings to George. As such, rather than highlighting how dangerous many of George's antics might be, the end of the story—when George predictably saves or discovers something—becomes the preoccupation of countless audiences. That is, Curious George holds different values and is understood differently for different audiences.

Gorsevski also offers a newer rhetorical reading of Pocahontas and President Trump's White supremacist memes. In doing so, she reminds the reader that "polysemy facilitates questioning" of hegemonic narratives (2018, 164). In my reading, the polysemic nature of cultural icons provides the conditions of possibility to revolve the axis backward to highlight Curious George's origin story not as a singular event but instead as an interior feature of this character's cultural iconicity that circulates as the foundation of future readings. By connecting the recurring image of the jungle tree and location of capture, George's obsession with jungle animals, desire to discover space and literally leave his current location, and emergence as perhaps the last known Holocaust hero, exemplify as polysemic readings of cultural icons how the matrices of colonialism advance.

The fandom of cultural icons is active and dedicated; often enthusiasts' power is strong enough to affect elements of programming (Brooker 2000). The 2006 *Curious George* film exemplifies the power of the audience. The transformation of The Man in the Yellow Hat from an explorer who captured George to an explorer, now named Ted, with whom George hid in a boat is a small, but important, detail that modernizes the enslavement narrative in a way that enhances audience digestibility. While audiences play an important role in the critical readings of cultural icons, so does the "cultural power and the role of these interpretations within the networks of cultural discourse" (Brooker 2000, 29). Thus, audiences who possess a nostalgic relationship with Curious George may read such critiques as a personal attack.

As cultural icons travel, they carry with them the needs of the audiences in various political environments. They carry mass-media appeal and serve as institutions that are offered as solutions to social problems (Heywood and Dworkin 2003). Curious George currently holds this type of institutional positionality. In his contemporary form, he serves as a heroic figure offered to US citizens as a coping mechanism for school closings and the US's current lack of STEM leadership and technological competition. Like most cultural icons, George plays the hero; as such, he is able to occupy a powerful motivational role in public discourse.

An understanding of how cultural icons change when interpreted through different ideological perspectives requires a critical lens that considers, at a minimum, race, class, gender, and sexuality as coordinates of colonization. This type of multifaceted lens can provide explanations for the polymorphous stages of a cultural icon. Readers should consider the ways in which icons can evoke "culture and social contexts of formally colonized countries" and often contain historical traces of colonization (Sturken and Cartwright 2009, 406). However, the conditions of postcoloniality not only result in the emergence of hybrid communities comprised of diasporic subjects who often interact through mediated networks; they also reflect a broad set of changes that have effected a complex form of dependence and independence (Sturken and Cartwright 2009). As discourses of globalization emerged, postcolonial scholars took up various approaches to the politics of occupation and oppression. While European scholars have produced far more postcolonial scholarship, the US has seen an insurgence of neocolonial, decolonial, and settler colonial scholarship. This project critically considers three veins of postcolonial theory: postcolonial children's literary criticism, postcolonial science and technology studies, and postcolonial nostalgia.

In the following section, I argue that colonization has much to do with how US citizens come to make sense of cultural icons such as Curious George. It begins by reviewing some critical new ways in which scholars of postcolonial theory and colonization have moved beyond the faded conditions that propelled the emergence of this scholarship in the 1980s.

Contemporary Postcolonial Studies

Postcolonial studies is an intersectional and interdisciplinary critical field of study offering intellectual, cultural, textual, political, and performative analysis. It includes theories and movements committed to critiquing and resisting inequities, power imbalances, Eurocentric research methods, master narratives, universal theories of culture, spatial homogenization, and temporal teleology, while locating the ways in which these legacies emerge in the globalized present. Rather than attempting to correct interpretations of the past, postcolonial studies are invested in troubling accepted accounts of history. Postcolonial studies is an interventionist and transformative project that actively challenges present knowledge, invites space for innovative theories of knowledge production not grounded in Western epistemology, advocates for human freedoms, and "anticipate[s] a future beyond colonialism in all its forms" (Zabus 2015, 1). Graham Huggan, a comparative postcolonial literary and cultural studies scholar, explains that intervention is a key postcolonial tactic in that it "operates in the interstices between cultural critique and political advocacy" to raise general consciousness of injustice rather than a special rational for struggle (Huggan 2016, 12). Postcolonial studies traces the past in order to understand the cultural conditions of the present. Though many connect the field to the disintegration of European empire, signaled by a series of independence movements in the twentieth century (and beyond), postcolonial studies considers the historical and contemporary ways in which discourses, language, and symbols continue to colonize knowledge, ideas, people, and communities. Most contemporary postcolonial theories are invested in understanding the ways in which violent and oppressive conditions of the past inform the present and possibilities for its transformation. Colonialism constitutes a distinct set of conditions, and different colonialisms function in myriad ways. Thus, the study of postcolonialism is not homogenous; the "post-" does not signify an end to colonialism, and it does not operate in the same way across spaces and temporal occurrences. I take up postcolonial theoretical frameworks as explanatory and normative frames through which Curious George can be read. Curious George narratives demonstrate that reading colonial texts requires multifarious approaches in order to offer compelling explanations for the distinctly different ways in which domination operates. Specifically, postcolonial readings magnify how dominant texts, like Curious George, maintain and promote Anglo/Euro narratives of progress and US exceptionalism by universalizing modes of Western modernity.

Colonial theories from various disciplines interact with postcolonial theory in complicated and often contradictory ways. These theories work to explain the tentacles of colonial pasts and futures that manifest in contemporary rhetorics of Whiteness (Alley-Young 2008), transnationalism (Hegde 2011), global communication studies (Kraidy and Murphy 2008), neocolonialism (Ono 2009;), environmentalism (Mount and O'Brien 2013), queering postcolonial politics (Hawley 2001), settler colonialism (Yang and Tuck 2012), and de/coloniality (Wanzer-Serrano 2015; Vats 2016). I argue that these theories have much to gain by working together. Seeking to understand how colonialism operates can productively work toward eliminating injustice, as Alley-Young suggests, so that marginalized peoples do not speak with a single voice but "they might continue to challenge each other to account for gaps" in hegemonic knowledge (2008, 319).

This project is evidence that working with various types of anticolonial philosophies yields a far more comprehensive and nuanced understanding of the present. Postcolonial studies has always rejected a definitive academic home, and this theme of rejecting disciplinary dogma should extend to emerging areas of anticolonial writing. Since colonialism often works in insidious ways, the field of study demands a willingness on the part of various theorists to work together contingently to represent interdisciplinary perspectives across history, literature, journalism, anthropology, sociology, gender studies, race studies, and beyond.

Postcolonial studies emerged in the 1970s and gained popularity in the 1980s and early 1990s. It provides a way to theorize the conditions and discourses of colonization and decolonization. By the turn of the twenty-first century, postcolonial studies became an established global field with no distinct disciplinary home. While some nations and cultures continue to suffer from territorial occupation, postcolonial studies offers important explanations of how "first world" conditions exist in majority world countries (referring to population size rather economic inequality) and the ways in which "third world" conditions continue to function in "first world" countries even when such countries are ostensibly "post" an era of territorial colonization.

Though anticolonial and postcolonial theories remain robust and vibrant areas of academic inquiry in much European scholarship, US scholars based in the humanities (outside of English) have seen a dip in the popularity of postcolonial studies, starting at the turn of the twenty-first century. Some scholars traded their postcolonial terminology for the more attractive lexicon of globalization and transnational studies (Loomba 2015). In communication studies specifically, postcolonial studies have faced a variety of critics caught up in the circuits of amplifying discourse of globalization (Nayar 2015). Yet postcolonial conversations and debates remained innovative abroad and among smaller circles of US scholars. "After experiencing this near-death experience," explains Chantal Zabus, a professor of postcolonial literatures and gender studies, "the ailing and still twitching discipline" was then relocated, redirected, and rerouted in effective ways. Now the study of colonialism (including postcolonialism, neocolonialism, settler colonialism, and decoloniality)[10] is vibrant and is being used by scholars to explain, and mount resistance to, numerous institutional injustices (Zabus 2015).

This momentary lack of interest was strongly refuted by Robert Young in 2012. Citing colonial opposition to indigenous people and the rise of religious fundamentalism as evidence (both of which increased during the Trump presidency), Young asserts that postcolonial scholarship is not only relevant but also necessary in the current moment: "The desire to pronounce postcolonial theory . . . [as] dead on both sides of the Atlantic suggests that its presence continues to disturb and provoke anxiety: the real problem lies in the fact that the postcolonial remains" (2012, 19). His claim is that the field of postcolonial studies has remained durable and open to interpretations that are salient to the contemporary global era. Postcolonial scholars have often returned to the writing of such foundational theorists as Edward Said, Homi Bhabha, Gayatri Chakravorty Spivak, and Frantz Fanon, and have applied their ideas to the current conditions. The various strands of scholarship working against imperial and colonial forces are not completely incommensurable and in fact have a great deal to offer one another in ways that work to explain the complexity of colonial contemporary moments. The divides in postcolonial studies are often between competing revolutionary and revisionist impulses (Huggan 2016).

This perceived lull in US scholarship might have been the result of frequent criticisms of postcolonial studies. Critics focus on the complexity of the field and its academic jargon, and have questioned its continued relevance. Huggan astutely points out that there are few areas of studies as capable of making sense of the present as postcolonial studies, and that

one of the discipline's greatest strengths is its continuing commitment to complexity—its studied refusal to seek easy solutions to the problems its raises, and its scrupulous attentiveness to the unstable relationship between aesthetics and politics, activism and academia, actions and words. (2016, xvii)

Those invested in understanding the histories of colonial occupation that undergird the contemporary context expand postcolonial scholarship to various areas of inquiry including environmentalism, settler colonialism, utopianism, migrations, queer politics, and science and technology studies, among others.

Deepika Bahri, a professor of comparative literature, skillfully highlights the ways postcolonialism can productively theorize modern colonialism precisely because it understands that contemporary discourses stem from discourses of colonialism in which a series of colonial moves has taken place. Bahri explains:

An examination of pre-modern colonial activities, in fact, may give us a more complex understanding of structures of power and domination and may illuminate the operations of older histories in the context of both modern colonialism and contemporary global relations. (1995, 56)

Bahri does not suggest that postcolonial studies should be singled out as the only way to theorize injustice, nor does she maintain that a total dismissal of European colonialism is possible. Postcolonial theory is fiercely contested among postcolonial theorists themselves (Lazarus 2016). The economic and ideological characteristics of present-day colonialism change the conditions of colonialism; in turn, postcolonialism offers many possibilities for intervention (Bahri 1995).

Multiple theories of colonialism continue to emerge; these include theories of globalization, neocolonialism, settler colonialism, and de/coloniality studies. Though my arguments about Curious George are US-based, I remain committed to postcolonial studies because its scholarship is expansive enough to contain competing interpretations. My claim is that Curious George is a colonial text that is magnified by readings that draw from emerging postcolonial scholarship; thus, rather than dismissing the significant work produced by scholars focused on competing interpretations of colonization, I argue that these areas of study should work together frequently and contingently. I acknowledge that some anticolonial scholars position themselves as incommensurable with postcolonial studies, but Curious George demonstrates that multiple rubrics, even if seemingly contradictory, are useful tools for understanding the ways in which this cultural icon operates both temporally and spatially through colonial and postcolonial narratives. This is not an exhaustive review of globalization studies, neocolonialism, settler colonialism, and de/coloniality. Rather, it highlights these four areas in order to demonstrate that each has important interventions to offer to the vast postcolonial canon. The ultimate goal should be for these areas of scholarship to come together in conversations, differences intact, in order to strategically combat hegemonic colonial powers.

An important relationship between postcolonial and globalization scholars has enabled them to learn a great deal from one another (Krishnaswamy and Hawley 2008). As such, postcolonialism remains a resistant theory that has the capacity to respond to the changing world order (Hegde 2005 and 2011; Kavoori and Chadha 2009; Lunga 2008; Parameswaran 2008). While postcolonial and globalization scholars sometimes advance divergent methods and priorities, together their dialogical possibilities consider both the colonial past and the globalized future. Loomba astutely argues that postcolonialism and globalization can indeed occupy the same discursive space and have a great deal to offer one another. In the more recent edition of her well-known *Colonialism/Postcolonialism: The New Critical Idiom*, Loomba confronts globalization scholars:

Postcolonial studies cannot be simply replaced by something called globalization studies. If it is to be equal to the task of analyzing our contemporary world and visualizing how it can be changed, globalization scholars will have to incorporate some of the key insights of postcolonial studies, especially its historical awareness of past forms of empire and the structural connections between colonialism and neo-colonialism. Only then will it be able to trace global inequities in the often-confusing landscape of contemporary economics, politics, and culture. Today, it seems that much of globalization's shine has worn off. (2015, 16)

Radha Hegde cites aspects of globalization as "new objects of inquiry for post-colonial scholars": "Reading globality against the grain," she continues, "has always been the purview of postcolonial scholarship. . . . The racial and social divides exacerbated by globalization have strong connections with colonial hierarchies. . . . The old patterns are now being replayed in new contexts and neoliberal configurations" (in Schwartz-DuPre and Hegde 2016, 29).

US communication studies scholars such as Hegde have been incorporating the lessons of globalization since the early twenty-first century (Shome and Hegde 2002; Buescher and Ono 1996; Ono and Buescher 2001; Kraidy 2002). Just a few years after Raka Shome (1996) offered central connections between the field of communication and postcolonial studies, *Communication Theory* devoted a special issue entirely to postcolonial scholarship that directly addressed its relationship with globalization. Radhika Parameswaran's (2002) reading of the colonial representations in *National Geographic* and Marwann M. Kraidy's explanation of the cultural dialectics of diaspora speak directly to discourses of globalization prior to the formal explosion of the field. In their lead article, Shome and Hegde (2002) chart the questions and problematics of postcolonial scholarship, its intellectual and historical development, and its important contributions to communication studies. They offer a provocative critique of globalization and multiculturalism, exploring how these dominant theoretical lenses warrant exploration from a postcolonial framework. Rhetoricians who study the circulation and reception of symbols, and media scholars invested in various facets of production, reproduction, and reception are particularly well suited to use the lessons of postcolonialism to make sense of the global past and future. While some argue that these areas of inquiry are incongruous, I maintain that there is much fertile ground for collaboration. In fact, the expanded lexicon of postcolonial studies increases its ability to explain injustice and the possibilities for emancipatory advocacy. For example, the terminology of neocolonialism offers a great structure for understanding US postcolonial conditions.

Kent Ono, an early champion of neocolonialist studies, argues that "neoco-lonialism is both the present form colonialism takes, as well as the strategies and means by which contemporary and historical colonialism are repressed and masked" (2009, 2). Ono uses an intersectional neocolonialist lens to make sense of and resist colonialist discourses in film, television, and various modes of US media culture. For Ono, "neocolonialism currently exists in the United States as a specter of the colonial past" (2009, 7). His focus on the United States directs Ono to reject the use of the term "postcolonial" because, he argues, it refers to societies "no longer controlled by colonial metropole" (2009, 13). He explains that in the US context, colonialism has moved underground and is rarely discussed; thus, neocolonialism is a more appropriate term for describing the current contemporary condition. Because neocolonialism circulates as "post-" traditional articulations of European colonialism, scholars consider how contemporary US narratives of migration and discovery build upon a colonial infrastructure that was never entirely dismantled and instead continues to litter media culture (Ono 2009). Importantly, Ono clarifies that the "primary function of an ideology critique of neocolonialism is to explain multiple levels of oppression (race, gender, class, sexuality) and their connectedness, or 'webbed-ness,' as historically produced within the United States" (2009, 73). Jenny Sharpe, a professor of English, gender, and comparative literature, adopts a similar perspective with a slightly different justification. While Sharpe affirms that violent colonialism undermines post–civil rights, women's rights, Chicanx people, Native Americans, migrants, and Black[11] Power activists, she warns that naming these injustices as postcolonial disavows its past as one of White settler colonies and abducted African slaves. Like Ono, she worries that the "post-" dilutes the awareness of the continued injustice in the US context (Sharpe 1995).

Importantly for this book, Ono explains that representations of colonialism do not often appear in ways that alarm audiences; this is certainly the case for Curious George. "Representations stand in for reality; they are illusions or fictions of what could be, not evidence of what actually exists" (Ono 2009, 73). However, postcolonial scholars such as Edward Said, Raka Shome, and others have read colonial representations of media culture for years under the rubric of postcolonialism. Further, understanding how and in what ways US audiences come to interpret other nations and cultures has also been an important project for postcolonial scholars (Parameswaran 2002; Mishra 2007; Schwartz-DuPre 2010; Stabile and Kumar 2005).

No longer a British colony, the United States has become one of the greatest colonizing powers in the world (Huggan 2016). Institutionally and intellectually, the US has become a leading imperial power as a site of knowledge production. Including the US in the rhetoric of postcoloniality is central to understanding that one can be both a victim of violence and a perpetuator of it. Just as Curious George tells a glorified story of enslaved Africans, so too does it attempt to draw on the icon of the Holocaust hero. Having both narratives within the rubric of postcolonial studies highlights these complexities, contradictions, and conflicting narratives without apology or desire for congruity. I am not looking to negate Ono's defense of neocolonialism and its linguistic value; instead, I highlight the ways in which neocolonial theories are useful in order to understand colonialism, both externally and internally. Most contemporary postcolonial scholars understand that those deploying postcolonial terminology are not wedded to strict interpretations of European territorial occupations and avail themselves of multiple types of colonial violence and resistance.

Ono privileges neocolonial terminology over settler colonialism, the violent displacement of indigenous people by an oppressive invasive setter society, because the latter, he argues, implies that Western migrants arrived gently and lived peacefully. Consequently, it masks the "slaughter, subjugation and disempowerment of indigenous peoples" (Ono 2009, 14). As the cultural and literary studies scholar Clare Bradford strongly argues, "the trauma and disruption of colonialization continue to impact on the material conditions of colonized peoples. . . . At the same time, it is misleading to construct Indigenous people as victim populations, suffering the effects of colonization without agency or capacity for opposition" (2007, 9). Some advocates of settler colonialism also critique postcolonial scholars for ignoring the contemporary violence that continues to be imposed on indigenous people and for implying that indigenous life began with European invasion. While both of these arguments are valid, they also rest on a homogeneous understanding of postcolonial scholarship. Alley-Young argues that the study of postcolonialism should include the transnational experiences of indigenous peoples because "many North American, Pacific Rim, and European nations have a history of genocide, forced assimilation, and/or forced re-education of indigenous peoples" (2008, 308). The inclusion of indigenous studies in postcolonial scholarship highlights the ways internal colonization works. I do not suggest that scholars ignore indigenous studies; instead, I advocate for the recognition that colonialisms are diverse and sometimes oppositional. For example, postcolonial theory may offer indigenous studies explanatory frameworks and/or expansive terminology.

De/colonial theorists make up another constituency of scholars who oppose colonization and promote resistance. Decolonialization advocates often position themselves against postcolonial scholarship. Advocates of decoloniality such as Ramon Grosfoguel (2011) and Darrel Wanzer-Serrano (2015) aim to disconnect themselves from modernity/coloniality and to challenge Eurocentric knowledges that postcolonial scholarship does not recognize. They claim that postcolonial scholarship, produced and institutionalized by Europe and the

United States for their own consumption, ignores other Western territories such as those in Latin America. They call for a decolonization of postcolonial studies. Nelson Maldonado-Torres clarifies:

> The de-colonial turn involves interventions at the level of power, knowledge, and being through varied actions of decolonization and "des-gener-acción." It opposes the paradigm of war which has driven modernity for more than five hundred years, with a radical shift in the social and political agent, the attitude of the knower, and the position in regards to whatever threatens the preservation of being.... (2007, 262)[12]

The overarching claim of decolonial scholars is that postcolonial studies is entrenched in a Western epistemology that reproduces the very domains of thought and practice that create and maintain colonial power and knowledge structures (Grosfoguel 2011; Maldonado-Torres 2007). This constituency of mostly Latin American scholars (Mignolo 2007) understands the world as made up of heterogeneous global hierarchies that constitute, in Quijano's terms, a colonial power matrix. This matrix rejects the cultural/economic binary, and consequently represents a critique of colonialism, postcolonialism, globalization studies, political economic studies, and world-system analysis. Wanzer-Serrano acknowledges that decolonial and postcolonial scholars often end up on the same side of a given issue, but the method of inquiry differentiates these two paradigms (2015). Decolonial scholars consider postcolonialism as distinct from coloniality because the latter understands the continuity of colonial forms of domination after the end of colonial administration (Grosfoguel 2011). Maldonado-Torres explains that postcolonial theory

> denotes a political and economic relation in which the sovereignty of a nation or a people rests on the power of another nation, which makes such a nation an empire. Coloniality instead refers to long-standing patterns of power that emerged as a result of colonialism, but that define culture, labor, intersubjective relation, and knowledge production well beyond the strict limits of colonial administration. (2007, 243)

These scholars contend that coloniality rejects the postcolonial myth that the Americas exist in a truly decolonized period, post- or beyond colonialism. Instead, it affirms that postcolonialism upholds ideologies of Western development, occupation, and domination. Coloniality dismisses discourses of globalization and world-system approaches because scholars claim these theories are laden with Eurocentric knowledge, gender inequities, and racial hierarchies, and that they foster the expansion of capitalism (Grosfoguel 2011). For this constituency, the terminology reflects a radical distinction. For example, Anjali Vats (2016) uses the concepts of decolonial vernacular and de-Westernizing restructuring to advance critical yoga studies. In her project, Vats reads legal texts that use narratives that are entangled with European colonization but do not rely on European readings. Maldonado-Torres clarifies that a purely postcolonial perspective "promotes a fundamentally genocidal attitude" in which "colonial and racial subjects are marked as dispensable" (2007, 246). Coloniality scholars read both the present and the past as periods following a Eurocentric trajectory of knowledge and power.

Though coloniality theory often provides a useful theoretical framework, I do not adhere to its terminology because it singles out a particular group—mainly Mignolo's followers—instead of including scholars who approach colonialism from a variety of perspectives. However, I appreciate the Eurocentric and US/European focus these critics direct at the field of postcolonialism studies. Decolonial scholars can offer a great deal in terms of providing citational evidence from scholars outside of dominant US/European university structures. The postcolonial project is interventionist, and I echo Hegde's declaration that "the global moment does indeed present spaces for postcolonial analysis and reflection" (2016, 30). My allegiance to postcolonial terminology is grounded in the radical transformative scholarship that operates within distinct fields, whose methods are different, and yet remains committed to a multiplicity of methods that promote democratic intervention. This scholarship includes: postcolonial children's literary criticism, postcolonial cinema studies, postcolonial science and technology studies, and postcolonial nostalgia studies. I am not convinced that these ideas are completely incommensurable with decoloniality. As the professor of postcolonial literatures and culture Robert Young argues, the postcolonial "lives on, ceaselessly transformed in the present into new and social political figurations" (2012, 22). To consider the histories that make the present relevant is central to challenging colonialism in its various manifestations.

By focusing on a seemingly unassuming cultural icon in Curious George, I aim to chip away at the clandestine, omnipresent, and material colonial practices that circulate in popular and ordinary ways. This book is both a critique of universalizing existing postcolonial scholarship and an invitation for future postcolonial scholars to advance theories that include reading the past into the present—not through a single lens but through a matrix of anti-colonial perspectives that offer the possibility of operationalizing those theories into praxis.

The durability and resilience of postcolonial theory as an area of inquiry provides important possibilities for the reading and understanding of cultural

icons. This book reads the Curious George assemblage as advancing the ideology of US exceptionalism—the claim "that the US, like the King, and like
the State stands above the law because it dispenses justice" (Loomba 2015, 7).

Accordingly, Curious George is an important icon of study because he has
evolved through several decades of colonialism. To embrace this entangled
junction, I illuminate George's relationship to representations of colonial narratives of the past in the context of this cultural icon's circulation within and
beyond an assortment of media texts. The nature of a cultural icon's space/
time continuum forgoes the possibility of ignoring the cultural economy of
globalization and how it came to be. Instead, it illuminates the ways in which
icons manifest as ambassadors of US exceptionalism.

The publishing industry, public libraries, and educational institutions
play a powerful role in promoting imperial rhetorics. Mainstream children's
texts enculturate youth into colonial practices as future citizen-subjects. To
push against this limitation, the English scholar Pamela McCallum insists
that postcolonial scholars "must intervene, must take on the anti-oppression
work … [as] an integral part of the postcolonial project" (1995, 14). Postcolonial
readings of children's cultural icons and the texts in which they manifest are
among the many ways that postcolonial studies embraces the contemporary
global moment.

My keenness for this project was reinforced by my Jewish community's
backlash. My experiences sharing this project seem to suggest that the US public (especially Jewish adults), by-and-large, consider critics of *Curious George*
to be sacrilegious. "How could you suggest that Curious George participates
within a racist narrative," they asked, "when you know his writers escaped the
Holocaust?" At best, they were asking "how can a victim of colonialism also
be a perpetrator of violence?" At worst, their point was "how can you compare
(or perhaps deny) that the violence of the Holocaust was not the worst atrocity
known to humankind?" I was further provoked by friends who suggested that
their children loved Curious George in much the same way they themselves held
childhood nostalgia for the "cute little monkey." I read these fears as sentimental colonial nostalgia. The hybrid colonized and colonizer, as well as nostalgia
for the colonial past, are questions of great interest to postcolonial scholars.
These conversations motivate me; yet I remain engrossed in the discomforts
experienced through my critiques and analysis. Postcolonialism has chutzpah[13];
it is skilled at sitting in discomfort and engaging the murky, the hybrid, and
the untenable tenets of identity. Importantly, I make no claim to write about
the histories of "enslaved Africans" or "Holocaust refugee narratives"; rather,
I examine how these media events underscore United States citizenship. This
book extends beyond a specific academic community and should be valued

by an intelligent public that is invested in, skeptical of, and enculturated in the current ways in which occupation, colonization, and emancipation are currently articulated through the nation's cherished cultural icons. The conditions of today are constituted in part by the colonial articulations of the past, and thus cannot be understood outside of such readings. As Bradford explains: "neither the past nor the present can be imagined without reference to the other" (2007, 9). The colonial coordinates of the past remain vital to the conversations surrounding the occupation of peoples, places, ideas, epistemologies, and histories. From this perspective, the postcolonial is affected by the practices and discourses of colonization—past, present, or future.

Organization of the Book

The four chapters that follow critically consider the possibilities illuminated by postcolonial readings of the ever-popular US cultural icon Curious George. I argue that George, the captive enslaved and diasporically colonized African monkey, is recast as a STEM educator in film, television, and museum exhibits during a time when the US government argues that the nation's lack of pre-paredness in science and technology is in part to blame for poor US interna-tional leadership. The policy operates under the assumption that lack of global leadership caused the Great Recession and the COVID-19 pandemic; this has led to increased funding for STEM education. As an ambassador for STEM education, the familiar Curious George can attract children to STEM. Parents simultaneously feel intrigued by their nostalgia for George, trust him as their homeschool science teacher, and invest in his recasting as a Holocaust hero. In unison the STEM and Holocaust narratives neatly situate George within protected categories, immune from criticism.

Each chapter takes up a subdiscipline of postcolonial studies as a theoreti-cal lens through which to re-read Curious George discourses and exemplify how they support US exceptionalism. By doing so, each chapter advances the claim that postcolonial theories are capable of robustly reading contemporary texts and that they have great value in explaining how cultural icons circulate to make sense to their readers. I begin chapter two by considering the history of children's literary criticism and the relative lack of attention to children's books by postcolonial critics. One of my chief objectives in this chapter is to argue for a more robust re-reading of children's literature through a post-colonial lens. Curious George functions as an exemplar, demonstrating the gravity of reading children's literature with the same critical rigor commonly devoted to classical novels. It also provides a means to teach children how to be critical consumers of knowledge. Children are influenced educationally, socially, culturally, and politically by the literature they consume (Hunt 1996). Postcolonial literary criticism has a strong history of re-reading—viewing old texts with new enlightened eyes—and rendering analyses and explanations for the taken-for-granted epistemologies advanced through their narrative and circulation (Ball 1997; Bradford 1997 and 2007; Cummins 1997; McGills and Khorana 1997; Nodelman 1992).

Chapter Two reviews the minimal but important scholarship devoted to Curious George. Using this scholarship as a point of departure, I end this section with a postcolonial re-reading of Curious George books. The series of books continues to position George as a diasporic figure who dreams of returning to the jungle of his capture, while The Man in the Yellow Hat plays the role of either the benign colonialist or the pathetic, yet sometimes empathetic, father figure. Drawing on the emerging field of postcolonial children's literary criticism, I hope to contribute to an understanding of canonical children's literature as an important education mechanism that teaches a benevolent narrative about both US slavery and contemporary diasporic citizens. Curious George highlights the value of postcolonial children's literary criticism, not to encourage censorship or banishment, as is the case with some Dr. Seuss classics, but instead to embolden educators, parents, and children to read with a critical sensibility aimed at discerning how young people are taught to participate in colonialism.

Chapter three reads Curious George's cinematic and televisual discourses with attention to the ways that the Public Broadcasting Service (PBS), and numerous streaming platforms, deploy George so that he operates as a tool for educating preschool children about science, math, technology, and engineering. George's curiosity is the basis for connecting each episode with a STEM lesson. By historically situating science education, I consider how Curious George supports a US policy of promoting democracy through technology education.

Considering George's central character trait of curiosity as well as his materiality as a primate, I explore how postcolonial science and technology studies (STS) can offer a critical understanding of colonial history and current relationships between curiosity, science, and the contemporary commitment to STEM. These Curious George tales invite a larger and pressing conversation about the ways in which the US political push for STEM education has often compromised funding for the very humanities-based disciplines that seek to explore the colonial discourses that underwrite the present. I use postcolonial science and technology studies (Anderson 2009; Eze 1997; Haraway 1990; Harding 2009 and 2011; Seth 2009) to read critically the colonial grounds through which cultural icons circulate within contemporary politics. I accentuate the importance of cultural icons, the histories they embody, and the essential roles they play in popularizing and legitimizing contemporary scientific research agendas. As a result, both George and STEM policy come to share a common public. George's iconicity positions him through the narrative of curiosity, which has often provided justification for US exploration and exploitation. I conclude the chapter by critically reviewing the relationship between curiosity, adventure, and colonialism, and by considering the role monkeys play in the US imagination as well as how the public understands nonhuman primates through the rhetoric of enlightenment. Recapping the current political push for STEM education as central to global competitiveness, these narratives exemplify how and in what ways cultural icons such as Curious George garner public support for US policy.

Chapter four offers a re-reading of the popular narrative of Margret and H. A. Rey's escape from Nazi Paris. I inquire as to how the desire to return to childhood may explain the allure of Curious George's Holocaust narratives. Pazornik reports that these Curious George narratives offer viewers the chance "to share something they had as children" (2010, para. 49). I consider four whimsical narratives that recast Curious George on another adventure—this time as a Holocaust refugee: Louise Borden's *The Journey that Saved Curious George: The True Wartime Escape of Margret and H. A. Rey* (Borden and Drummond 2005); the Nebraska-based Institute for Holocaust Education's traveling museum exhibit entitled the *Wartime Escape: Margret and H.A. Rey's Journey from France* (Dotan 2009); the New York Jewish Museum's limited special feature titled *Curious George Saves the Day: The Art of Margret and H. A. Rey* (Jewish Museum 2010); and the documentary by filmmaker Ema Ryan Yamazaki, *Monkey Business: The Adventure of Curious George's Creators* (Yamazaki 2017). These accounts present George as a Holocaust hero and model US immigrant. While these narratives provide possibilities for education, they are regrettably foreclosed by their lack of attention to the horror of the Holocaust and their commitment to American power. I read these narratives as Americanized versions of World War II that privilege only a certain type of immigrant survivor. It not only promotes pride through a remembrance of strong US ethics, but also simultaneously expunges the small but articulate group of literary critics whose writing highlights the slavery narrative within which the story of Curious George first emerged.

I read the twilight aesthetics evoked by these discourses through a triad of nostalgic longings. The first claim is that Curious George's popularity can be attributed in part to the desire to ignore the terror of the Holocaust by replacing it with a jubilant memory of childhood innocence. Second, I consider imperial nostalgia in order to explore the public's yearning to dilute the horrors of the Holocaust into a whimsical tale of George's adventures while promoting a US reading of the Holocaust. Finally, a theory of postcolonial nostalgia throws into focus the curious and very troubling relationship between the modern-day George as Holocaust hero and George as benevolent slave. Here it is essential to remember that the violence the Reys endured does not justify the violence their books reproduce. The significance is that people can be victims of colonialism and simultaneously profit from it as well. While this hybrid colonizer/colonized relationship has been, and continues to be, false, the common insistence that individuals and communities constitute only one side of the binary is a dangerous form of deception that needs to be interrogated and expunged. Taken together, these readings defend the contemporary currency of postcolonial nostalgia theory, explain audiences' likely aversion to critiques of Curious George, and maintain that after decades of scholarship committed to identity politics and postcolonialism, the erroneous public sentiment remains that one cannot simultaneously escape the violence and perpetuate colonization.

I close the book by suggesting that George exemplifies the ways in which postcolonial theories can continue to advance vibrant and imperative conclusions of both oppression and opportunity when read in concert with cultural icons. Read as simultaneously a figure of children's education, an essential ambassador of STEM education, and a Holocaust hero, George's present circulation situates the cultural icon as a promoter of the current rhetoric of US American exceptionalism. While Curious George plays a huge role in this book, he also stands in for a host of popular cultural icons that circulate nationally. This reading offers audiences a way to map the complexities of cultural icons, the possibilities of postcolonial reading practices, and an opportunity to illuminate how contemporary colonization continues to pervade even our most delightfully curious childhood friends.

Chapter Two

Curious George Explores the Diaspora: Postcolonial Children's Literary Criticism

In 2016, Curious George fans around the globe celebrated the 75th anniversary of their beloved curious monkey and paid tribute to the myriad ways he has entered their hearts and enriched their lives (Dirda 2016). Classrooms for children of all ages lauded the broad circulation and celebrated Curious George books. As early as 1953, the New York Public Library Superintendent of Children's Work, Mrs. Eulalie Steinmetz Ross, reported that "all of the Curious George books have proved 'naturals' for the most handicapped (mentally and physically) of the deaf children" (letter from Ross to H. A. Rey, para. 2, in H. A. and M. Rey n.d., Box 64, Folder 4 [cited hereafter as Rey Papers]). The librarian also reported that the series "made an instant appeal with a different restless and sad group of displaced children from Central Europe" (para. 3). John A. Miller, Vice President of Teaching Resources Films (an educational service of the *New York Times*), wrote to the Reys recommending that Curious George stories be made into educational films because the books offered "innovative concepts," making them "unusually attractive and entirely practical in the classroom" (letter from Miller to the Reys, para. 3, in Rey Papers, Box 93, Folder 2). In 1977, Lucky, a Scholastic Book Club, listed Curious George as recommended reading for all second- and third-graders (magazine cover of Lucky, in Rey Papers, Box 110, Folder 10). In 1979, elementary teacher Annette Jaussig of Evanston, Illinois, typed a letter to Curious George illustrator H. A. Rey, asking him to reply to her "remedial reading" class's letters regarding their "special friend" George (letter from Jaussig to H. A. Rey, 1979, in Rey Papers, Box 68, Folder 3). In Hattiesburg, Mississippi, the de Grummond Children's Literature Collection maintains the H. A. and Margret and Rey Papers, which

Curious George doll in crib with baby. Courtesy of the author.

include thousands of similar letters from teachers, librarians, politicians, parents, and students, documenting and sending awards that signal their love and appreciation for the Houghton Mifflin series. From the original in 1941 to its current iteration, the Curious George series has been both popular and widely read in US classrooms, homes, and libraries.

This chapter makes the case that the Curious George book series, both past and present, fits neatly into the genre of colonial literature and accordingly benefits from a postcolonial re-reading. I make the case that postcolonial children's literature offers a significant theoretical lens for academics, educators, parents, and children to make sense of the cultural icons that they hold dear. One of the most important elements of this colonial genre is a subset of books highlighting a boy's hero/adventure novel (Shaddock 1997). This approach is especially relevant to the Curious George series because both The Man in the Yellow Hat and George play the role of adventurer: The Man in the Yellow Hat upholds a colonial narrative by traveling to the "dark" African continent, where he captures a brown figure. Historically, the Curious George story can be read as a slavery narrative. In its more contemporary form, Curious George can be read as a diasporic tale in which the central figure, George, performs his desire to return to his jungle home and place of capture. Using Curious George as an example highlights the value of applying postcolonial critique to popular children's literature. This re-reading process does not advocate for censorship or banishment; rather, it is designed to embolden educators, parents, and most importantly children to read with a critical sensibility aimed at discerning how US audiences are socialized and habituated to participate benevolently with colonialism. Reading texts through a postcolonial lens demands that readers make sense of these texts as integral in the fabric of ideologies. By considering a literary series with such extensive readership and longevity through a critical lens, readers can learn about how the beliefs, values, and practices of US American culture are manufactured and produced. The communication scholar Clare Bradford maintains that readers should begin to understand how texts position audiences to embrace imperialism, especially texts that situate young readers "as citizens of nations marked by the violence of colonialism" (2007, 225). Instead of defending Curious George as dismissive nostalgia or a sign of the times, I read Curious George as a colonial book starring George, a cultural icon who since 1941 has played an important role in training children about the customs and conventions of US citizenship and colonialism.

The first section of this chapter explores the significance of children's literature in teaching young citizens prejudice. In doing so, I attend to some of the racist US history of children's literature through the lens of postcolonial literary criticism rather than traditional children's literary criticism. This distinction highlights historical aspects of US literary criticism that are relevant to postcolonial studies, but often not explicitly named as such. This move places postcolonial studies at the forefront of critique. The primary audience of this section is not those well versed in the US history of children's literary criticism—these first few pages do not offer a distinct intervention. Though this review of citizens and organizations that advocate against racist narratives (primarily, though not exclusively, in the US context) is not exhaustive; it traces the early development of children's literary criticism to aid readers who lack familiarity with this history.

The second section considers the scholarship of Edward Said in order to review the important role critical readings of novels play in the construction of a postcolonial canon, and then offer a summary of the modest, yet momentous, genre of postcolonial children's literary criticism. The focus is primarily on postcolonial readings of dominant colonial books rather than resistive indigenous texts or counter-narratives. I do this not to downplay or dismiss the importance of colonial resistance or the tradition of children's literature as subversive (Mickenberg 2005), but to reflect on the ways in which a colonial book series, starring a cultural icon, can circulate for seventy-five years in US culture without significant critique. Doing so underscores the important role postcolonial studies can play in situating and critically considering children's literature.

In the third section, I attend specifically to the very limited critiques that consider the colonial narratives of the Curious George literature series. Reviewing these previous works outlines how and in what ways my reading of George as a diasporic subject and noble slave marks an important distinction from past readings. The final section draws on previous readings of George as a point of departure for my own postcolonial reading—one that differentiates itself by attending to the way past and present Curious George books might resonate with and replicate dominant ideologies. This critical re-reading situates Curious George within the canon of children's colonial literature by critically examining the literary series as a traditional colonial narrative—one in which young children can be taught to relate benevolently to the history of US enslavement of Africans and the contemporary role of diasporic individuals and communities. Through the re-telling of slave captures (in the first Curious George book), this series can do the ideological work of explaining, interpreting, and inculcating colonial histories for young children; consequently, it deserves and demands a postcolonial re-reading by both adult and young audiences.

The series stars George as a diasporic subject and features The Man in the Yellow Hat as a Western explorer who plays both captor and pathetic father figure. George's diasporic identity—a hybrid position that actively participates in a rhetoric of resistance—is illuminated by analyzing his profound love for animals, his continued desire to recreate jungle imagery, and his troubling yet enduring relationship with The Man in the Yellow Hat. This reading emphasizes the often overlooked commercial messages of benevolent colonialism that are reproduced in children's literature. Participating in such postcolonial re-readings enables parents and educators to introduce young readers to the important techniques of reading critically.

Few children's series have approached the scope and sales of the Curious George series. Despite its longevity and fame, just a handful of children's literary critics have focused on this series. The lack of critical attention is surprising, given that Curious George provides such a rich example to consider the influence of this beloved and ostensibly benevolent cultural icon of children's literature. Teachers have used George as an important pedagogical tool for US children learning about their national culture. While the cultural iconicity of Curious George has changed across time, space, and medium, the book series has remained relatively stable—the unaging curious African monkey is left alone in the United States to experience successive adventures. Each adventure affirms Curious George as an exemplar of colonial literature staring a beloved diasporic monkey. Yet, with the exception of the first 1941 publication, George's capture in Africa is never mentioned directly.

My intention is not to correct a wrong or to reimagine a history and replace it with a more accurate account of events. Instead, I acknowledge that no text is innocent or free from ideology. The *Curious George* series circulates alongside a plethora of past and present US narratives and tropes of colonialism—the enslavement of Africans, diasporic resistance strategies, scientific evolution, nostalgic narratives of World War II, post-9/11 tourism, and current US political and economic investment in Africa. This reading offers a potent example of using postcolonial children's literary criticism as a lens through which we can understand how a cultural icon, such as Curious George, performs through traces of the past while simultaneously ignoring the narrative's historical violence.

The term "children's literature" denotes literature written for children, not by children.[1] The larger purpose of this chapter is to use Curious George as an example that demonstrates the importance of reading cultural icons of children's literature with the same critical rigor devoted to classical novels. The ideologies that justify racism, sexism, and identity-based entitlements are not natural; they are learned. For many, this education begins with the ritual of story time. While the public reveres Curious George, his popularity demands intelligent critical and cultural attention. Postcolonial literary criticism has a strong history of re-reading—viewing old texts with new enlightened eyes—and rendering analyses and explanations for the taken-for-granted epistemologies that its narrative and circulation advance.

Intentionality

Some scholars argue that the intention of the authors (in this case, the Reys) should be considered when doing an analysis of the storyline or narrative. Yet the intention of the writers is not necessarily what audiences take away. Thus, the Reys' intention lacks relevance to a critical reading of the public's relationship with George. Whether these narratives coincide with the intentions of the Reys, or Universal Studios, or various reproductions is of little significance. I am instead invested in understanding both how this cultural icon has upheld its popularity through the various iterations of Curious George and why this incredibly pervasive figure remains relatively free of academic or popular critique.[2]

By unpacking how Curious George nurtures imperialistic narratives, I am not foreclosing other possible readings, nor do I aim to uncover any intentional colonizing practices by the Reys. This monograph focuses on the study of cultural icons and how they come to constitute and be constitutive of colonial archetypes and ideologies. My commitment to the text, context, and circulation of Curious George extends previous critiques not only because it attends to books written after 1966[3] (which other critics, such as June Cummins, do not), but also because it offers a reading that may or may not have been the Reys' objective. Instead, I follow a critical rhetorical model that rejects intentionality, as articulated here by John Sloop:

> Critical rhetoric places its focus on doxastic rather than epistemic knowledge. That is, rather than being concerned with knowledge of the essence of objects … or philosophical discussions about meanings, critical rhetoric is concerned with public argument and public understandings about these objects … critical rhetoric views its own writing as a political practice, an attempt to alter or shift public knowledge by illustrating how that knowledge has been constructed. (2004, 18)

Rather than the intention, critical rhetoric practices direct scholars to help explain how texts can position audiences. Accordingly, I understand a postcolonial rhetorical reading of George as a means to analyze and evaluate contemporary knowledge construction.

Like other popular literatures, cultural icons warrant readings that emerge from various genres of postcolonial scholarship; Curious George invites one such reading. I do not begin with positions like those held by the literary scholar Jennifer Shaddock, who claims that some children's literature authors are racist (1997). Instead, I contend that, "like a genetic imprint passed on from generation to generation," the narrative tropes and synecdoches of adventure in Curious George's book "cannot fully escape the vestige of sociopolitical meanings that the narrative structure" has historically served (Shaddock 1997, 156). The goal is not to uncover George's "real" story, but to read it with the desire to understand the ways in which cultural icons come to constitute rhetorically neutral, yet nostalgic representations of the US in the past and present.

Children's Literary Criticism

Children's books play a significant role in interpolating young citizens into the world in which they live. Critical scholars of children's literature encourage adults to continue to ask hard questions that undergird a reflexive reading: who is represented and how, who is absent, and what are the implications of their absence? While a complete account of children's literature is beyond the scope of this chapter, this section emphasizes that children's literature provides a significant, informative way young people learn who they are and what roles they play, or are expected to play, in their culture (Perrot 1997).

The ideology of the American Dream dominates most US-produced children's literature, and these books all too often negatively represent characters through inequitable narratives of class, race, sexuality, and gender. If books are to give children[4] a means to understand the world in which they actually live, then children need to become aware at a young age of the notion of social location by "uncovering systems of meaning that perpetuate social inequities" (Botelho and Rudman 2009, xv). Because children often desire to "see themselves reflected so as to affirm who they are and their communities are" (Botelho and Rudman 2009, 1), children's books offer important opportunities that create the conditions of possibility for producing socially conscious citizens.

Given the importance of children's literature, scholars, teachers, and parents should not only attend to their children's books, but also direct their attention to and re-read with a critical lens any series that span generations. The American studies and children's literature scholar Julia L. Mickenberg argues that children's literature has the capacity to "point towards solutions that affirm the possibility of reshaping American society and institutions to embody the nation's democratic promise" (2005, 57). Similarly, Jean Perrot, a French critic and emeritus professor of comparative literature, explains that the new international order highlights the need for more critical readings of texts designed for children (1997). Children's literature is all too often devalued (Hunt 1996). As such, highlighting and crediting pioneering individuals and organizations for developing the rich field of children's literary criticism is essential.

Formally, children's literature emerged around in the eighteenth century, although writing for children existed long before that. With exceptions, educators and librarians have historically considered children's literature to be outside or on the fringes of the literary establishment (Mickenberg 2005).[5] The period spanning the late nineteenth and early twentieth centuries is known as the Golden Age of Children's Literature. During this time, there was a surge in children's literary publications, including magazines and books. Though difficult to define, the concept of children's literature was and remains a powerful tool because it models knowledge for individuals who lack life experience. Literature interpolates children educationally, socially, culturally, and politically as citizens.

Just as educational policy and customs upheld the racism of the era, so too did children's literature. Scholars have documented the depiction of African Americans in children's literature back to the 1850s (Williams and Carver 1995). In response to the profound racist depictions in children's books, W. E. B. DuBois and A. G. Dill started a monthly magazine in 1919 titled *The Brownies Book*, designed for Black children to read about themselves and their culture (Ashmore 2002, 44). Even well-intentioned authors often perpetuate harmful stereotypes. Racism against African Americans in children's literature thrived during the 1920s and 1930s, and continues to be a problem (Ashmore 2010; Mickenberg 2005). Many contemporary children's books all too often eliminate characters of color altogether.

In the 1920s, Bertha Mahony and Elinor Whitney Field, early pioneers of children's literature, founded *The Horn Book*, one of the first magazines committed to children's books and reading (Horn Book Magazine n.d.). *The Horn Book* began as a timely effort to catalog children's literature and is cited as one of the oldest sources of children's literary criticism. However, critiques of negative portrayals of minorities continued to be ignored prior to the 1940s (Mickenberg 2005).

In the 1940s, the decade in which Curious George was first published, overt racism was prevalent in children's books. Literary critics did not widely recognize the racial bias that characterizes those texts, and several contemporary critics are still reluctant to draw attention to the racism. In 1949, African American parents appealed to education boards to discontinue the use of such overtly racist books as *Little Black Sambo*, though most literary critics did not recognize the problem. While many cities and states refused to discontinue use of these books, Toronto, Canada, and Lincoln, Nebraska were notable exceptions (Goncalves 1994). By the 1950s, *The Horn Book*'s third editor, Ruth Hills Viguers, recognized cultural bias in children's books and published Frances Clarke Sayers's famous critique of Walt Disney books, "Walt Disney Accused" (Sayers 1965). The critique represented a response to California's then Superintendent of Public Instruction, Max Rafferty, who had claimed that Disney was "one of the great American educators of the twentieth century" (Wojik-Andrews 2002, 36). A year later, Joanna Foster, biographical editor of *The Horn Book*, established a volume of select recommended children's-book illustrators that contained "biographies of the artists who have made significant contributions to the field" (Foster, 1966, in Rey Papers, Box 45, Folder 1). Interestingly, in February 1966, Foster wrote H. A. Rey requesting that his drawings of Curious George be included in the collection. The inclusion of H. A. Rey's illustrations in *The Horn Book*'s list marks an early distinction between books with negative messages and implications, such as those cited in Sayers's critiques of Walt Disney, and those with more celebrated narratives, such as Curious George. Early critical readings of children's literature published by *The Horn Book* set the stage for what has become the small but significant field of children's literary criticism. However, not until years later was there sustained attention to racism, sexism, and colonialism in children's books.

Some of the most important critiques of children's literature emerged from work promoted by the Association for Library Service to Children (ALSC). The ALSC has roots that date back to the 1900s (Association for Library Service to Children n.d.), but its policy focus elevated its status in the early 1950s. This division of the library association recognized the importance of children as an audience. The ALSC's mission was to empower librarians to become powerful advocates for children by providing them with library services and materials. Beginning in 1922, the organization began giving awards to authors of children's literature, most notably the Newberry Award. Named after the British bookseller John Newberry, this medal was one of the first US children's book awards, and it increased the prominence of children's books by recognizing "the author of the most distinguished contribution to American literature for children" (Association for Library Service to Children n.d.). Since then, the ALSC has expanded the number of their awards to include the Caldecott Medal, which honors the most distinguished American picture book, and the Pura Belpre Medal, which honors a Latino/Latina author whose works best portray, affirm, and celebrate the Latino/a cultural experience. Charlemae Hill Rollins, a member of the Newberry-Caldecott awards committee from 1956 to 1957, was an early critic of negative portrayals of African Americans in children's literature and taught one of the first US children's literature classes (Ashmore 2002). The sentiment was not that popular and in 1960 *Curious George Takes a Job* won the Lewis Carroll Shelf Award—given by the University of Wisconsin to books worthy of sitting on the self with Lewis Carroll's *Alice's Adventures in Wonderland* (1865).

While awards recognizing quality children's literature remain, some early critics continued to devote attention to books featuring oppressive representations. In 1965, Nancy Larrick published one of the most popular pieces of children's literary criticism, "The All-White World of Children's Books." Larrick argues that children's literature was predominantly racist and describes the whitewashing that characterized children's books and the books' flawed racist perceptions of African Americans at the time. She documents that only 0.8 percent of the 5,206 children's trade books published between 1962 and 1964 included an African American character (Larrick 1965). In her canonical essay, Larrick asks where the people of color were in children's books and spurred the "We Need Diverse Books campaign" (Nel 2017, 1). Also, in 1965, motivated by the civil rights movement, and concerned by the racist portrayals in school textbooks, Mississippi Freedom School teachers established the Council on Interracial Books for Children. The objective was "to promote a literature for children that better reflects the realities of a multicultural society" (Social Justice Books n.d., para. 1). This pioneering group took on issues of racism and sexism in children's literature. The Council developed *The Bulletin of Interracial Books for Children*, which served as a guide for school and library purchases of trade books and textbooks (Banfield 1998). As the organization grew, it established the

Racism and Sexism Resource Center for Educators, which provides guidance about ways to counteract racist and sexist attitudes and to promote cultural pluralism (Banfield 1998). While this organization has changed in form and scope, it remains an important advocate for quality children's literature. Founded in 1969, the Coretta Scott King Book Award is "given annually to outstanding African American authors and illustrators of books for children and young adults that demonstrate an appreciation of African American culture and universal human values" (American Library Association n.d.).

In the 1960s and 1970s, the growing influence of race consciousness demanded that public and educational institutions remove racist images. A small fraction of scientists and educators began to speak out about the harmful effects of racist children's books on the development of African American children (Goncalves 1994, 5). The impact of organizations protesting discriminatory children's literature led to the slow disappearance of some blatantly racist books; regrettably, the majority of these emptied shelves were filled with books that lacked images of Black people entirely. Invisibility should be equally unacceptable.

Children's literary criticism as a mode of resistance became increasingly popular in the 1980s, with the resurgence of the postmodern turn in literature (Jones 2006). Since then, multicultural children's literature has spent three decades advocating for more diverse representations of race and ethnicity (Mickenberg 2005). In the mainstream, children's books were not considered to be all that influential. They were not banned, censored, critiqued, or attended to, thus making them an effective way to "sustain cultural and political sensibilities" (Mickenberg 2005, 6). These books continued to enjoy a measure of protection and freedom from scrutiny. While some children's books offered positive representations of race and gender, most narratives continued to reaffirm the existing racist, sexist, and imperial social order. Much of the familiar children's literature of the twentieth century implicitly supports the individualist values of capitalism in the United States, as well as traditional gender roles, White racial hegemony, and middle-class norms. Some of it "is strikingly racist" (Mickenberg 2005, 7). Even when presented with alternatives, the general community often failed to read the more progressive books promoted by children's literary critics.

Increasingly, small groups are beginning to document racism in children's books and to promote alternatives. For example, since 1994, the Cooperative Children's Book Center at the University of Wisconsin has been documenting children's books by and about people of color. In 2019, they documented that more children's books featured animals as their main characters than featured children of color as protagonists (Black/African 11.9 percent, First/Native Nations 1 percent, Asia/Asian American 8.7 percent, Latinx 5.3 percent, Pacific Islander 0.05 percent, Brown skin 9.2 percent, White 41.8 percent, LGBTQIAP

3.1 percent, Disability 3.4 percent, and Animal/Other 29.2 percent—Cooperative Children's Book Center 2020). In 2006, the American Indians in Children's Literature organization was established to provide a "critical analysis of
Indigenous peoples in children's and young adult books" (American Indians
in Children's Literature n.d.). In 2014 the We Need Diverse Books organization formed out of frustration with the lack of diversity (diversebooks.org).
As the children's literary scholar Philip Nel explains, by 2017 the number of
multicultural books for children had plateaued. Only about thirteen percent
of children's books feature people of color—a statistic that has stayed fairly
consistent since 2002 (Nel 2017, 2). This absence is significant because it means
that many children only read stories about children who are unlike themselves.
Further, the whitewashing of children's literature is often the first place children
learn prejudice. The lack of representations of people of color leaves children
ill equipped to notice and critically respond to racist tropes. As Nel argues,
"children's toys, books, and culture are some of the most important influences
on who we become—and on what biases we harbor . . . or don't harbor" (2017,
16–17). What children learn from books informs the roles they play and expect
others to play in their society. Though as critiques of children's literature slowly
grew, so did postcolonial literary criticism.

Postcolonial Readings of Children's Literature

Postcolonial theory emerged not only by offering critiques of believed-to-be
great canons of literature, but also by emphasizing intersectional identities
and matrices of oppression to offer a vital foundation for re-reading children's
literature. Literary critics often aim to track "the meaning," "authorial intentions," and "historical accuracy" of texts. By contrast, scholars of postcolonial
literary studies

> consider how texts inscribe the shifting relations of power and knowledge
> evident in colonial and postcolonial societies, and in their discussions of tradi-
> tional narratives; postcolonial literary studies resist universalizing interpreta-
> tions, preferring to focus on the local and the particular. (Bradford 2007, 8)

Postcolonial readings offer constitutive criticism that strives to make sense of
how the cultural production of texts participates in the politics of colonialism.
Postcolonial scholars are determined to untangle and visualize the colonized
structures that situate understandings of culture, society, and politics. They
are interested in how "children's texts represent the experience of colonization

in the past and its effects in the present" (Bradford 2007, 8–9). Postcolonial scholars are skilled at articulating how texts construct the world (McGills and Khorana 1997). McGills and Khorana point out that the ways in which issues of "difference remain a backdrop hardly impinging on our consciousness . . . [and] the privileging of one group over another as natural. Postcolonial literary readings consider the construction of cultural identity; in doing so, they seek the acceptance of the Other" (1997, 12).

One of the originators of postcolonial studies, Edward Said, famously defines colonial discourse as "a text purporting to contain knowledge about something actual . . . such texts can create not only knowledge but also the very reality they appear to describe" (1978, 94). I have argued elsewhere that colonial discourses are not lies; rather, they provide an ideological apparatus that constitutes seemingly natural truths that in turn produce material realities (Schwartz-DuPre 2014). Postcolonialism does not create political movements that break from the colonial past; instead, it represents a "philosophical-cultural departure from the larger homogenizing logic of European modernity" (Ray and Schwarz 1995, 150). Don Randall argues that the knowledge system works "in part, by exclusion, and through exclusion it falsifies" (2010, 32). Rather than being understood as experience, the postcolonial lens is articulated as language (Bradford 2007, 9). Said's critical readings of classic literature provide important groundwork for the emergence of postcolonial critique (Bradford 2007, 6). His scholarship is useful for unpacking the ways in which literature produces a trajectory of realities that readers come to believe without suspicion.

Said's perspective on the importance of postcolonial readings of literature is a useful context for the emergence of postcolonial critiques of children's literature. In his major work, *Orientalism* (1978), he develops theoretical foundations for postcolonial readings of literature that claim to document "knowledge" about the Middle East. In *Culture and Imperialism*, Said expands arguments from his earlier works by extending postcolonial readings beyond the Middle East to "describe a more general pattern of relationships between the modern metropolitan West and its overseas territories" (1993, xi). Said argues that in nearly all cases involving Africa and the Far East, the West believes that it was bringing civilization to primitive, barbaric lands and its peoples. "They" (the colonized Other) were depicted as in need of the "gift" of Western development, evolution, and progress. While acknowledging the colonial practices of ethnography, historiography, philosophy, sociology, and literary history, Said devotes much of his critical reading to literary novels, which he believes "were immensely important in the formation of imperial attitudes, references, and experiences" (1993, xii). *Culture and Imperialism* documents the ways in which narrative fiction is intertwined with the urges to build empire.

Said argues that stories "are at the heart of what explorers and novelists say about strange regions of the world," (1993, xii), as well as a tool that colonized peoples use to assert their identity and resist occupation. The battle over imperialism, he maintains, is determined by the narrative: "The power to narrate, or to block other narratives from forming and emerging," is central to the constructive nature of people, cultures, and nations (1993, xii). Importantly, he admonishes scholars who maintain neutrality and suggests that not to "look at the connections between cultural texts and imperialism is therefore to take a position" (1993, 98) that supports and bolsters the dominant power. In short, to let the narrative stand unchanged and unexamined is to be complicit in a powerful constitutive act that supports the status quo.

The assumed ideological neutrality of literature enables imperialism, the belief structure that supports the literary occupation of people, places, and ideas, to flourish. These occupations, otherwise understood as colonialism, are facilitated, enabled, and promoted by an imperial mentality that cultural texts often advance. For example, Said critiques a commonly critiqued novel, Joseph Conrad's *Heart of Darkness* (1899), as well as works by not-so-obvious authors William Makepeace Thackery and Jane Austen, in order to highlight the deeply embedded ways in which novels are "fundamentally tied to bourgeois society" and central to imperial conquest (1993, 70). Said does not argue that these novels caused imperialism; instead, he argues that they functioned as cultural artifacts of social references that depend on the authority and power of existing structures. He explains that narratives have a

> regulatory social presence in West European societies. . . . Novels are pictures of reality at the very early or late stage in the reader's experience of them: in fact they elaborate and maintain a reality they inherit from other novels. . . . Today's critic cannot and should not suddenly give a novel legislative or direct political authority. (Said 1993, 73–74)

Said focused on nineteenth- and twentieth-century novels from imperial England because of their cultural affiliations to the domestication of India, Africa, Ireland, and the Caribbean. He extends the value of literature as a political and economic regulatory enterprise to genres that sustained the novels' imperial promises, which included travel writing, ethnography, and poetry. Along with other postcolonial scholars (Achebe 1977; Childs 1999; Jameson 1982; Rhys 1992; Spivak 1988 and 1999), Said cultivates in literary critics a growing commitment to interpreting the postcolonial project as a re-reading of literature in order to expose imperial infrastructures. His commitment to adult novels is significant to the development of children's literary criticism but not without critique.

Peter Hulme (1995) critiques Said's work by highlighting his preoccupation with the "Old Worlds" of Asia and Africa and his neglect of the European settlement of the Americas that began in 1492. A critique of United States colonial history helps to explain its current position in the world (Hulme 1995, 120). This critique is similarly true for Canada and Latin America. For Hulme, the postcolonial refers "to a process of disengagement from the whole colonial syndrome" (1995, 120). Hulme's reading provides an important means of expanding postcolonial theories to include US literature. Though Said and Hulme maintain their focus on the great works of literature and accompanying counter-hegemonic books, Perry Nodelman maintains that they devote scant attention to the role of children's literature and the constitution of the child as citizen.

Known for his 1992 article, "The Other: Orientalism, Colonialism, and Children's Literature," Nodelman gained public attention for applying Said's work to the narratives of children's literature. Arguing that children's literature is a site worthy of postcolonial attention, Nodelman claims that the production of children's literature benefits adults by teaching them how to engage with children. Mirroring Said's claim that novels serve the interests of the Western colonization of the Orient, Nodelman proposes that children's literature is dictated by adults, for adults, with the intention of "mastering the subject" (1992, 31). In calling for a critical reading of children's books, Nodelman includes works on children's psychology, as well as popular books adults read when they were young. He argues that adults use these books to restore their lost childhood and return to their image of ideal childhood. Nodelman ends his essay with a request—to ask of children's literature, and scholars writing about children's literature, "what does it do?" (1992, 34). This notion of doing avoids a consideration of authorial intention and instead directs attention to the ways in which children identify with literature.

Postcolonial scholars call for re-reading children's literature, especially those texts that protect and promote the colonial enterprise. Scholars may have overlooked these texts because most children do not engage with lengthy narratives or novels. Yet, as soon as young children begin listening to stories, they are likely to engage books that secure the imperial mentality and perpetuate colonial ideologies. Modern imperial contexts shape the representation of children. Don Randall, an English language scholar, explains that it is not surprising that "modern literature for children does much to shape and specify the child's being, doing, and becoming. In many texts ... children readers are called upon to learn and adopt certain sociocultural ideals and aspirations" (2010, 30). Simply, children's literature interpolates children to understand what it means to be a successful citizen. Children learn quickly what the expectations of their assigned gender are, how their socioeconomic environment directs them to behave, and what opportunities and obligations their skin color affords them.

Not all children's narratives come to constitute benign colonial mentalities. Yet, I contend that books such as those in the Curious George series should have a principal place in the canon of colonial children's literature. The series' longevity and broad circulation have done a great deal to teach children how to ignore the colonial narratives of African enslavement and diasporic identities that underwrite the collection by focusing instead on the wild adventures of a curious monkey. A postcolonial reading of this book series can focus more clearly on the assumption that cultural icons can teach young children and adults to participate in contemporary colonialism.

Postcolonial theory has much to offer a critical reading of children's literature (Ball 1997; Bradford 1997; Cummins 1997; McGills and Khorana 1997; Nodelman 1992). In some cases, scholars view children—the ostensible reading and/or listening subject of children's literature—as colonized subjects of adults (McGills and Khorana 1997; Nodelman 1992). This perspective is especially insightful when considering texts such as Curious George, because most children share with George a lack of agency. As McGills and Khorana describe in their introduction to *ARIEL*'s special issue on "Postcolonial Theory and Children's Literature," the role of postcolonial critics of children's literature is not to change a child's agency, but instead to clarify for children, and the adults in their life, how colonizing forces operate within literature (McGills and Khorana 1997, 8). *ARIEL*'s special collection was among the first to apply contemporary postcolonial criticism to canonical children's books, including June Cummins's reading of the first seven Curious George books.

Instead of reading children as colonized subjects, some scholars are more concerned with places: colonized, decolonized, or colonizing (Bradford 2007; Cadden 1997). This position is also crucial to a reading of Curious George because George's new home, in the US with The Man in the Yellow Hat, and his previous home, the African jungle, both influence his hybrid identity as a diasporic subject. Beyond subject and place, this re-reading offers possibilities of resistance produced by the literary narrative. Resistive texts have recently become a more prominent part of the relatively small genre of postcolonial children's literature. Yet, the vast majority of postcolonial critiques of children's literature are concerned with discerning the ways in which children become constituted as members of a colonialist culture. Curious George books offer a partially resistant perspective because George's affection for the jungle and other animals signals his refusal to fully assimilate into US culture. Curious George is a particularly interesting series to consider in this regard; while the overall narrative of enslavement and captivity is oppressive, George's adventures often pose as acts of resistance.

Though resistance is of vital importance, the vast majority of postcolonial children's literary criticism is committed to discerning how books constitute people as subjects who participate within and frequently extend colonial discourses. Postcolonial re-readings aim to analyze how children's books participate in the colonizing enterprise by offering powerful Eurocentric biases and patriarchal lessons (McGills and Khorana 1997, 8). Simply put, criticism can help people learn. By engaging with adults who ask children questions about the curious, troubling, or resistant aspects of texts, they can enable even the youngest child to have insights that expand beyond their initial encounter with books. Herbert Kohl's famous book *Should We Burn Babar?* insightfully explains that "children quickly come to understand that critical sensibility strengthens them. It allows them to stand their ground, to develop opinions . . . living according to conviction and understanding rather than being subject to the pressures and seduction of others" (1995, 16). The opportunity to expose children to criticism is reason enough not to ban canonical books like *Curious George*, even if they do advance colonialist narratives.

Banning books removes them from circulation and takes away the opportunity to read them critically. For example, Laura Ingalls Wilder's *Little House on the Prairie* (1935) not only remains popular but was honored by the Association for Library Studies to Children (1952) with an award in her name. At the time, a reader complained to the publisher objecting to the deeply offensive statements about Native Americans. In response Harper changed "people" to "settler" to satisfy critics and continues to publish Wilder's offensive descriptions of Native Americans and White settler manifest destiny. Recently, after years of complaints the Association removed Wilder's name from the award (Flynn 2018), but the book still remains wildly popular. Like *Little House on the Prairie*, Dr. Seuss's collections, and *Babar*, *Curious George* is a best seller, a children's classic, which adults often purchase uncritically, without meaning to impose colonialist narratives on children. Adults are hoping to share the experience of reading a familiar story with children (Kohl 1995, 17). While children may not be able to understand the various complexities implicated in these critiques, they should be introduced to strategies for challenging the texts they read, thus giving them the seeds to become what bell hooks describes as the enlightened witnesses (Jhally 1997).

Some scholars advocate amending racist books to make them more digestible and less offensive to contemporary audiences. However, this strategy is not only difficult, but typically fails because the altered versions rarely remove all of the insidious, microaggressive, or blatant racism imbedded into the narrative. Thus, it is important to challenge the erasure and/or amending of colonial characters, narratives, and chapters, because to do so is always already a problematic and ineffectual act. The benefit of keeping these books in circulation is that they offer readers the opportunity to cite and name imperial thinking and colonial acts. Working through the pain and pleasure of critically reading books that rely on institutions of bigotry and oppression is a way to teach young people to become critically sensible adults. "Teaching the original versions of these books," Nel maintains, "can help young people targeted by racism learn how to direct their anger," and it can "also make white readers aware of racism's pervasiveness and their own racially embodied selves" (2017, 26). Critically re-reading is especially important in the case of classics whose central character is already an icon that children and adults regard as innocent. I am not suggesting that writers should compose offensive books for critical practice; plenty of examples of problematic children's texts already circulate. Reading the classics in their original form but through a postcolonial lens can help young people understand how racism and injustice is taught from infancy. If parents and other educators encourage children to ask questions, then they can teach future citizens how to engage consciously in the critical process of unpacking colonialism. In the case of the Curious George series, adults could ask young readers "where do you think monkeys might want to live? What are the traits of a good father? Do you think The Man in the Yellow Hat is a good friend to George? How would you like to be George?" The answers to these questions provide the foundation for critical discussion. As children age, the questions change and the conversation can deepen. Asking questions about pictures and illustrations is another valuable way to engage children in critical thinking.

The Power of Pictures

Illustrations are important elements that differentiate most children's books from adolescent, young adult, and adult novels. Whether pictures anchor, relay, or contradict the words, children's literature relies on images to enhance narratives. In the instrumental early years (birth through three years) when most children cannot read, visual representations imprint stories in their minds.

Curious George, as a US cultural icon, focuses on a subset of children's literature characterized by its illustrations—picture books. Understanding illustrations in children's books is critical to understanding how children envision their literary friends. Some picture books contain written text, but the images anchor the words through illustration, and thus this is often children's (and even parents') sole reason for selecting favorites (Goncalves 1994). Images provide interest and connection between books and children in early childhood before they can read. These young audience members engage in a common practice of forming relationships with the pictures that capture the story and make it memorable. Illustrations are representational—they teach children about the world through their messages (Lechner 1995). In the early years, picture books fill a central place in children's education and enculturation; they connect the signified to signifiers, which in turn become the foundation of their cultural knowledge.

James A. Erekson, a professor of literacy, explains that the images in picture books tell a "complementary version of the story" (2009, 148). Peter Hunt (1996) further explains that pictures may be accessible to children, but the meanings derived from them are not situated in context. This insight becomes particularly important in the Curious George series. For example, in the first book, an explorer captures George, forcibly takes him to the United States, and happily sells him to a zoo. The image of African slavery might be apparent to some adult audiences, but for other adults and most preschoolers the association to African slavery may be ignored or missed entirely. Yet, the image of George choking in the burlap bag in which The Man in the Yellow Hat trapped him can direct even children to know that George is not happy about his capture. After reading through hundreds of letters sent to Margret Rey on her ninetieth birthday, I learned that writers of all ages were far more likely to recall the image of George swinging from a jungle palm just before his capture in the first book, than to remember the specifics of the written narratives that accompany it. The English literature scholar Robyn McCallum explains the value of picture books in cultural production:

> As both cultural products and cultural constructions, picture books reflect the culture that produces them, and they actively construct and canonize images of that culture. . . . Insofar as children's texts seek to enculturate their readers within mainstream society, these texts are an index of the ways that the dominant images of the culture are ideologically reshaped. (1997, 101)

While McCallum writes specifically about Australian children's books, her claim that picture books represent and construct dominant cultural values holds true for young audiences in most nations. Ideologically, images guide children to constitute their culture, nation, and community. In turn, pictures direct children to construct understandings of the roles they play or are fashioned to play as citizens.

The dominant impact of images is particularly germane to the Curious George series because of the ways in which George's articulation has shifted over time. Though children might first meet George in a picture book/literary series, since then he has starred in PBS's popular television series,[6] has appeared in four motion pictures, and has been central to games, products available on the internet, museum exhibits, and musical productions. Teachers, librarians, and parents regularly consider him an important educational figure. However, remarkably and perhaps suspiciously, Curious George has garnered very little critical attention from postcolonial or cultural critics more generally.

Understanding children's literature and specifically illustrations as an important structural vehicle for education is central to using postcolonial theory to re-read Curious George as a cultural text across space and time. Tracing both colonial and resistant signifiers embedded within Curious George narratives provides children with an example they can employ with other cultural icons they hold dear.

Existing Critiques about Curious George

Despite the popularity[7] of Curious George, only four notable academic critics,[8] June Cummins (1997), Joseph Zornado (2001), Daniel Greenstone (2005), and Ann Mulloy Ashmore (2002, 2010, 2012) have addressed this icon through critiques that focus heavily on the original seven books (H. A. Rey 1941b, 1952, 1957, 1958, 1963; Rey, Rey, and Children's Hospital Medical Center 1966). Their work constitutes the Curious George scholarship, but their arguments do not significantly attend to books published after 1966. Still, their critical analyses offer a launching point for my argument that in both past and present books George continues to live the life of a diasporic figure. My intervention extends and significantly develops the arguments advanced by previous scholars by proposing that Curious George's colonial history was not a sign of the times; instead, the colonialist scripts of the series reflect a current and evolving element within the canon of children's literature.

The literary critic June Cummins offers audiences the first and most comprehensive critique of the first seven books. She details the parallel between North America's cultural ambivalence toward slavery and the original Curious George book. She judiciously argues that the first book

> recalls the accounts of capture and enslavement undergone by Africans during the era of the slave trade. George's association with slaves allows us to position him as a colonial subject, and his relationship with his captor, the Man in the Yellow Hat, brings to mind parallel relationships, notably of slaves to masters and children to parents. Viewing George from a postcolonial perspective allows us to see how the book series reflects American cultural ambivalence towards its own colonial history. (1997, 69)

Cummins then explains how the original seven Curious George books adhere to a parallel narrative structure: George creates mischief because he lacks discipline, obedience, maturity, and civility; he saves the day in some way and receives praise; he then learns a lesson and assimilates to convention.

Daniel Greenstone, an English scholar, offers a similar reading of the first book, though he uses a stronger tone, describing The Man in the Yellow Hat as a "gun-toting" kidnapper (2005, 221). Like Cummins, he considers the limited life experiences of a child and explains the first volumes in the series as portraying "a protagonist who eagerly, and almost entirely without apprehension, confronts some of the most profound childhood fears imaginable, including physical danger, illness, abandonment and exploitation by adults" (Greenstone 2005, 221).

Training children to respect the authority of adults is a lesson that Joseph L. Zornado, a children's literature scholar, echoes. He argues that one of the implicit messages of Curious George is "that Western culture can fabricate a reality more suited to George's needs than nature itself" (2001, 127). For Zornado, the adult knows what is best for the child, for the child is, after all, just a little monkey, or an ignorant savage, and cannot possibly understand what he needs (2001). Thus, George reproduces the paternalist logic that predicates colonialism; if subjects are unable to parent themselves, in the name of the civilizing mission, others should forcibly do so. Cummins and Zornado agree that the first seven books have the potential to lull children into being complacent with their own and others' colonization. Yet Cummins's analysis extends beyond that of Zornado and Greenstone, because she considers the interaction between imperialism and civilizing practices of citizenship in the original Curious George books.

Cummins suggests that Curious George enlists young readers to the civilizing mission of their nation (1997). Linking Anne McClintock's (1995) study of imperialism, in which "savages" and "negroes" occupy the same space as male children, and Ariel Dorfman's (1983) reading of the popular children's book Babar, Cummins argues that Curious George books rely on the slippage between these categories—adult/child and master/slave—in order to encourage children to identify with George. Readers must, Cummins directs, "view how the books make use of those blurry comparisons to assuage American ambivalence" to our colonial past (1997, 72). Her connections fundamentally explore the ways cultural texts reify colonialism by teaching children, parents, educators, and librarians to ignore and/or rationalize the oppressive acts of its country's past and present.

Cummins identifies four ways in which the Curious George original series performs a sanitized and ambivalent slave narrative. First, The Man in the Yellow Hat tricks George into leaving the African jungle by enticing him with objects belonging to the White man—"many captivity narratives recount similar trickery" (1997, 72). Next, The Man in the Yellow Hat captures George and forces him into new circumstances that position George between horror and wonder. Third, just as slaves attempting to escape from bondage were shackled as their ships journeyed through the Middle Passage, so too is George shackled when he jumps overboard. Finally, as was the case with most slaves, George is restrained and imprisoned, first in a jail and then in a zoo. Cummins acknowledges that the conditions of George's capture were better than those of most slaves; however, George's tale provides a means for readers to interpret slavery as tolerable, if not acceptable. "Such ambivalence," she maintains, "marks the George series" (1997, 73). Drawing on Henry Louis Gates Jr.'s discussion of African American literature, Cummins proposes that George maintains elements of satire, irony, uncertainty, disruption, and reconciliation, yet fails to communicate them because he lacks the ability to speak (1997, 74). She draws parallels between the Curious George narratives and slavery by highlighting George's inability to communicate, suggesting that this deficit marks him as an Othered colonial subject. While many children's books anthropomorphically grant animals speech, George is "rendered voiceless precisely at the moment of capture" (1997, 74). Using similar strategies, slave traders separated slaves from other members of their language groups. George's "lack of speech is a constant reminder of his lack of power and place" (1997, 74). While I agree that George's muteness may limit his agency, Cummins neglects to mention the role of the omniscient narrator who conveys George's thoughts and feelings to readers. Though the narrator does not report the synecdoche of George's origin, the following section demonstrates that pictures and synecdoche do a great deal of that work.

For Cummins, the notion of place is also central to George's figuration. Like most slaves, George embodies a hybrid colonial subject. Cummins argues that "[b]ecause he is cute and cuddly, he is partially acceptable" (1997, 77). "But his blackness, or animalness, ultimately point[s] to and maintain[s] his difference" (1997, 77). While George continuously performs heroic tasks, his hybridity marks him as Other as his mood fluctuates between his longing to return home and his desire to fit in. Cummins cites instances in which George's escape is not literal, but takes place in his mind. In these moments, he is yearning for home through images and dreams. Finally, Cummins points to George's infatuation with African scenery, specifically his tree in the first book.

Greenstone's critique focuses on George's desire to return to the jungle. He points out that Curious George Takes a Job (1947) begins with George escaping from the zoo, jumping and leaping on and off a bus, running through a restaurant to steal food, scaling skyscrapers, and then returning to The Man in the Yellow Hat, from whom he takes a paintbrush and "paints a jungle scene with himself climbing a tree" (Greenstone 2005,). The book also illuminates George's former life when The Man in the Yellow Hat takes him to a movie studio and George signs a contract to make a film about his life in the jungle. The narrative essentially asks George to remember and relive those jungle memories. In his analysis, Greenstone points to the picture of George's jungle tree over the breakfast table as a reminder of George's capture. In spite of this obvious manifestation of homesickness, the Reys never explore these feelings. "Instead the scene is played for comedy" (2005, 223). Greenstone points to the evolution of the first Curious George series, suggesting that George's adventures become tamed or subordinated in order to teach children to adhere to the larger social aims of society (2005, 226). Greenstone's astute exploration of George's feeling about his jungle home and capture points out that the narrative of loss is central to the early books.

Ann Mulloy Ashmore, former Rey collection specialist at the de Grummond Children's Library, is likely the most well-published scholar regarding Curious George books and their authors (Ashmore 2002, 2010, 2012). Concerned about critiques directed at the series, Ashmore uses her historical knowledge of the Reys to defend what she believes was their anti-racist intention. The Rey Papers collection, Ashmore explains, "affords access to information earlier critics lacked . . . clues to their intentions, and . . . their testimony as to their motivations and goals" (2010, 358). By highlighting the Reys' mentoring relationship and great friendship with Jesse Jackson, Ashmore attempts to guard the Reys' reputation: "Of particular significance," she claims, "is the impact his [Jackson's] friendship had on the Reys understanding of the consequences of racist attitudes throughout America and within the postwar world of children's publishing" (2010, 358). What is remarkable is how the Reys' friendship with a prominent Black public figure (Jesse Jackson) becomes a reasonable and responsible alibi to defend the books' innocence and lack of complicity with African enslavement. The (patently absurd) logic is that a positive relationship with a person of color must necessarily negate the possibility of racism. This logic rests on a naive and simplistic view of identity that critical race theory and postcolonial studies, among other theoretical orientations, dismissed years ago. While Ashmore's desire to protect the Reys extends well beyond that of the other Curious George scholars, even Greenstone and Cummins try to make sense of the Reys' motivation. This is one essential distinction between their work and my own.

In divergent spatial and temporal contexts, Curious George functions well outside his creator's desires. Whether the Reys had conscious or unconscious beliefs about race when they designed George is of little consequence to the reading of a public perception. The Reys were heavily committed to progressive social and political causes including literary education, environmental and biodiversity preservation, and health and science education. However, postcolonial scholars such as Spivak (1988, 1999) have demonstrated the value of elaborating critiques regardless of the Reys' best intentions. These practices are instructive here, and support the proposition that regardless of purpose, Curious George books reflect and maintain a colonial narrative. While past readings of Curious George and the Reys are split in their interpretation of the books, both ignore the role Curious George plays as entertainment for children diachronically. The continuation of George's desire to return home positions him as more than an adventurous monkey. George is also a diasporic figure who is not assimilated to his current home and desires to return to the jungle.

George the Diasporic Monkey

Though Cummins argues that the original seven books resurrect racist slave narratives, I maintain that George's traumatic removal from the jungle continues to haunt him throughout the series. George's refusal to forget, and desire to return to, his jungle home positions him as a diasporic figure with the potential to resist. This longing is an essential part of the story that persists through subsequent retellings and recasting. Longing to return to a place or time that no longer exists as it once did is a central aspect of diaspora.

Diaspora is an ambiguous term burdened with context (Braziel and Mannur 2003). Although some claim it means to "disperse," the term comes from Greek, where it refers to "the voluntary or forcible movement of peoples from their homelands into new regions" (Ashcroft, Griffiths, and Tiffin 2007, 61). Its etymological root is *diasperien*, meaning "across" and "to sow or scatter" (Braziel and Mannur 2003, 1). The term "diaspora" is used to describe people displaced from their homeland as a result of colonization, migration, or immigration, often referring to Jews living in exile from Palestine in the third century BCE (Brubaker 2005). Scholars have also adapted the term to describe the Black African experience resulting from the slave trade (Braziel and Mannur 2003; Gilroy 1995). The theoretical discourse of diaspora has further expanded to include movements resulting from war or ethnic conflict, indentured labor, the postcolonial brain drain, and skilled and unskilled migrant labor in the global circuits of decentered capitalism (Bardhan 2011). The English scholar Jonathan P. A. Sell reads diaspora as a state of mind, an imagined state in which identity is discursively constituted to produce identities that appear likeable to ourselves (2012, 10). The immigration sociologist Rogers Brubaker argues that "one can identify three core elements that remain widely understood to be constitutive of diaspora"—the dispersion in space, orientation to the homeland, and boundary maintenance (2005, 5). Brubaker suggests rejecting diaspora as an entity, due to the changing condition of the nation state, globalization, and transnationalism. Dispersion, Brubaker explains, is the primary condition of diasporic identity. In his framework, the diasporic subject is forced—physically or otherwise—by conditions to relocate spatially. While I agree with Brubaker's rationale, Curious George, even in his more contemporary books, regrettably lacks such sophistication.

This reading of George's diasporic identity throws into focus both his captivity and his resistance to his captive condition. As Radha Hegde (2016) explains, the diasporic space "decenters binaries" of insider/outsider (2016, 17). This tension is evident in George's cultural identity; his initial muteness is continually performing stupidity for the comic enjoyment of his largely hegemonic audiences. Like the very young children who love him, George is rendered mute and lacks agency. Three resounding themes mark George as a diasporic subject. First, his longing to return to his African home and his inability to fit in to US culture spark his desire to be among and to free animals. Second, he maintains a preoccupation with the jungle environment in which he lived in advance of his abduction, namely the jungle tree he was swinging in prior to capture. Finally, his precarious and undefined relationship with The Man in the Yellow Hat, who is neither his master nor his father nor his owner nor his "friend," as the book repetitively directs. Read congruently, these three themes position George, both past and present, as a diasporic figure longing to return to his jungle home.

In the literary series George's diasporic subjectivity emerges through his affinity with and yearning to be with animals. Several Curious George books have a plot that centers on George's confinement, eventual escape, and search for some sort of freedom, either for himself or for other animals with whom he seems to share a special kinship. This theme continues from the early books to the present. For example, in Curious George Rides a Bike, from the original series, The Man in the Yellow Hat wants to celebrate the three-year anniversary of the occasion when he took George from the jungle (H. A. Rey 1952, 4). In this early tale, George is actually "stolen" once again, and forced to ride a bike in an animal show. In Curious George Flies a Kite, George gravitates toward a neighbor's bunny cage, freeing the rabbits from captivity (H. A. Rey 1958, 16). George's preoccupation with animals extends to more recent books, thus underscoring his standing as a diasporic figure.

In Curious George Visits the Zoo, he is intent on watching the monkeys in the cage taunt the little children (M. Rey and Shalleck 1985, 19–23). In a more recent book designed for toddlers, Curious George Hide-and-Seek, George only plays with the cat, dog, bunny, and squirrel (H. A. Rey 2008). Children's literature often anthropomorphizes animals; Curious George books resist this trend and the nonhuman animals are silent and often caged. At the aquarium, George climbs trees to be close to the fish (M. Rey and Shalleck 1984, 6). In *Curious George and the Puppies*, George is so fascinated with the puppies that "he had to pet one," so he opens the cage door slowly and they all escape (H. A. Rey and M. Rey 1998a, 14). In the end, George emerges as a hero for finding the last puppy and is subsequently allowed to take one home. Thus, when George is able to model his control by locating and returning the puppies, he is rewarded with the human characteristic of owning a pet. In other words, he gets positive reinforcement for signs of his assimilation. In the Curious George books adapted for television, George's only friends are animals.

In the Public Broadcasting Service's (PBS) nine serious television renditions of the later books, George becomes allies with the doorman's dachshund, Hundley. PBS's character descriptions consider Hundley and George as allies because they "have to work together" ("Character Descriptions," in PBS Parents n.d.). George's other regular animal friends include: Charkie, the cocker spaniel, who is "happy to get involved with anything George is up to"; Gnocci, the free-spirited cat; Compass, the homing pigeon; and Jumpy, the daredevil squirrel who "shares George's love of discovering new things" ("Character Descriptions," in PBS Parents n.d.). If animals are caged, George tries to free them, if they are free George regularly teams up with them. George's simian nature often overcomes him and he continually sympathizes with and works to free other animals. Read alone, each instance of animal camaraderie is part of George's many adventures; together they suggest an alignment with other colonized and displaced groups. Like so many diasporic subjects, George may never really escape or be able to help others in similar situations; yet he retains his desire to be with other displaced or caged subjects. In addition to being with animals, his diasporic identity is also performed by George's love for the jungle location.

Diasporic conditions presuppose a homeland orientation, suggesting a subject's value, identity, and loyalty toward his land of origin. George's infatuation with the jungle palm tree where he lived prior to his capture is the second theme, and it is perhaps the most striking element of his diasporic character. As the iconic reminder of George's homeland, the tree is a synecdoche for the jungle in its repeated representations. Maintaining collective memory or myth of the homeland and "regarding the ancestral homeland as the true, ideal home, and the place to which one would (or should) return" is a guiding principle that constitutes diaspora (Brubaker 2005, 5). The iconic image of the jungle tree remains the most memorable image of the series and is featured prominently in other iterations of George in museum exhibits, coloring books, memorabilia,

and in displays advertising his literary collections. The jungle tree appears
continually through the entire book series. Sometimes it is images of George in
his jungle palm eating a banana just before his capture. Other instances show
framed pictures of George being captured near the tree (these are common
throughout The Man in the Yellow Hat's home), and in other scenes George
is attracted to trees (in the park, zoo, or aquarium) that resemble his jungle
palm. The jungle palm is featured repeatedly throughout the entire Curious
George series and brand. This metaphor can stand in to mark George's lack
of assimilation to US culture and his continued desire to return to the habitat
monkeys are accustomed to—the jungle.

The visual rhetorician Elisabeth El Refaie importantly argues that

> the modes and media we use to communicate foreground or background par-
> ticular aspects of our embodied experience, a process that in turn has a profound
> influence on the metaphors we create. Artists working in the visual medium of
> comics, for example, are compelled to engage with the nature and limitations of
> human vision, making it more likely that they will use metaphors that draw on
> the experience of seeing or not seeing things clearly, regardless of whether this is
> an explicit theme in their stories. (2019, 4)

El Refaie divides visual metaphors into three types. For her, pictorial metaphors
refer to images of concrete, recognizable objects, scenes, and people that are
used to stand for something else. In the Curious George series, the visual representation of a monkey stands in for an enslaved African, and a jungle tree for
his desired location. She uses the notion of spatial metaphor to describe how
the position of and distance between elements in the story, and their relative
size, arrangement, and orientation on the page, may be exploited to convey
thoughts, emotions, or social relationships. For example, George is often looking up at the image of the jungle tree—above his bed or the breakfast table.
El Refaie considers stylistic metaphors as visual features such as color, form,
level of detail, quality of line, and/or visible traces of the means of production,
which are used to indicate an abstract concept or a nonvisual sense perception (2009, 16). In the Curious George series, a yellow jaundice color pervades
and presumably stands in for both the happiness George appears to have and
also the diseased relationship he has with his captor, The Man in the Yellow
Hat. Through the series there are several instances in which multiple visual
metaphors are used in tandem.

In the initial story, the jungle tree represents George's site of capture (H. A.
Rey 1941b). In *Curious George Takes a Job*, the monkey takes over for painters
on lunch and paints a whole room "into a jungle with palm trees all over the

walls and a giraffe and two leopards and a zebra" (H. A. Rey 1947). George even paints himself climbing the iconic tree from which he was swinging when he was first introduced to readers. Finally, George gets a job as a movie actor in a jungle, featuring his own captor. *Curious George Rides a Bike* begins with George getting out of bed in black-and-white-striped jailbird pajamas (H. A. Rey 1952). On page two, George is featured in just brown fur at the breakfast table with The Man in the Yellow Hat. Above the table is a framed image of George, the jungle tree, and the yellow hat. The framed scene is right out of the first Curious George book. The Man in the Yellow Hat points to the image. The text reads "Today we are going to celebrate because just three years ago today I brought you home with me from the jungle. So tonight, I'll take you to the animal show" (H. A. Rey 1952, 2). The references to George's abduction and desire to be with animals is direct and framed, most literally, with the jungle tree.

In *Curious George Gets a Medal*, after freeing the pigs from the farm, George jumps into the dinosaur exhibit in the museum to climb the iconic jungle tree (H. A. Rey 1957). In *Curious George Flies a Kite*, George frees bunnies and flies with a friend's kite into a tree (although the tree is not a palm), from which he has to be rescued by The Man in the Yellow Hat (H. A. Rey 1958). When *George Learns the Alphabet*, the letter "J" features a jaguar looking up at the iconic jungle tree. The caption reads "Jaguars live in the Jungle. George knew Jaguars. He had lived in the Jungle once" (H. A. Rey 1963). In the last of the original books, *Curious George Goes to the Hospital*, George literarily swallows his past (M. Rey, H. A. Rey, and Boston Children's Hospital Medical Center 1966). During the initial scene, The Man in the Yellow Hat helps George put together a puzzle, featuring an image from the first book in which George is being tempted by the Man in the Yellow Hat's hat (he had placed it on the ground to coax George out the jungle tree so that he could capture George). Watching himself gazing at the scene in his past, George decides to eat a piece of the puzzle. George gets sick because he swallowed a piece of the puzzle depicting this past. Even his consumption of the past does not rid him of its memory.

In the more recent books, George continues to be obsessed with the jungle environment, a memory of the homeland. *Curious George Goes to an Ice Cream Shop* begins by telling the reader "George and his friend [referring to The Man in Yellow Hat] were cleaning the house" (M. Rey and Shalleck 1989a). Near the written text there is an image of George and The Man in the Yellow Hat sweeping a bedroom. Everything in the bedroom is yellow, peachy-brown, and blue except the framed picture image of the jungle tree above George's bed. It is likely George's room because there is a bowl of bananas on the table. As it was in the original 1941 book, the picture is the same—a green and brown depiction of the iconic palm tree. Representations of the jungle emerge as subtle reminders of his past, typically when George is engaged in "civilized" activities in the modern world, such as watching a movie or participating at school.[9] Whether picking out a Christmas tree or fishing, George repeatedly gives in to his instinctive need to swing through trees (Hapka, Rey, and Young 2006; H. A. Rey 2001). On his birthday, George's animal friends decorate The Man in the Yellow Hat's house with jungle tree decorations and invite George to play pin-the-tail-on-the-zebra (H. A. Rey and M. Rey 2003). In *Curious George Goes to a Movie*, The Man in the Yellow Hat suggests they see a dinosaur movie (M. Rey and H. A. Rey 1998). As usual, the man leaves George alone (in this instance, he leaves to get some popcorn). George, who was watching the film alone, gets spooked by the on-screen dinosaur. Seemingly, George's affinity for animals does not extend to prehistoric predators. In the book's illustration of the movie screen, readers can see the dinosaur's big tail whisk past and nearly hit a jungle tree just like George's. Once again, the iconic jungle palm tree appears. Three pages later, after George makes his way up to the projection booth, he scares the boy in charge of the film reel. The boy jumps, knocks the reel down, and George leaps into the movie window, using the light from the projector to create shadow animal puppets. George uses his hands to create shadows of less threatening animals—a bunny, a duck, dogs, a bird in flight—and finally he uses his own shadow to entertain the movie audience. This tale exemplifies, once again, the enduring, recurrent trope of the African jungle tree. Yet, this instance of discomfort is eased by creating shadow images of animals. There are many other instances in which his love for animals helps ease George's grief at the loss of his jungle home.

In *Curious George's Dream* (H. A. Rey and M. Rey 1998b), George sits down to eat after a disappointing day at the amusement park. He had been too small to ride the rides unaccompanied (which leads the reader to assume that The Man in the Yellow Hat was once again absent), and his hands had been too small to hold the bunnies at the petting zoo. After dinner, The Man in the Yellow Hat surprises George with a movie. Judging from the illustration of the television screen, George is watching a movie resembling *King Kong* (Cooper and Schoedsack 1933). The narrator explains: "George was enjoying the movie, but it had been a full day and now he had a full stomach. Soon he could not keep his eyes open," and just as the movie shows the large gorilla holding up a screaming lady next to the iconic palm, George falls asleep. The movie imagery is important; it is a scene of familiarity, another primate and the beloved jungle palms. As George sleeps, readers are positioned to watch his anxiety play out in his dream.

George "was back at the petting zoo" (H. A. Rey and M. Rey 1998, 7–10)! "But this time something was different. The petting zoo was too small. In fact everything was small" (1998, 10). The illustration shows a big Curious George sleeping and propped up against a tree.

> Maybe he was big . . . then he remembered the bunnies. Why, he was not too small to hold a bunny . . . he went to the bunny hutch. Now George could hold LOTS of bunnies, and he cuddled them to his face. The bunnies liked George . . . but the manager of the petting zoo did not. "Put those bunnies down," she said. "You'll scare them. You are too Big." (1998, 11–13)

In his dream, George's greater size enabled him to find comfort with other animals; his size also became a problem, as it does for the gorilla in *King Kong*. Even in George's dream he did not fit in. He was still not allowed to be with other animals; in fact the people at the park became frightened of big George and ran away from him. He "felt awful" and "lonely" (1998, 13–15). When The Man in the Yellow Hat appeared in the dream, George was at first relieved, only to realize then that he was too big to go with the man. George was disappointed again—until he wakes up from his dream to realize he is no longer big. The tension between his desire to be with his protector/captor, The Man in the Yellow Hat, and the denial of his access to the animals to which he is akin, replicates a colonial theme of the complex colonizer/colonized relationship.

Though big George is positioned as his dream, a scene of the apes and the jungle palm continues to mark George's diasporic anxiety of not fitting in, of being unassimilable, of being too alien. Readers learn of his fear, the inability to be comfortable and be the right type and size. Arguably, this is a point of connection with diasporic individuals and with some young readers who may feel uneasy about their inability to do what bigger people can do. George's dream suggests that growing up is not a solution to diasporic loss. One moral is perhaps that readers who are different might never fit in—unless of course they are the tall, white-skinned, and male explorer type. The theme of assimilation to nonnative home continues.

Curious George Says Thank You tells a tale of all the people to whom George can send Thank You cards (H. A. Rey, and Margret Rey 2012). He gathers tons of paper, envelopes, crayons, and stickers. On the second page, the text reads at the top "The Man in the Yellow Hat walked in to find George covered from head to toe . . . 'Oh-oh, George! What are you doing?'" (2012, 8). The illustration from left to right features a concerned-looking man dressed in yellow, a green desk, George covered in stickers, his supplies strewn all over, and a familiar image above the desk. Framed in yellow, there is the scene from the 1941 book of George and his jungle palm and the yellow hat. The placement of the desk chair suggests that the framed picture would not face The Man in the Yellow Hat when he sits at his desk, as a beloved family picture often does. Instead, it faces whomever The Man in the Yellow Hat is talking to across the desk, as would a diploma, certificate of accomplishment, or trophy. The idea of showing off a trophy or animal bust, in this case George, captured on an adventure is a common trait of explorers. It is also evidence that though The Man in the Yellow Hat may at times be nice to George, the book upholds a common colonial narrative in which George figures as The Man's captured trophy, a noble slave with intelligence inferior to the White man. In many cases, George's "adventures" and "curiosity" literally become the White man's burden. The Man in the Yellow Hat agrees to help George with his Thank You cards. The man sits in his desk chair with George on the other side of the desk, facing the framed illustration. While the image is not mentioned in the book, it is a subtle inclusion (as it is in most books). After delivering all his Thank You cards, "George has one more very special Thank You card to deliver. He had saved the best for last!" On the last page of the book George hands The Man in the Yellow Hat a card. Though there is no mention of what it says, the gesture that while George may love his jungle palm, like a noble diasporic icon, he is making efforts to assimilate. Further efforts to assimilate can be read in other Curious George books.

In *Curious George Goes to School*, George paints a jungle palm with a simple and small bald-headed figure at the tree's trunk (Rey and Shalleck 1989b). The art teacher hangs it on the wall next to a picture of a blonde White girl riding a white horse. The contrast of the girl riding a white horse and the jungle once again illuminates the colonial conquest of White explorers riding into the native jungles. In *Curious George Visits the Library*, he is intrigued by the librarian who is reading a book about singing bunnies (Rey, Rey, and Weston 2003). He climbs up on a table of books, bypasses the book about the jungle, and instead opts for a book about dinosaurs. After collecting other books about trucks, elephants, and planes and engaging in some antics, he checks the books out. Another girl checks out the book titled *Jungle*. In both the book and the television version, when faced with the decision to choose a library book with a picture of himself in the jungle or a picture of a dinosaur, George opts for the latter. This library encounter marks a distinct sign of diasporic identity, one in which the subject sometimes resists its own desire for a return to the homeland that the rational mind knows cannot take place.

In a more recent volume, *Curious George's Big Adventures*, the only human is The Man in the Yellow Hat; all of the other characters are jungle friends (Anderson et al. 2006). George's room is painted to look like the jungle; however, the author describes the monkey as experiencing adventure only after he left his animal friends in Africa. In these instances, George presents for readers the conditions of possibility of choosing to be happy, situating him neatly in a long history of the cheerful slave trope, popular in US children's literature (Nel 2017, 218) and colonial novels such as *Uncle Tom's Cabin* (Boulukos 2008; Stowe 1852). When George chooses against his jungle book, he vacillates between depictions of freedom and oppression throughout the narratives; he embarks on new adventures in the modern American landscape while simultaneously gravitating toward what reminds him of his former life and land.

The jungle, the place The Man in the Yellow Hat or narrator describes as George's place of origination, has traditionally pejorative connotations. Derived from the Hindi (from Sanskrit) term *jangala*, "jungle" is defined by the *Oxford English Dictionary* as "waste or uncultivated ground ... as the dwelling-place of wild beasts." This connotation is important to the colonial narrative in which George is "saved" from the wild. The original images may have been representative of the 1940s and 1950s, when jungle pictures were particularly popular in the United States (Foster 1999, 42–43). However, midcentury fashion does not explain the continued deployment of George's obsession with jungle imagery.

As with many colonial representations, the inclusion of the iconic jungle palm remains a subtle marker of George's origin. Yet the Reys' fan mail suggests that children think otherwise. Starting in the 1950s, the Reys where inundated with fan mail, most of which Margret Rey kept. While mail came from everywhere, elementary school students, teachers, and librarians sent the majority of letters and drawings. Throughout the years, the letters covered a range of topics and book titles; the bulk of students writing to the Reys focused their drawings on George and the iconic tree from which he was first taken. Later examples (from after the 1980s) demonstrate that George's relationship to the jungle was not a memory of the past, but a recent connection made by contemporary readers. For example, in 1988, a second-grader named Adina[10] sent a drawing of George in a palm tree, with The Man in the Yellow Hat approaching. Her classmates, Melissa, Greg, Ashley, and Brent sent similar depictions (Rey Papers, Box 69, Folder 2 [Ashley], Box 68, Folder 1 [Brent, Greg, Melissa]). In 1991, students Sean, Marie, and Mathew, from various schools, wrote Margret to wish George a happy birthday and sent similar drawings (Rey Papers, Box 68, Folder 4). As late as 1994, Margret Rey got fan mail with a drawn picture of George's capture near the iconic jungle palm from Wisconsin kindergartener Bobby Parkinson.

These examples demonstrate that even seventy years after his original capture, his youngest fans still understand George's love for the African jungle. George in the jungle tree is arguably the most iconic image in the series. Houghton Mifflin's free teacher guide and learning materials "Curiosity Kit" includes a connect-the-dots activity featuring George in his jungle tree Houghton Mifflin Harcourt 2015b). The publisher's Teacher Vision program, which offers teachers lesson plans to help their students explore this literature, also includes a George's Mural printable resource (TeacherVision 2008.). Featured prominently on Curious George collections' covers and in students' drawings, illustrations continue to focus on George's capture by The Man in the Yellow Hat and jungle images of the tree where George swung in the vines and happily ate a banana before the moment of his capture. The pride exuded by The Man in the Yellow Hat at framed images of the capture provides a digestible way for audiences to justify George's capture as acceptable if not admirable. This type of reading offers Curious George fans a benevolent acceptance of colonialism. Such benevolence is especially dangerous because its echoes historical violence, yet repositions it as for the good of the colonized. Understood as a gift, the desire to be kind, generous, or charitable, benevolence's roots (according to the *OED*) stem from "the desire to promote the happiness of other . . . [or] contribution for the support of the poor." The rhetoric of benevolence is integral to the practice of colonialism because it categorizes the occupation of peoples homelands as necessary and inherently good for its subjects. In this rhetoric, occupation of people and land are almost always justified as for the good of the colonized. Benevolence is integral to the imperial project and thus is the ideological justification for the physical colonization of the Other. Gilbert and Tiffin trace the history of benevolence, arguing that "benevolence has been a rather expansive and even ambiguous concept over centuries, as benevolent practices and principles have been adapted to respond to particular cultural, political, social, religious, and economic imperatives" (2008, 7). Colonizers have an extensive list of "gifts." Such reprehensible "gifts" include the 1924 Supreme Court decision of Buck v. Bell, which justified the forced sterilization of the poor, mentally ill, and disabled to promote eugenic initiatives, claiming "It is better for all the world, if instead of waiting to execute degenerate offspring for crime, or let them starve for their imbecility, society can prevent those who are manifestly unfit from breeding their kind" (Disability Justice 2020). Another repugnant "gift" example is the sexual enslavement of Japanese women, commonly known as "comfort women," who were forcibly raped by Japanese and American men in the 1930s and 1940s to "ease the anxiety of soldiers before and after battle" (Soh 2009). Even the US invasion of Afghanistan was rhetorically posed as a moral obligation to "save victimized women" (ironically, something the US only cared about during the retaliation for 9/11). Simply, the vicious suggestion of colonial benevolence is that once occupied people give their new circumstances a try (by choice or by force), they will assimilate and appreciate that the colonizer did them a favor.

This brief understanding of benevolence is central to a reading of Curious George books. George's original capture, a recurring theme in the series, can be read or viewed by young children as an effort to free George from his life in the jungle, or even an opportunity for The Man in the Yellow Hat to bring the monkey to the promises of the American dream. Named by The Man in the Yellow Hat after the US's first President, George maintains an obsession with the jungle tree, which is, as I understand it, a sign of his diasporic longing to return to his homeland. A benevolent reader might read the jungle tree as evidence of his primitive life prior to his capture. The Man in the Yellow Hat could even be read as doing George a favor, since he assured the little monkey that he would be "happy in the zoo" (Rey 1941b). These benevolent readings could dangerously extend to almost all of George's adventures because his jubilant attitude and friendly demeanor can be, and often are, read by immature audiences as a sign of his successful assimilation. All too often, adults and even educators have been acculturated to support these benevolent colonial readings of Curious George, or perhaps they would rather not be burdened by offering children, who love the curious adventures, the metaphorical reading of George the diasporic captive stuck in the US against his will.

The remedial reading of George as jubilant upholds an extension of the benevolence of colonialism. Though some academic critics have attended to the first book as problematic, the vast majority of the attention given to George from the 1940s to the present has been positive. His cuddly demeanor and silly antics either disavow his introduction or position audiences to understand this icon as a joyful recipient of US life. However, my reading of George as a diasporic icon supports an extension of colonialist benevolence by suggesting that George's assimilation to life outside the jungle is not only imperfect, but is rather repetitively problematized. The very coordinates of George's cultural iconicity uphold the disingenuous nature of benevolent colonialism. First, he is a monkey, understood by Western standards as an inferior mammal, and though he is the protagonist of all his adventures, he is entirely denied a voice, and his thoughts are presented by an all-knowing narrator. Second, George is consistently curious about even the basic aspects of life. These narratives, in my reading, reject a benevolent colonial position by detailing how George performs a denial of contentment with US culture. The monkey's desire to free animals, his fixation with jungle palm trees, and his tumultuous relationship with The Man in the Yellow Hat are evidence of his dissimilation to US life. Yet, the metaphor of George as slave is powerful because it supports a whitewashed and repulsive reading of slavery often articulated by US cultural icons. The suggestion is that the White man's colonial acts are "not so bad" because they are for the benefit of burlap-bagged beasts.

A benevolent reading of George is also likely to resonate with young children who, while sometimes disagreeing with their parents, grow up to understand

the benefits of parental control. The images of George's playfulness and innocence mimic those of a child. As such, he lacks agency. Like his young readers,
he is controlled and contained because his lack of capacity to care for himself
require others to care for him. However, unlike children who grow to perform
obedience, George, is perpetually infantile. He never ages and remains contained in a youthful state of innocence in which he embarks upon numerous
adventures, taking on American activities that habitually get him in trouble
Thus, he is forever indebted to his captor, The Man in the Yellow Hat, for saving
him. Importantly, this effort to persistently try to do as others do (fish, cook,
work, vote, etc.) can be read as a performance of benevolent assimilation—an
honest submission to his current condition in exchange for protection by The
Man in the Yellow Hat.

Benevolent assimilation of colonized people has long been a guiding principle
of US foreign policy. For example, in 1898 after US forces had defeated Spain,
President William McKinley issued the Benevolent Assimilation Proclama-
tion, declaring that the "inhabitants of the Philippine Islands" would benefit
from the United States' "benevolent assimilation." "In fulfillment of this high
mission," McKinley pronounced,

> supporting the temperate administration of affairs for the greatest good of the
> governed, there must be sedulously maintained the strong arm of authority, to
> repress disturbance and to overcome all obstacles to the bestowal of the blessings
> of good and stable government upon the people of the Philippine Islands under
> the flag of the United States. (Cadden 1997)

A similar message remains central to US immigration policy in 2020. President
Trump's merit-based immigration policy denies entry to individuals who are
unwilling or unable to enhance the US economy and conform to the US's ideologically technical growth mentality. Assimilation into US culture, even if by
force, remains a mission of the colonial project. George's refusal to assimilate
fully positions him as a diasporic figure with a troubled relationship to his owner.

Since tricking George into a burlap bag and taking the monkey from Africa
to the United States, The Man in the Yellow Hat is the only other primary
and recurring character in the series. Yet curiously, none of the scholars who
examine the series devote much attention to The Man in the Yellow Hat as the
quintessential colonial explorer. As George's captor and negligent paternal
master, The Man in the Yellow Hat provides George with a third constitutive
criterion of diaspora—boundary maintenance. According to Brubaker, boundary
maintenance involves "a preservation of a distinctive identity vis-à-vis a host
society" (2005, 6). George's condition never changes; he never speaks directly to

readers, he never gets more skilled in the traditions and habits of the US, and, what is more, he never ages. He never overcomes his hybrid existence when each episodic narrative begins with a new story, independent from the last. The Man in the Yellow Hat never treats him differently; George never learns the language and never grows in body or mind. Static in both time and age, George finds himself reiterating the same mistakes and failing to learn the same assimilative moves. In the literature series, George's relationship to The Man in the Yellow Hat never changes.

As is the case with many colonial narratives, the male explorer stands in for the heroic father and master of the land that he is brave enough to traverse and to which he has the courage to return. While some explorers take an indigenous treasure or woman, The Man in the Yellow Hat takes a monkey which he names George, after George Washington. Characterized by his wide-brimmed yellow hat, he is the companion and (often ineffectual) caretaker of Curious George. Featured in every book, The Man in the Yellow Hat always appears the same. He is a tall, White man with dark hair and eyes, and he always wears a bright yellow, *National Geographic*–style explorer ensemble. If he is not wearing a yellow jacket, The Man in the Yellow Hat's sunny yellow collared shirt is almost always accompanied by a yellow tie or scarf, a belt, and three-quarter length safari-style yellow pants, with brown, antique army-style, calf-length boots.

The Man in the Yellow Hat lives alone (until he moves George in), and his New York doorman-attended apartment, house in the country, convertible car, and frequent visits to Pisghetti's Ristorante suggest that The Man in the Yellow Hat is wealthy. In the book series, he is never working and never with friends or romantically involved. The Man in the Yellow Hat represents an exceptional character. He replicates his role in book after book as the quintessential White hunter/savior of the colonial narrative, always present at the end of the book to rescue George or celebrate his heroic act. The narrator or other characters refer to The Man in the Yellow Hat as George's "friend," but his role is more that of a deadbeat fatherly character who provides a continued reminder of George's curiously persistent diasporic condition. George is never completely his slave, nor entirely his child, and he is too functional to be a pet. However, echoing other diasporic figures, George is noble and seems to care a great deal for The Man in the Yellow Hat, even though The Man in the Yellow Hat is continually absent. As is true for most colonial missions, the mother country "becomes valorized as a place of 'positive values, good climate, harmonious landscape, social discipline and exquisite liberty, beauty, morality and logic'" (Ball 1997, 176). Instead of citing The Man in the Yellow Hat's continued absence or negligence in his role as educator or parent, fans of Margret Rey write numerous letters to her advising George to do a better job of listening to The Man in the Yellow Hat's instructions.

Fans read The Man in the Yellow Hat as George's parent or as a stand-in for a parental figure. For example, when a second-grade teacher from Lockport, New York sent a package to Curious George (care of Margret Rey), she included letters from her students documenting "advice from each student telling George how he could keep out of mischief" (Letter from Lynne Fletcher to "Curious George," Rey Papers, Box 69, Folder 2). What could have been a moment of rupture was foreclosed when readers asserted that George should do a better job adhering to the rules of his parental figure: "George, ask The Man in the Yellow Hat if you can do stuff before you do it," instructed Ashley Boots. One classmate advised: "George you should wait and ask The Man with the Yellow Hat if you can do something." Another classmate extended these arguments: "George don't be by yourself. Stay with a grown-up." Still others suggested that "if you have a Mom or Dad listen to them." (Letters from Ashley, Megan, and two unidentified writers, Rey Papers, Box 69, Folder 2.) This fan mail suggests that readers understand The Man in the Yellow as standing in for a paternal figure. While the children direct their recommendations to George, critics might question what type of father The Man in the Yellow Hat exemplifies.

The absence of The Man in the Yellow Hat offers a double reading. On one hand, it is not common for colonizers to leave their subject/slave alone unless they trust their subject will not misbehave or run away. On the other hand, if readers position The Man in the Yellow Hat as a loving, or at least responsible father figure, then it is curious that the same audience seems habituated to accept him as an absent father. George's situation is explained by the natural conditions of colonialism. George knows nothing of this world and is completely dependent on The Man in the Yellow Hat for food and accommodations. As such, there is no logical reason for George to resist. As with many diasporic subjects, while they long for home, they also long to fit into their current conditions and not to disrupt any benefits of their dependent condition. This state of difference and confusion exemplifies the reasons that while habitually left alone, George's rebellions are rarely targeted at The Man in the Yellow Hat.

One wonders if Curious George's popularity and publication would endure if the series featured a Woman in a Hat. Historically, the treatment of women travelers or explorers strips them of their feminine characteristics in the public eye. Those such as Jane Goodall who retain their gender identity do so by taking on the traditional caretaker role of protector and savior. In order to service those whom they accompany, most maternal figures are often expected to disavow their own personal needs and desires. Audiences might be unwilling to accept a Goodall-like character that steals George or any animal from its natural habitat unless it is in obvious danger. For the narrative to be palatable, George would have to have been rendered helpless prior to capture. Equally problematic is the way in which some maternal figures are explained by children's literary critics. For example, in popular readings of Sendak's famous book, *Where the Wild Things Are* (1963), the character of the mother is the subject of scathing critique. This comparison between *Curious George* and *Where the Wild Things Are* is important because these books share extreme popularity and are indebted to male-centered adventure/explorer narrative (Shaddock 1997, 155). An important difference in these boys' adventure tales is that the adult figures in these respective books are distinctly gendered.

Shaddock explains that *Where the Wild Things Are* "relies on a frame of feminine domestic and masculine voyage" (1997, 156). Max has a dinner-time conflict and his mother sends him to bed without supper (Sendak 1963). The book's narrative depicts the wild adventures that Max has in his dreams, which stand in for journeys that all children can take in their minds. The book sparked mixed reactions. Literary critics, such as John Clement Ball (1997), insisted that the book deserved scholarly attention because of its imperial narrative. Some popular critics read Max's mother as delinquent because Max was sent to bed without supper (Huget 2011). Curious George books also feature a narrative of delinquency. At the start of each book, The Man in the Yellow Hat, consistently demonstrating poor judgment, leaves George. Unfailingly, George causes trouble, and The Man in the Yellow Hat returns in the end. Thus, if Max's mother is disgraced for sending Max to sleep without dinner, one can only imagine what would happen to a "Woman in a Hat" who habitually left George for hours without any supervision. Sadly, US culture seems to willingly accept and often applaud subpar fathers while scorning women whose maternal responsibilities and gender roles extend to even fictitious novels. This comparison highlights two important elements of Curious George's diasporic condition: first, his relationship with The Man in the Yellow Hat maintains some central elements of the Master/slave dichotomy; second, and relatedly, it is unlikely that their relationship would be accepted if a strong female character took the place of The Man in the Yellow Hat in the series.

Nevertheless, Margret Rey's enormous volume of fan mail implies that many readers readily accept The Man in the Yellow Hat as a paternal figure for George despite his continued absence. Rather than incompetence, the fans' biggest frustration with Margret Rey was that they do not know The Man in the Yellow Hat's "real" name. In 1965, Houghton Mifflin held a contest inviting Curious George fans to submit the "real name" of The Man in the Yellow Hat. Anti-colonial texts such as Toni Morrison's *Beloved* were applauded by audiences and recognized with awards for leaving the colonizer unnamed to draw attention to the enslaved protagonist. Yet this possibility is foreclosed in the case of Curious George, as fans demand that the Man in the Yellow Hat not remain nameless. Instead, the insistence on a proper name suggests that audiences are unwilling to let the metaphorical colonizer remain anonymous and stand in for the practice of White colonization. Letters full of predictions and justifications came from all over the US. Suggestions included Harry, Balloon Man, Ed, and The Ephirata. School districts in Pennsylvania suggested The Man in the Yellow Hat should be or was named Al. The Atlanta Public Library submitted Mr. Nevada, and The New York Board of Education argued that The Man in the Yellow Hat was also named George (letters from Clarice Cooper, Dorothy Frey, Bernadette Johnson, and Dorothy Scofield, in Rey Papers, Box 5, Folder 6; letter from anonymous fan to Margret Rey, in Rey Papers, Box 69, Folder 5). To my knowledge, Margret Rey did not write back to anyone letting them know if The Man in the Yellow Hat had a real name. The Reys did not reveal that his name was Ted until the publication of *See the Circus* (1988). Audiences that missed this publication would wait until the 2006 film debut *Curious George*, staring Will Ferrell as The Man in the Yellow Hat, to see the "real" Ted in action (O'Callaghan 2006).

A Literary Conclusion

After re-reading the original series, I expected to find that the endurance and esteem of *Curious George* would have yielded many critiques. Disappointingly, there are relatively few. Not only does the series continue to sell, but it is also more popular today than it ever was. While the original series has received little critical attention, between 1941 and 2014, 172 books[11] have been published, and more books continue to be written. In more than seventy-five years, only a handful of scholars have raised concerns about George's abduction from Africa. Even after Dr. Seuss's public cancelation, little attention was direct toward George. To my knowledge, this monograph represents the first in-depth critique of George's continued discomfort and diasporic relationship with his new "home." George's obsession with freeing caged animals, his desire to be among them, his preoccupation with the jungle environment, specifically the palm tree, and his inquisitive relationship with The Man in the Yellow Hat position audiences to understand that George is not comfortable in his American home. In fact, George's diasporic subjectivity can be read in a majority of Curious George books. The lack of critique is particularly concerning because Curious George is designed for young readers.

When books are introduced to pre-readers, and then reintroduced in classrooms and libraries, children come to understand those books as written for them as a primary audience. However, too often their lessons are rehearsing the colonial tropes of White imperialism. The narratives do not raise concern about the history of African enslavement or assimilation. Read in concert with the postcolonial lexicon, Curious George narratives should invite a resistive reading that extends beyond the adventures of a cute monkey.

Children's literary narratives form and teach children about their own history, about the people with whom they share their environment, and about their understanding of and predispositions about people's values. They are just as important as popular books geared toward adults. Children's books impart upon young people what is expected of them, a benign tool teaching them how they are expected to behave. These lessons get multiplied by a book series with high circulation over a long time in which adults share similar stories and perhaps long for the same understandings.

Re-reading popular works with a postcolonial sensibility illuminates the ways in which racist and colonial ideologies are constituted and circulate. Further, if adults help children navigate a re-reading of previously engaged narratives, they can invite them to learn the value of critical reading practices. In the decades since George's emergence, the conditions of colonialism have changed, and so too has George. No longer confined solely within the pages of literature, George has grown into a cultural icon. The public's experience of Curious George is unlikely to end, given his ubiquity. While Curious George's appeal, short films, and toys were developed almost immediately after the original book, George's esteem erupted in 2006 with the debut of his first movie, a popular Public Broadcasting Service series, and a contemporary colonial narrative of scientific discovery.

Chapter Three

George Teaches Science: Postcolonial Science and STEM-based US Leadership

> The detached eye of objective science is an ideological fiction, and a powerful one. But it is a fiction that hides—and is designed to hide—how the powerful discourses of science really work.
>
> —*Donna J. Haraway*, Primate Visions

In August 2012, Google attempted to challenge the Apple-dominated tablet market by releasing the Nexus 7. In its debut advertisement, the "Google Nexus" commercial invites viewers into the sunny living room of a blond-haired, fair-skinned woman. Comfortably, she simultaneously holds her daughter and her tablet while reading the classic *Curious George gets a Medal* (Rey 1957). In anticipation, the young, blond-haired, blue-eyed, barefoot girl listens attentively. The mother reads softly: "This is George, he is a good little monkey and always very curious" (Google Nexus 7 2012). The theme of curiosity begins to mold the narrative. Dressed in the yellow palette of Curious George, the young girl listens on the couch, then moves to the kitchen table and blows into her straw until the milk overflows in a cloud of bubbles. As the soft music plays, she offers the Nexus 7 tablet to her mother to read. "George," the mother continues, "built a rocket ship to travel into space." Viewers watch as the child carefully places her broccoli, peas, carrots, and cauliflower around the edges of the Nexus to construct a fantasy rocket ship in her living room. "Do you want to go to space, George? You will have to be very brave," the mother recites. Audiences observe the young girl jump on her bed, wearing a shirt of yellow, similar to the book's cover and The Man in the Yellow Hat's hat. She covers her head in a brown blanket, which is reminiscent of the monkey's fur and the burlap bag in which George was first captured.

The advertisement then cuts to the girl's play area, where she has set up her stuffed animals for a virtual tea party with her grandma, who welcomes her granddaughter on the screen of the tablet. "Hello my little monkey," Grandma says. The music intensifies while the mother continues reading: "everyone got on and they were off to the launching site" (Google Nexus 7 2012). Now running barefoot through her sizable house with a tablet in hand, wearing a SCUBA mask and water-bottle backpack, the young girl prepares her curiosity to take flight. She slows down to check her coordinates and asks: "Google. How far is earth to the moon?" The living room's rocket-shaped lamp provides a visual reminder for viewers as the mother resumes: "The great moment had come." Carefully putting on her improvised rocket helmet, the girl speeds out the door onto the sunny grass of the yard, where her makeshift rocket ship and tricycle–decorated moon rover await. Google closes the advertisement by telling potential consumers: "The playground is open" (Google Nexus 7 2012).

Built around a Curious George narrative, the Nexus advertisement implicitly connects the power of curiosity and science, portrayed as a playground—a substantial and safe structure designed for children's exploration. The absence of men in the advertisement presents the historical placement of women in the home, specifically the kitchen and living room. Through the nostalgia of Curious George, the mother is able to empower her daughter, include her own mother, nourish her family, and promote Google's newest technology. The mother and grandmother play along as the carefree girl pretends to be George. The young girl covers herself in a brown blanket, surrounds herself with stuffed animal friends, and plans an adventure to the moon. Like a minstrel skit—a racist history of White actors pretending to be Black—the lighthearted advertisement starring a playful, affluent, young, blond-haired, blue-eyed girl and her relatively youthful mother displaces for most audiences any potential concern about the White girl emulating the brown monkey. Instead, the scene celebrates the possibilities that technology and curiosity can bring to young White girls. Here, the future citizen offers potential consumers the possibility that innovation in science and technology is accessible, if not necessary, to inspire a curiosity that neither limits nor endangers girls. The advertisement implies an endless opportunity for discovery and exploration. The articulation of Curious George with science and technology is premised upon George's archetypical attribute of curiosity and adventure. This advertised exploration is one of many media texts uniting the cultural icon of Curious George with ideological colonial beliefs of manifest destiny and scientific discovery. The connection between space, technology, and curiosity makes the Curious George stories logical promoters of science.

Given the ubiquity of STEM discourse in contemporary US culture, as well as the seemingly automatic acceptance of STEM as essential to the United States' global competitiveness, I suggest that Curious George works as a citation that gestures toward a mode of soothing public anxieties and popularizing STEM. George does not directly engage STEM policy or tell readers what to think. Instead, Curious George's promotion of STEM lessons invites readers to take part in a legacy in which the proliferation of science is promoted as progress at any cost. Whether by design or coincidence, the Curious George educational boost of STEM functions as a reference toward current policy trends. Through postcolonial Science Technology Studies (STS), I read the iconography of George as a curious monkey and STEM ambassador. This chapter considers the ways in which George can trigger audiences' support for a political agenda that is both promoted and popularized through the colonial roots of curiosity. These roots include the Western desire to tame and slay primates and a colonial frontier mentality predating STEM education. This reading advocates for a rethinking and questioning of STEM as a value-free solution to global competitiveness that encourages young people to "get curious." A postcolonial reading of the cultural iconicity of Curious George demonstrates the ways in which the historical relationship between curiosity, primates, and science is deeply ambivalent. While it may prove productive in some instances, it also evokes colonial connotations that should provoke a healthy dose of skepticism toward the current educational push that encourages young learners to emulate a curious monkey. While I agree that STEM education has resulted in significant accomplishments, I suggest that several of those accomplishments bear traces of their colonial histories. This reading is designed to unearth a colonial icon that provides justifications for many of STEM's achievements. Further, I maintain that the public—Curious George lovers and policy makers alike—will be well served to pause, chronicle, consider, and commemorate the grave injustices of previous educational agendas driven by scientific curiosity and primates.

In the midst his popularity, Curious George has become more than a literary figure; he has become a cultural icon of curiosity. His brand of curiosity is positive, fun, and adventurous, which consequently enables him to promote STEM-based education. While Curious George has multiple material adaptations, his role as STEM ambassador remains predicated on his two essential iconic signifiers—his curious mind and his monkey-like body. As a cultural icon, his curious mentality and primate materiality are his fixed markers. Importantly, George's distinguishing signifiers are also the foundation of colonial scientific histories and contemporary scientific policies.

In what follows, I make five interrelated moves. First, I engage postcolonial STS as a reading practice that is invested in both the colonial past and the contemporary present. These discourses work together to engage cultural icons theoretically and articulate the way they constitute and are constitutive of the political economy of ideas. In this first section, Curious George is grounded by reading him as a cultural icon whose features locate him as a historical nodal point in contemporary science. The second move highlights a historical re-reading of George's affection for curiosity in the positivist sense, then reads the roots of that curiosity as a means through which powerful nations and White bodies justify occupations of seemingly foreign lands and Black and Brown bodies. A logical extension of this argument follows, throwing into focus historical narratives of primate evolution as a justification to colonize in the name of scientific progress. Next, I critically consider media texts, specifically films that reinforce the barbaric, intellectually naïve, and dangerous myth of primates[1]; then return to Curious George and situate his curiosity and monkeyness within a larger narrative of scientific colonialism, reading George as a cultural icon with the capacity to "civilize" the nation's children through curiosity. As such, I take up George within the broader context of US scientific discovery—a discovery predicated on discourses of curiosity. Finally, I affirm the significance of a postcolonial STS approach, and accent the historical legacy of cultural icons in their current circulation toward public policy. In an effort to prioritize a skeptical examination of the billions of dollars thrust into pre-school education in the name of STEM, my reading of Curious George calls into question the US government's political push to educate future citizens about the promises of unquestioned curiosity.

Postcolonial Science and Technology Studies

George's central character trait of curiosity and his materiality as a primate provide opportunities to explore how postcolonial STS can offer a productive reading of colonial history and its current relationship with curiosity and science. Recognizing how the US has come to make sense of this iconic monkey affords a better understanding of how the trope of curiosity, essential in US scientific discourse, positions George within a history of primates. As a cultural icon he is equipped to direct citizens to read contemporary STEM educational policy as ideologically neutral.

Samuel K. Bonsu, a scholar of African socioeconomic subjectivities in contemporary markets, explains ideology as "a system of thought that maintains particular forms of power relations, which are often invisible to those who are actively involved in its dispensation" (2009, 1). Further, communication scholar Kent Ono argues, ideological critique is the process of working to make sense of and understand the system of "ideas, beliefs, attributes and values underlying" what audiences see and hear (2009, 72). Using postcolonial STS to read *Curious George* offers a way to highlight the ideological circuits that cultural icons and the histories they embody play in popularizing, citing, affirming, and legitimizing institutional ideas.

Ideological critiques are central to postcolonial interventions. The postcolonial theories outlined in previous chapters have driven postcolonial analysis in innovative and stimulating directions within the contemporary coordinates of globalization. Professor of English Pramod K. Nayar stresses the importance of postcolonial attention to the current politics of globalization. He maintains that "postcolonialism has never been as relevant as it is today" (2015, 1). Similarly, in their introduction to *Textual Practice*'s 2013 special postcolonial issue, Loh and Sen state that "Postcolonial studies—with its vast theoretical engagement with the uneven effects of globalization's vicissitudes alongside a commitment to the continued intimacies with colonization—is propitiously placed to offer a critical role in this new world order" (2013, 353). While postcolonial scholars have historically focused on world literature, these authors claim that postcolonial reading practices should also be invested in global shifts of political and economic power. Postcolonial scholarship should invest not only in science, but also in the ways in which science and technology are communicated, defended, and historically situated.

Postcolonial scholars have long had a critical interest in science (Anderson 2002 and 2009; Chakravartty 2004; Eze 1997; Haraway 1990; Harding 1998, 2009, 2011; Krishnaswamy and Hawley 2008; Seth 2009; Young 2003). In *Is Science Multicultural?* Sondra Harding suggests that science devalues the beliefs and practices of non-European cultures. She writes:

> commitment to the difference in the kind of beliefs and practices advanced by European science is central to the self-conception of many people around the world as modern, enlightened, progressive, and guided in our beliefs and behaviors by the highest standards of objectivity and rationality. (Harding 1998, 9)

As early as the 1700s, scientific rationale provided "knowledge" that justified the occupation and cataloging of non-Europeans as a subhuman species. The entire fields of botany and biology would not have been possible without colonial missions that collected the specimens from non-European lands for European study (Haraway 1988; Loomba 2015; Seth 2009). Through discourses of biology, scientists proclaimed that race was marked by the color of one's skin and systematically determined the inferior intellectual capacity of non-Whites. Scientists proclaimed that Black skin, skull shape, hair type, and facial features signified a low-grade primate (Loomba 2005). Such "science" invited figurative and literal occupation. The core of these "knowledge" claims rendered dark-skinned people colonial subjects and subhuman savages (Bonsu 2009). These imperial beliefs created a colonial mentality that led to the horrors of the global slave trade.

Phillip Wander argues that "science and all it represents stands at the center of our civilization" (1976, 223) and champions the rhetoric of science as a moral necessity. Kenneth Burke, in *Permanence and Change*, calls "trained incapacity" "the inability of professionals to see beyond their own specialty" (1984, 7). In the early to mid-1990s, rhetoricians, often influenced by Wander and Burke, discussed the ways in which scientists' persuasive strategy fell prey to the rhetoric of science that complements postcolonial STS. These subdisciplines share a desire to question the ways in which science is articulated to the public and pursued in the name of progress. While the rhetoric of science is sometimes interested in the rhetorical strategies and tactics used to move the public's relationship with sciences, postcolonial STS is explicitly committed to questioning the ways in which different intersectional identities and groups are affected by the history and colonialism of scientific persuasion. Together, these fields of study supplement one another and inform how science is packaged and delivered, often working to support the scholarship of researchers whose results advance the production of capitalism. Championing the postcolonial principles of dismantling systems of oppression, postcolonial STS focuses on asking questions about the colonialist mentalities that underwrite the assumptions of past, current, and future claims of scientific progress.

Colonialist mentalities credit science as a productive theory of human development rather than a system of exploitation. STS professor Suman Seth explains:

> the idea that science and technology were among the gifts that western imperial powers brought to their colonies was an integral part of the rhetorics of a "civilizing mission," one vaunted by both proponents and critics of the methods of colonialism. (2009, 373)

In Western efforts to civilize the "barbaric" and occupy the world, science became the language of civilization and progress. The empire's power relies not only on the science of medicine, the green revolution, and the wheel, but also on steamships, machine guns, gas chambers, and ultimately biological, chemical, and nuclear power. Seth goes on to argue that "in the wake of the social turn in the history of science, scholars of science and colonialism have emphasized not only the discursive or ideological power of science, but also the ways in which western scientific knowledge has been co-constituted with colonialism" (2009, 374). As science develops, it all too often aggressively displaces other knowledge systems by promoting the lens of objectivity. The belief that science is moral, rational, universal, value-free, and ideologically neutral makes it difficult to dispute the historical construction of racist beliefs and representations based on science. Historical postcolonial readings of scientific determinism offer strategies to counter the universality of present-day scientific knowledge because they challenge the pervasive paradigm of productive progress.

Postcolonial scholars have promoted examining the science of race and the pursuit of particular sciences. While some contemporary scientists reject race science in the traditional sense, Seth stresses the importance of recovering race science as "once-objective" science, as a means to provide

> important resources for those wishing to deconstruct contemporary scientific projects. One thinks automatically of the human genome diversity project and attempts to market racially-specific pharmaceutical products which are reinstituting race as a central popular and technical concept in the biological and medical sciences. (2009, 375)

This example highlights the fact that while humanities scholars commonly understand race as a social construction, many natural scientists still see it as biologically determined. Historical postcolonial readings of scientific determinism play an important role in contemporary inquiry because they function as counterevidence to the universality of scientific knowledge. Past accounts challenge science as the foundation of progress. These narratives should encourage a healthy and visceral skepticism of contemporary scientific rhetoric.

STS is occupied primarily with how science travels, becomes transformed, and interacts with other knowledges. Warnick Anderson, a historian, accurately argues that "any critical account of how science travels and interacts, whatever its assumptions and theories, is *implicitly* postcolonial" (2009, 390). Anderson's concern is not a new one; in the early 1990s, Stuart Hall lamented the isolation of globalized accounts of science and technology, claiming they lead to a false distinction between culture and economics (Hall and du Gay 1996; Hall et al. 2000). Hall's complaint is that globalization scholars should not only challenge how science interacts and travels, but also consider the colonial histories that indoctrinate the authority that science currently embodies. In order to theorize the characters and consequences of globalization, critics should consider histories of the colonial occupation that inform the present. The American philosopher of feminist, postcolonial epistemological and scientific studies scholar Sandra Harding does exactly this.

Since the early 1990s, Harding has been championing a postcolonial feminist theory of STS, grounded not only in science, but also in a history of colonialism and its postcolonial aftermath. Rather than focusing on the rational/European man as subject, she maintains that postcolonial STS is invested in non-Western cultures and the implications of science policy for the growth of knowledge and social welfare on a global scale (Harding 1998). Postcolonial STS scholars provide critical reading practices that reconsider scientific pasts in concert with both the present and the future and have much to offer the fields of postcolonial studies as well as science and technology studies. Harding explains that "postcolonial studies provide valuable resources for current public debates about science in a multicultural and global society—what kinds of sciences I have had and have now, what kinds I can get, and what kinds I could or should want" (1998, 9). For Harding, a postcolonial STS understands science as a political struggle in which questions of who benefits from policy and economics are intertwined with almost any scientific endeavor. For her, it is essential to confront the universal and political entitlement claims made in the name of science (Harding 2011). Since Harding's early works, the field of postcolonial STS has expanded to include considerations of postcolonial technoscience, a critical mode of analysis that engages the political economies of capitalism and science (Anderson 2002; Harding 2011; McNeil 2005). Postcolonial science and technology studies have taken on scientific information including, but not limited to: alternative medicine research (Adams 2002), nuclear power (Hecht 2002), global health (King 2002; Rottenburg 2009); and space (Redfield 2002).

Re-reading cultural texts through the lens of postcolonial STS enables readers to see how traces of colonial legacies are embedded in contemporary practices and how cultural formations embodied in scientific practice, history, and policy refigure colonial traditions of imperialism. Drawing on postcolonial STS, my reading of Curious George considers the significance of cultural icons in order to create the possibility of engaging in colonial histories with contemporary scientific education policies, and illuminates the ways in which the past informs present policies of scientific rationality. George's reconfiguration as a STEM educator suggests that some cultural icons, such as Curious George, have yet to separate from their colonial roots. Curious George exemplifies the importance of taking seriously the cultural icons that serve to rhetorically constitute US identity and colonial science.

Curious George is thus an exemplary case on which to use postcolonial studies' theoretical trajectories of STS, because this icon represents and reproduces the legacies of scientific colonialism in present cultural and political contexts.

As a cultural icon, Curious George brings colonialist traces of scientific ratio-nality of curiosity and the racialized body to bear on contemporary STEM discourses. Curiosity has a long history of being adopted by colonizers as an alibi for the "discovery" of lands as well as the occupation and exploitation of dark-skinned bodies. I do not suggest that all STEM research is necessarily colonial; rather, I introduce a healthy skepticism of the overwhelming, popular contemporary investment in STEM education. My aim is not to provide a "grand critique" of STEM; instead, like the technology scholar Anne Balsamo, I intend to "manifest the connections between what seems to be on the surface disparate practices and knowledges" (1998, 297). A critical application of postcolonial STS calls for historical perspectives applied to the global present. Discourses of Curious George evoke two grand narratives of colonialism—the Western positivist and colonial paradigm of curiosity, and its related yet distinct nar-rative of the primate.

Curious about Science

Long before the publication of *Curious George* (Rey 1941b), discourses circulated identifying curiosity as the driving force of scientific discovery (Ball 2014; Groen and Smit 1990; Parrish 2006). While the idea of curiosity traces back to the sixteenth century, it was not until the seventeenth century that curiosity began its connective bond with science. Since then, as the award-winning science writer Phillip Ball writes in *Curiosity*, scientific discourse remains grounded in a modern, positivist reading of curiosity as the "eagerness to know or learn something" (2014, 7). The *Oxford English Dictionary* defines "curiosity" as the "neutral or good sense . . . the desire or inclination to know or learn about anything, *esp*. what is novel or strange." These affirmative denotations throw into focus the inclination to articulate Curious George with science education. If the public believes curiosity to be a positive drive or attitude that pushes the STEM fields to produce new and productive knowledge, then those who, like George, teach STEM become embodiments of these positive manifestations of curiosity.

Meanings and values associated with curiosity have not always been as virtuous as those in contemporary discourse. In dissonance with a desire to learn, the *OED* also offers a definition of curiosity "in a blamable sense" as the "disposition to inquire too minutely into anything; undue or inquisitive desire to know and learn." In other words, to be curious can also suggest qualities of excessiveness. Ball describes curious objects that are "usual and intricate but which offer little purchase for the enquiring mind that wants to understand

and explain the world" (2014, 7). Aristotle understood curiosity with such skepticism, suggesting that it was an "aimless, witless tendency to pry into things that didn't concern us" (Ball 2014, 10). These definitions imply that curiosity is neither attractive, nor sufficient, nor always directed to the object of investigation. These denotations, which contrast with discourses about science, suggest that to be curious is to meddle and become a nuisance or hazard to society. The uptake and explanations of Curious George narratives ignore Aristotle's concern and instead retain a remarkable capacity to emphasize and celebrate the positive articulations of curiosity. While George definitely is mischievious—he monkeys around, so to speak—there are never negative consequences to his curious and usually dangerous endeavors.

In each story, George's curiosity is often described as being adventurous, deriving not from malice but from a comical inquiring sensibility. More often than not, he breaks rules (assuming he was ever told the rules), does what he is told not to do, and is frequently a hazard to himself and others. While these adventures seem humorous to readers, they are taken up by parents and educators as an acceptable example for George's productive investment in curiosity and scientific investigation.

A significant number of Curious George books begin the same way:

This is George
He is a good little monkey and
Always very curious.
One day . . .

For Curious George readers of all ages, the story is familiar. In 1941, George's curiosity about The Man in the Yellow Hat's hat is what enables The Man to capture the monkey. George's curiosity motivates every book, movie, and product. George's curiosity about animals provokes him to jump into animal cages, climb on museum sculptures, and travel to space (Rey 1957; Rey and Shalleck 1985; Rey 2015b). In 1989, Margret Rey opened the Curious George Foundation to fund programs for children that "share Curious George's irresistible qualities—ingenuity, opportunity, determination, and curiosity in learning and exploring" (Curious George 2019). In 1993, Scholastic Publishing sent a letter to Margret Rey suggesting that Curious George could be a new instructional symbol for delivering science to children (1993 letter from Scholastic to Reys, in Rey Papers, Box 110, Folder 10). While George is curious about almost every facet of US culture (such as foods, places, institutions, religious holidays, and sleepovers), George's curiosity about science began with his interest in space.

The excerpt from the aforementioned Nexus advertisement featuring *Curious George Gets a Medal* (1957), which was published in the midst of US anxiety about the Soviets launching Sputnik—the first artificial satellite to enter into the earth's orbit. Nine years before the Reys' publication, the US sent an aeromedical laboratory rhesus monkey named Albert to space (Gray 1998). "American and Russian scientists utilized animals—mainly monkeys, chimps and dogs—in order to test each country's ability to launch a living organism into space" (Gray 1998, para. 1). Over the past fifty years, hundreds of animals, many of which were various species of monkey, were killed in human experiments designed to further space travel (Gray 1998). But in 1957, the fictional Curious George survived.

Curious George took flight. The premise of the narrative is George's first trip to space. The "good little monkey" was "curious," and when a letter was delivered to The Man in the Yellow Hat's home, unsurprisingly George was even more curious (Rey 1957). After a series of mishaps, George learns that a professor had built an experimental spaceship small enough for a monkey and was hoping that The Man in the Yellow Hat would give George permission to try it out. He did, and George traveled to and from space. As in many of the other stories, George becomes a hero. Since 1957, George has been curious about space a number of times; yet, in each instance, the dangerous risks are dampened and remolded as both adventurous and comical.

In addition to books, television, and film appearances of George in space, George's curiosity for the science of space remains a central narrative theme, even in books that are not ostensibly about space. For example, in *Curious George Makes Pancakes* (M. Rey, H. A. Rey, and M. Weston 1998), his bedroom wall features a framed picture of a rocket ship, and in *Curious George's First Day of School* (H. A. Rey and M. Rey 2005), George is illustrated eating breakfast, prepared for his school day adventure with a rocket ship lunch box.

Two newer books feature George's explicit curiosity about the galaxy. *Curious George and the Rocket* (H. A. Rey and M. Rey 2016) is a board book and abridges the narrative of the space journey in which George gets a medal for being the first space monkey. The second, *Curious George Discovers Space*, begins by asking the reader "Are you curious about outer space? George is too!" (H.A. Rey 2015b, 1). Here George visits the International Space Center and then helps solve a problem with the Mars rover. As of 2021, NASA has five rovers on Mars: Sojourner, Spirit, Opportunity, Curiosity, and Perseverance. Using real photographs, the publishers claim to teach readers about "space travel, gravity, the solar system, and Mars" 2015b). The book is filled with "Did you know" bubbles that cite facts about space and about STEM more generally. The books make numerous connections between George, curiosity, and STEM, a theme that extends to Curious George's animation.

2006 marked George's formal refiguration from a popular literary character into an ambassador of STEM education in both film and television.[2] Ono explains that "television can be a very powerful and persuasive civilizing instrument, for television lets audiences know what actions, behaviors, and beliefs are and are not acceptable to others" (2009, 75). Because the Children's Television Act of 1990 requires "licensee to support or enhance educational and informational programming," networks are required to demonstrate that their programming includes educational material that is "good for children" (Nussbaum 2012.). When the Public Broadcasting Service (PBS) premiered their *Curious George* television program, they marketed the educational philosophy that George's curiosity "embodies the preschool child's potential in the field of science." The philosophy states:

> Many parents and caregivers know how to support language literacy development in their children: they read aloud to them, and fill their environments with letters, words, and labels. But few are aware that by embracing children's natural curiosity, they are supporting their educational potential in the fields of science, engineering, and mathematics. So, while George is nurturing children's innate tendencies toward inquiry and hands-on exploration, he is also motivating parents and caregivers to do the same. (PBS Learning Media n.d.)

Unlike the Google advertisement, the agent of curiosity is undoubtedly male, and his parents presumably lack a teaching capacity that George fills. Christine Paulson, a senior researcher at the Concord Evaluation Group (an organization heavily funded by the National Science Foundation), concluded that George teaches the essential skills of curiosity, and children who read and watch Curious George regularly score significantly higher on math and science evaluations (PBS Learning Media n.d.). The Concord Study also confirmed that 84 percent of parents engaged with Curious George felt "more confident helping their children learn math and science" (Concord Evaluation Group 2012). *Education World*, a publication for K-12 educators, postulated that Curious George "encourage[s] inquiry and curiosity" for STEM-based learning (Tomaszewski 2012). The *Huffington Post* reported, "The *Curious George* educational impact evaluation comes on the heels of a brief that urges policymakers to invest in high-quality preschool education, citing its universally acknowledged economic and social benefits" (Huffpost Education 2012). In addition to a regular Curious George program, PBS offers teachers instructional resources to teach STEM such as the "Curious George STEM Collection" (PBS Learning Media n.d.).

The collection instructs professionals to use George's materials to promote the curiosity needed to encourage STEM education. The animated television series and films' narratives are similar to the books and maintain the themes of curiosity, science, and space.

The episode of George's animated series "Grease Monkeys in Space" (Fallon, Bennett, and Romano 2007) has a curious title. A grease monkey commonly refers to a blue-collar mechanic, but is thought to have stemmed from the Industrial Revolution in Great Britain when children, because of their small size, greased various parts of large machines like automobiles. The episode features Curious George and The Man in the Yellow Hat heading to space to repair a large telescope, and George has the unique small size that enables him to be successful. Starting in 2006, George traveled alone to space on film in "Curious George's Rocket Ride" (Miller and Fallon 2006). In this narrative, the International Space Station's food supply has run out, and George is the only one who has the particular skills (four hands) needed to fly the rocket and deliver supplies. In 2014, George is curious about other planets and takes a trip to Mars (Fallon, Bennett, and Romano 2014). If viewers missed the episode, they can review it on the PBS video app. Fans can engage in various "space activities" with Curious George online. The connection between space and curiosity is a common theme in science-fiction programming.

The spaceship is a central trope of science fiction. While little scholarly attention is devoted to children's visual media and science fiction, a great deal of overlap exists between science fiction and fantasy (Rankin and Neighbors 2011). Some children's films, such as *Monsters, Inc.* (Docter, Silverman, and Unkrich 2001), are what Rankin and Neighbors call "sci-fi fantasy." In their introduction to *The Galaxy is Rated G*, they contend that fantasy contains magic or some other supernatural phenomenon, whereas "science fiction is technologically-based (no matter how impossible or not-yet possible) and grounded in the sciences" (2011, 10). Science fiction became a popular genre in the late nineteenth century in response to advances in science and technology. The cinema scholar Susan Hayward explains that science fiction "relies on the audience's willingness to suspend disbelief and does so by playing on our fears of science" (2012, 315). Originally understood as a sub-genre of horror, science fiction plays on audiences' fear of alien invasion and apocalyptic death. It reflects the ambivalence between doom and possibility.

In the 1960s and 1970s, science-fiction films "revealed how intolerance, chauvinism and racism continued to reign" (2012, 317). Hayward points to examples such as the Planet of the Apes series, the Matrix series, and the Star Wars series. *The Matrix* (Wachowski Brothers 1999) and *Star Wars* (Lucas 1977) lift the bar of science fiction to marvel at the wonders and possibilities of science (it is worth noting that *The Matrix* could be read as displaying a dystopian future). The genre's popularity soared in the 1990s, and since 2002 an average of thirty sci-fi films are released yearly, most of which are made in the US (Hayward 2012).[3] The genre generally affirms the status quo of the policy moment; thus, when science is popular with the general public, the films portray science that way. As such, with the strong promotion of STEM technology, George's numerous journeys to space promote science to audiences (the younger the better) by highlighting the strengths of STEM while simultaneously shading its limitations. In this science fiction narrative, space exploration is attributed to Curious George's curiosity about space, perhaps revealing a desire for him to leave his current location. The relationship between science and curiosity is important because it locates George within the science fiction script of the colonial frontier.

The colonial mentality of the frontier justifies the murder and displacement of indigenous peoples in the American West in the name of manifest destiny (Haskins 2018). Curiosity and tales of adventure uphold such narratives. Starting in the 1950s and 1960s, after the USSR launched Sputnik, the exploration and colonization of space became a necessary pursuit to guarantee the survival of the species and the drive to conquer, occupy, and inhabit planets beyond Earth (Williams 2010). Space exploration is often motivated by a belief that environmental catastrophes on Earth are inevitable and that the new frontier is the moon or Mars—places many humans believe will provide alternatives to Earth. Funded by the federal government and corporate investment, space exploration is portrayed as a heroic conquest. Space exploration is a logical mission for George, who is always curious, adventurous, and heroic. John F. Kennedy deployed discourses of the "New Frontier" in his 1960 acceptance speech and again 1962 when he advocated for the US to join the Cold War space race and put a man on the moon. While budgets for NASA have fluctuated over time, in 2019 Vice President Mike Pence, head of the National Space Council (disbanded in 1993 by George H. W. Bush but reestablished in 2017 by Donald Trump), announced that the US government would commit $21 billion to NASA. President Trump envisioned a "space-dedicated military branch, complete with space warfighters and weapons, by the year 2020" (Haskins 2018). Speaking in 2019 on behalf of NASA's Moon to Mars mission, senior NASA administrator Jim Bridenstine announced: "We will go to the Moon in the next decade with innovative, new technologies and systems to explore more locations across the lunar surface than ever before. This time, when we go to the moon, we will stay. We will use what we learn as we move forward to the moon to take the next leap—sending astronauts to Mars" (Bridenstine 2019). President Biden made an early commitment to continue Trump's deep space human exploration

(Davenport 2021). In 2020 the first commercial spaceship designed and build by SpaceX (owned by Elon Musk) launched the first human spaceflight since 1981. The successful launch of SpaceX's Dragon Crew spacecraft was the first step in a plan to pursue interplanetary space travel (Clark 2020).

Curiosity is central to the goals of government- and privately-funded space travel. NASA's newest space laboratory, the Mars Science Laboratory, features as its centerpiece the rovers Curiosity and Perseverance, which carry the "most advanced suite of instruments for scientific studies ever sent to the Martian surface" (Howell 2018). NASA's four-step goals end with "knowledge of Mars sufficient to design and implement sustained human presence at the Martian surface" NASA n.d.). Their goals are furthered by the ideological commitment to colonize another planet, an updated form of manifest destiny—a history enabled only by violence and the slaughter of others. Curious George and NASA share a commitment to scientific curiosity made possible by dedication to and investment in the science, technology, engineering, and mathematics of space travel.

In the film *Curious George 3: Back to the Jungle* (Weinstein 2015), Universal Pictures featured George's curiosity to set up a narrative that unites his love of space and his promotion of US technology, when George lands back in his African home. The film depicts George making new animal friends, reuniting with old friends, rescuing a baby rhino riding on top of the giraffes (as George did in the original book *Raffy*), and trying to fix a dam to save his drowning animal friends. The dam, a figuration of Western engineering, features prominently as the gift George brings from the US to save his inherently doomed and primitive homeland. In this film, George saves Africa from flooding by locating the missing RDS (Realistic Disaster Scenarios) control, and works with Mission Control in Houston (presumably the Johnson Space Center) to find the satellite tower in order to fix the leaky dam that threatens to flood all of Central Africa (no country is specified).

In this narrative, space extends to a broader topic, explaining the importance of technology. Importantly, the technology is based in the United States and is used to save the entire continent of Africa, whose inhabitants are positioned as inferior and lacking the capability to save themselves. Back in the United States, The Man in the Yellow Hat plans a trip to Africa to save George, exclaiming ironically, "the jungle is no place for a monkey" (Weinstein 2015).[4] While George can save all of Africa from impending flooding, the narrative puzzlingly situates him in need of saving by the Western Man in the Yellow Hat. This fleeting moment is missed by all too many fans, who understand The Man only as George's friend rather than his captor. In these scenes Africa is depicted in its colonial frame described by Bonsu as "an inherently wild and dangerous location, plagued by" its lack of progress, in the Eurocentric sense (2009, 5). Once he arrives, The Man in the Yellow Hat says, "I want to go home to my city where it is nice and safe" (Weinstein 2015). As with all Curious George texts, George is celebrated at the end of the story, and his curiosity, though dangerous, emerges as heroic. After saving his homeland, George happily returns to Chicago with The Man in the Yellow Hat.

In step with most Curious George narratives, *Curious George 3: Back to the Jungle* suggests that misbehaving and breaking the rules in the name of curiosity, especially in the name of Western technology, is ultimately justified. In fact, the lesson for children seems to be that employing curious means will not produce negative consequences as long as they justify a positive desire to learn about the unknown. Similarly, contemporary scientific colonialism suggests that such practices, though perhaps outdated and problematic in hindsight, are nevertheless helpful in bringing about novel scientific knowledge and discovery. Importantly, Curious George narratives extend space and technology to position George as an ambassador of STEM technology.

In 2019, *Curious George: Royal Monkey* debuted as the fourth film in the cinematic series. Here, George is confused with a royal monkey named Phillippe. While they look alike, His Monkeyness is stern, serious, and nothing like George. During a royal visit to the museum where The Man in the Yellow Hat works, George and Phillippe mistakenly trade places, and George finds himself in the land of Simiana (a made-up country whose name bears a linguistic similarity to "simian"). In this land, monkeys are kings, and although George briefly holds a superior status to many humans, his stay is limited and he is once again retrieved by The Man in Yellow Hat and brought back to the land where monkeys are an inferior species and humans control their activity.

On film, George gets a taste of an independent life in the jungle and in the land of simians; yet, each time he gets the opportunity, The Man in the Yellow Hat appears and returns George to the US, where he is confined with his original captor. The narrative never questions George's reluctance to return, and as such, the films, much like the books, absolve The Man in the Yellow Hat of any blame and reposition him as the benevolent colonizer. In September 2020, the newest film debuted on Peacock: *Curious George: Go West, Go Wild*. As new George spin-offs emerge, so does the franchise merchandise. Learning/gaming platforms, museum exhibits, astronaut George dolls, toys, and clothing keep the relationship between George, colonialism, space, and STEM strong. For example, the $70,000 national traveling children's museum exhibit, "Curious George: Let's Get Curious," promotes itself as a "top-notch" educational exhibition, offering children "Key concepts in science, technology, engineering and math" (Minnesota Children's Museum 2015). In each instance, George's mode of curiosity invites young minds to participate.

Postcolonial STS scholars such as Sandra Harding resist the notion of curiosity as value-free as it pertains to science. She finds the proposition that curiosity has motivated most scientific successes and fosters all future hopes for progress deeply concerning. While the achievements of scientific curiosity have been plentiful, so too have been its costs. Extensive and often unreflective readings of curiosity as models of humanity that are omnipresent are exceptionally dangerous (Ball 2014). I endorse Ball's call for a contained reading of scientific curiosity that is "wary of general statements" and favors the particular and contingent (2014, 398). In this logic, George is more than simply curious about rocket ships, as the Google Chrome advertisement might suggest. In fact, because he privileges certain ideological frameworks, he teaches only a positivist ideology of scientific discovery. The various resources provided to parents and educators as to how to teach science with Curious George offer remarkably little critical consideration of curiosity, save for a few remarks on material safety. The Curious George message is clearly stated on the PBS site: "Active Learning Begins with Curiosity!" (PBS Learning Media n.d.). George, as a resource, can help "establish the science skills and 'habits of mind' that lead to academic success and lifelong learning." The young citizen-subject that Curious George resources aim to cultivate is one whose "habits of mind" are inordinately curious and who is encouraged to ask endless questions. However, those questions do not extend beyond those tied firmly to the affirmation of scientific rationality that presumes a value-neutral orientation, is freely available, and is an objective discovery of natural phenomena.

Pardon the Primates

While George's curiosity marks an obvious connection with his roles in promoting STEM education, an equally important consideration is the way his curiosity is housed within his illustrated bodily form—the familiar figure of a little brown monkey. A consideration of the public's material and mythical relationship with primates helps situate the cultural icon of Curious George within a grand narrative in which humans understand apes and monkeys as inferior, primitive animals that are appropriate (and ethical) objects of scientific practice. Primates share a significant history with racist scientific metaphors of Africans. These symbols and metaphors permeate the body within which George is encased. This review of historical narratives surrounding primates is not exhaustive, nor is it designed to summarily dismiss science.[5] Instead, in this section I render visible the connotative value of the scientific primate discourses and the ways in which they get "served up for use in corporate and nationalist policies" (Harding 2011, ix). These historical narratives provide a contextualization of George as a monkey within a colonial lineage of scientific discovery. While George's monkeyness might contribute to his cuddly and lovable nature, it also echoes a history of racist colonial depictions of dark-skinned bodies dating to the science of the Enlightenment. The ways in which his monkeyness evokes a colonial past should move audiences to remain skeptical about the ways in which his body is deployed in contemporary STEM policy.

The West has maintained a great deal of historical and political investment in primates as proof of human progress. As an acclaimed American professor emerita in the history of consciousness, Donna Haraway elucidates that science is a practice of storytelling—a history whose methodological practice is embedded in stories based on testimony and interpretation (1990). Monkey comparisons used to dehumanize people of African descent can be traced back to antiquity when Christian and Muslim scholars viewed apes as demons (Campbell 2019). In the sixteenth century, primates were central to the birth of modern science and the narratives of taxonomic order that accompany it. By the mid-eighteenth century, the binaries that ground the current foundations of modern scientific thought—nature/culture, animal/human, body/mind, and origin/future—upheld the human-over-primate order (Haraway 1990). The nonhuman primate plays an especially important role in the history of Western civilization: scientists, enculturated to believe that primates came prior to humans, felt justified (or at least not guilty) in subjecting the animals to experimentation that might otherwise be considered torture, and that often resulted in the animals' death, in the name of human progress. (PETA estimates that over 106,000 primates are imprisoned in laboratories, where most of them are abused and killed in invasive, painful, and terrifying experiments—People for the Ethical Treatment of Animals n.d.)

Literally and figuratively, Haraway argues, "primate studies were a colonial affair, in which knowledge of the living and dead bodies of monkeys and apes was part of a system of unequal exchange of extractive colonialism" (1990, 19). Though these primates often look like George, and share his primitive nature, Curious George stands in contrast to the common Western relationship with monkeys because he is not read as threatening. Instead, George is cute and loveable—"a good little monkey." However, despite being good, this little monkey bears traces of his African past.

The negative connotations of the monkey, as an analogy for African primitivism and racial hierarchy, are uniquely Western. The primate is understood by Western audiences as pre-human, undeveloped, and evidence of humans' superior evolution. Globally, according to the science and philosophy scholar Hans Biedermann, some ape characters carry various positive connotations. In

Ancient Greece, the ape, known as the *pithekos*, was a "pejorative epithet" and a symbol of "malice and physical ugliness" (Biedermann 1994, 14). Monkeys commonly appear in East Asian and ancient Jewish art (Wecker 2010). Throughout the world monkey gods are worshipped as both warriors and tricksters. In ancient Egyptian culture apes were treated with great respect, since they were believed to be very intelligent. For Hindus the ape is understood as a holy animal represented by Hanuman, the powerful and loyal assistant to the god Rama. In South China and Tibet, the well-known Sun Wukong, or Monkey King, is famous for his supernatural powers, strength, speed, and bravery. In Mexican culture, the mythical Howler Monkey is a respected patron of the arts. Yet, in Christian semiology, since ancient times, the ape was a pejorative epithet, a symbol of malice, greed, and physical ugliness (Biedermann 1994).

In US culture, the racist "Negro-ape" metaphor was concurrent with the European discovery of apes and the continent of Africa (Lott 1999). The representation of distant and foreign people led to the belief that Africans were a distinct species. Early scientists, such as Edward Tyson (2014 [1699]) and François Le Guat (1891 [1708]), disputed whether Black people were animals or primitive humans (Oliver 2010; Tyson 2014). Enlightenment thinkers, such as the naturalist Linnaeus (1760), noticed the close resemblance between great apes and Africans, and were inspired by this "new species," thinking they had found an evolutionary link. Linnaeus developed "taxonomies ordering the European's scientific world by classifying different species of humans" (Campbell 2019, para. 10). Associate education librarian Edith Campbell explains:

> This converged with Peter Camper's work on physiognomy, a pseudoscience using the shape and size of the head, face, and brain to determine character and intelligence, and Charles Darwin's theory of evolution. These theories developed while European imperial powers pursued global colonization and sought cheap, unlimited labor to fuel growing economies. Scientific racism, which viewed Indigenous people in Africa and in the Americas as non-humans void of souls and humanity because they were likened to apes, justified enslaving these people not for a period of servitude, but in perpetuity, as chattel. (2019, para. 10)

By the 1860s, evolutionary anthropology was open to considering that Africans were human, but undeniably an inferior breed (Brantlinger 1985). In the absence of scientific knowledge, some classified Black people as the "hybrid offspring of ape-human mating" (Lott 1999, 8). African American Studies scholar Patricia Hill Collins (2005) discusses the deep commitment that Western natural and social science has to categorizing the natural order—a process that placed Africans closer to animals than to humans. Africans were understood as a primitive species "ripe for colonial conquest.... Thus, within western science, African people and apes occupied a fluid border zone between humans and animals" (Collins 2005, 99). While not all audiences necessarily read George as African, the ways in which spectators understand George might draw upon their cultural familiarity with primates and how they should interact with them.

By considering the narratives within which George's archetypical body is embedded, audiences are offered the possibility of seeing that the scientific narratives he currently serves are steeped in many of the same colonial logics as his original storyline. These logics mark the form of George's body as African, dark, childish, lacking speech, deficient in intellectual maturity, exhibiting poor judgment, and in perpetual need of a White male savior. Curious George, the dark-furred monkey, is celebrated for his naughtiness and delinquency. However, his cute, lovable, and silly nature offers up a sanitized scientific agenda full of adventure. As such, he conveys the notion that scientific investigation is rightfully and ethically practiced on the inferior primate, whose body serves to motivate the necessarily proper and ethical curiosity of the child. As evidenced in the Google Nexus 7 advertisement I used to introduce this chapter, George is the motivator and body on which the little girl's scientific curiosity is sparked and practiced. In other words, George does not profit from the curiosity he sparks; rather, the White blonde-haired girl reaps those benefits, and by extension the US populace at large.

Although Curious George is always referred to as a monkey (in literary, animated, and performance figurations), great interest and controversy remains over his actual and more accurate species identification. For most of history, Westerners have used the words "monkey" and "ape" interchangeably, although they are distinctly different. The most significant difference is that most monkeys have tails and apes do not (Wonderopolis n.d.). Margret Rey's fan mail has volumes of letters preoccupied with whether or not Curious George is truly a monkey, and if so, why he does not have a tail. The Reys' initial version of George (first named Zozo), had a tail. While George is definitively fictional and is clearly a primate, scientific and public audiences dispute whether his physical characteristics resemble more those of an ape, a chimpanzee, or a monkey. Pop culture internet posts also take interest in George's classification (Straight Dope 2011; OMG Facts n.d.; Mommyofdoom 2011; Broome 2015). *USA Today* settled on a tailless monkey or unidentified chimp (Breznican 2014). Greg Laden, an archaeologist, biological anthropologist, and *National Geographic* scientific blogger, argues that George's lack of a tail suggests that he is an ape. There is only one monkey, he continues, without a visible tail—the barbary macaque (Laden 2014, para. 1). Further, the relative proportion of the forelimbs and hind limbs (apes have short legs and long arms) seems to suggest that George is an ape, if not some other form of undiscovered primate (2014, para. 2). Kristina Killgrove (2013), a bioarchaeologist who, through a review of scientific nomenclature, supports Laden's tail theory, adds that barbary macaque monkeys live in the mountains and not in the jungle, as George did. Killgrove, knowing that the Reys owned marmosets (relatives of the monkey that have claws rather than nails) while they lived in Brazil, proposes that George was modeled after a South American marmoset. She adds that "At the time Curious George was created, the term 'monkey' was commonly used to describe any number of primates (and arguably, it still is today)" (Killgrove 2013, para. 3). Historically, the original scientific classification system did not distinguish between apes and monkeys (Killgrove 2013).

The debate about Curious George's species far outweighs the lack of discussion of his material appearance. In contrast, there is little speculation about whether Winnie the Pooh bears a resemblance to a bear, whether Kermit is an authentic frog, if Babar is truly elephant-like, or if Mickey is a well-proportioned mouse, and there is little popular or scientific interest in the species identification of Big Bird. Perhaps this is because Curious George is typically not anthropomorphized to speak, and the other icons clearly are. Yet, when George is given a voice (George's television voice is provided by Frank Welcor—well known for his role as the voice of the villainous Transformer Megatron), it is more of a whine or childish, broken English (Blair 2016).

Here I use the terms monkey, ape, and primate interchangeably because, unlike Laden and Killgrove, I am not invested in the scientific distinctions between species. Nor is this review designed to contribute to the narratives of discovery occupied with discerning Curious George's "true identity." Instead, I am interested in the ways in which US audiences constitute themselves in opposition to the primate narratives that ground modern science. A consideration of the material and mythical relationship the public has with primates helps situate the figure of Curious George within the grand narrative in which humans understand apes as inferior, primitive animals upon which science is ethically practiced.

Although George has always been curious about science, as evidenced by his interest in space travel, he was not an official STEM educator until television regulations required educational philosophies for programming. However, Curious George was made a physical emblem of science in 1996. In honor of Margret Rey's death, a donation from her estate helped establish the Margret and H. A. Rey Institute for Nonlinear Dynamics in Medicine at Beth Israel Deaconess Medical Center, affiliated with Harvard University Medical School. The ReyLab (as it is commonly called) website—strewn with Curious George icons—articulates the Institute's mission to create "a laboratory without walls, in the spirit of that playful primate who serves as a most fitting emblem of scientific curiosity and exploration" (Margret & H. A. Rey Institute for Nonlinear Dynamics of Medicine n.d.). These characteristics also figure George, and the objects of scientific research and study, as subservient to the broader paradigm of scientific discovery and its contemporary reiteration, STEM. As an African monkey, stolen by the White Man in the Yellow Hat, George becomes materialized through the visual representation of his body. His innocence and fuzzy, cuddly figure are essential to his cultural capital, commodification, and cultural iconicity.

George's figurative body and primitive curiosity serve as a vehicle for motivating the ReyLab and its vision of children's curiosity. The Curious George resources unwittingly invite parents and children to uphold colonial homilies of primatology. George's primate body signifies his inferiority in part because of its juxtaposition to the ways in which his fans and parents are addressed. For instance, in the "Curious about Space" resources, parents are instructed to "Ask your child to pretend that he or she is going into space to gather information about the moon. Like George, create a checklist of what he or she should bring" (Curious George n.d.). Whereas parent resources describe George as engaging in "memorable adventures" which emphasize the comedic nature of his curiosity and give parents and children alike "plenty of laughs along the way," they ask parents to become invested in "supporting [their children's] educational potential" and using George to "help children appreciate [STEM] disciplines" (PBS Parents n.d.). While marketed as a way of making science fun, these modes of address rely on a continuation of colonialist rhetorics about an inferior primate whose substandard body serves as a vehicle for legitimizing the rational and superior knowledge of Western science for children's entertainment. Parents are unwittingly prodded to encourage their children to see themselves as new colonists, embarking on a seemingly harmless adventure of curious discovery. The monkey's irrational comedic mishaps in deploying his own curiosity motivate this discovery, in contrast to the ostensibly more rational curiosity of most children.

The metaphor of monkey as pre-human is not simply a figure of historical record; it is, in Haraway's words, a "persistent western narrative about difference" (1990, 377). Even as the scientific myth linking Black people to apes has been disproved and shown to be wildly absurd, the hegemonic belief in the body as a reliable marker for biological and evolutionary racism persists. Extensive clinical trials for new drugs continue to be performed on "willing trial subjects motivated by poverty" in Africa (Rottenburg 2009, 424). The narrative of primatology and the myth of the "Dark Continent" occupied by a "subhuman species" is a misperception linked to science, but also constituted, reinforced, and promoted through popular culture.

Monkeying with Media

The colonial rhetoric of myths about Africans, race, and primates in contemporary media reinforces racist mythologies of primates in popular culture films, shows, and games. While each of the Curious George films and the television series deserves its own analysis, I treat them collectively to explore how these mediated texts support the colonial history of science and deeply imbed tropes of curiosity and monkeyness. A substantial body of literature demonstrates that exposure to media has a profound influence on beliefs and attitudes, and that young people learn a great deal about race through media (Klein and Shiffman 2006). Media does an essentially violent job of double capture. Films captivate audiences as well as the bodies they seek to exploit. Postcolonial theory merges with cinema studies in rich and illuminating ways that attend to, and move beyond, the history of capture (Ponzanesi and Waller 2012; Weaver-Hightower 2014).

Postcolonial film studies invest in "recent histories and on the lingering (instead of immediate) effects of colonialism" (Weaver-Hightower 2014, 3), while also assuming "the intertext of anti-colonialist writing and activism" (Stam and Shohat 2012, 297). Postcolonial film/cinema studies are central when making sense of the connections Curious George enables for audiences. For example, George's situatedness in a jungle habitat is something adult audiences have seen in movies dating back to the 1930s.

Famous films depict Westerners traversing the dark and dangerous jungles of Africa (countries are rarely specified) on a colonial journey. In many of these tales, the protagonist is on a quest for something belonging to the land or people of Africa. In *Tintin in the Congo* (Hergé, Cooper, and Turner 1931) it is diamonds in the Belgian-controlled Congo, in *Tarzan the Ape Man* (Van Dyke 1932) it is the ivory from tusks in an ancient elephant burial ground, and in *Kid 'in' Africa* (Hays 1933) it is to rescue Shirley Temple's character from a group of savages. These racist films are often characterized as part of the jungle craze (Terhune 2015). The film scholar Gwendolyn Audrey Foster offers a theorization of "jungle pictures." She traces the genre's roots back to the silent era and notes an increased popularity of the genre in the 1940s and 1950s. She goes on to suggest that "jungle pictures may be viewed as captive narratives, themselves appropriations of slave narratives" (Foster 1999, 57). Unsurprisingly, media are flushed with science fiction thrillers featuring a dangerous jungle ape that requires extermination, colonization, rehabilitation, reintegration, or recovery. Some examples include: *Murder in the Rue Morgue* (1932); the six sequels and reboots of *Tarzan the Ape Man* (1932, 1934, 1936, 1939, 1941, 1942, 1999); *Planet of the Apes* (1968) and its sequels and reboots (2001, 2011, 2014); *Gorillas in the Mist* (1988); *Avatar* (2009); *George of the Jungle* (1997); and *Godzilla* and its sequels and reboots (1954, 1956).[6] In 2021, after COVID-19 left theaters vacant for over a year, Warner Brothers banked on the legendary collision of *Godzilla vs. Kong* to lure audiences back to the movies. The use of jungle ape images to represent people of color is sadly conventional in US culture. The philosopher Tommy Lott explains that beast image representations dominate culture xenophobia about Black people (1999, 7). Ono brings the idea to bear on media, explaining that as "television representations help maintain colonialist relations and practices, [US] television also creates and reproduces degrading images of people of color . . . through codes and cues" (2009, 76). However, these codes and perceptions are not inherent; they are historically learned, rehearsed through science, and reinforced through popular media. Culturally, the history of science is presented through media's portrayal of primates as the enemy of humans. In addition to the cruel and dangerous conditions that real apes endure while performing, the dominant representations of apes reify the dangerous mythologies of past science. A comparison of *King Kong* (1933) and Curious George yields thought-provoking similarities and distinctions.

In 1933, the science fiction ape King Kong, a wild beast who falls in love with a White woman, made his movie premier. One of the most famous ape icons, Kong has been the star of nine films, a musical, and countless books and other memorabilia. The promotional image of the 1933 film features a silhouette of Kong towering over the New York City skyline with a helpless White woman dangling from his left hand. The portrayals of Curious George and King Kong are both distinct and similar.

Kong is feared while George is loved. Kong is geared toward an adult audience while George is marketed toward much younger viewers. Kong is chilling; George is cuddly. The *Wall Street Journal* critic Meghan Gurdon notes that George was "cutesified" in the 2006 movie and PBS series—"the little monkey's body appears lower slung and more babyish, his eyes wider and more winsome, than at his debut in 1941" (Gurdon 2016). Unlike Curious George, King Kong has been the topic of countless quality critiques, including readings suggesting that the frightening gorilla is a metaphor for the enslavement of Africans (Anonymous 2013; Bates 2015; Haraway 1988; Lott 1999; Rosen 1975; National Public Radio 2009).

The critic David Rosen explains:

> It doesn't require too great an exercise of the imagination to perceive the element of race in KING KONG. Racist conceptions of blacks often depict them as sub-human, ape or monkey-like. And consider the plot of the film: Kong is forcibly

taken from his jungle home, brought in chains to the United States, where he is
put on stage as a freak entertainment attraction. (1975, para. 3)

In addition to spurring a string of influential scientific, popular, and primate
films,[7] the Kong narrative shares some important similarities with George.
Both animals are forcibly taken from their jungle home, transported to the
United States, locked up and used for entertainment. However, this colonial
commonality of origin is marked by an essential difference—Kong's ferocious
portrayal perhaps justifies his enslavement, while George's childish curiosity
and accommodating attitude position audiences as complacent with his capture.
As a racist symbol, the capture of Kong affirms the historical, colonial, and
scientific perception that subhumans are dangerous beasts in need of taming.
Conversely, George's capture coupled with his curious cuteness offers audiences
a benign narrative more compatible with contemporary scientific colonialism.
In George's narrative, a rhetoric of curiosity is upheld as a justification for the
colonial quest. George's youth also explains his distinction from traditional
primate-in-jungle films. Because children are often perceived as nonthreatening
and innocent, audiences are likely to trust that their childhood antics will pass
as they grow into civilized and productive citizens. Curious George is likely
recognized by adult viewers as a citation of or reference to Kong. Yet, when in
Curious George Goes to a Movie George jumps in front of the movie projector
and amplifies his shadow, "the audience cheered" (1998). Though George was
momentarily likened to Kong, his recognizably small figure eases viewers' fears.

What George shares with many cinematic primate subjects is their removal
from the "wild" jungle of "Africa" to civilization, where they are artificially
endowed with human characteristics (Foster 1999). The structure of jungle
narratives—the great White hunter travels to dangerous and exotic landscapes,
and makes his triumphal return with an artifact of his imperial pleasure who
then falls hopelessly in love with his captor (Foster 1999)—fits neatly into the
original narrative of *Curious George* (Rey 1941b). Even animated representations
of nonhuman animals can lead to their physical abuse. The media studies and
animal ethics scholars Carrie P. Freeman and Debra Merskin argue that media
representations are the leading way children, and audiences more generally,
learn about other species. Yet these representations are typically stereotyping
and lead to a distorted view of the species:

Re-presentation (real or animated) is a tool of power.... When other animals are
rendered symbolically (such as in animation), the circumstances and conditions
of their real lives are made invisible. As a result, they are even more vulnerable,

particularly when they are presented as comic fodder or used as symbolic stand-ins for human emotions.... (Freeman and Merskin 2016, 209)

Thus, for viewers of King Kong, primates are commonly assumed to be predators, whereas Curious George offers viewers an equally flawed understanding of primates as cute, funny, intellectually defective, and reckless. These understandings of nonhuman animals create unrealistic expectations for how real animals should behave and can result in material harm for animals (Freeman and Merskin 2016). Therefore, Freeman and Merskin recommend that creators of animation, such as those producing films and movies of Curious George, should avoid "formulaic, romanticized, cutesy approximations ... and instead attempt to more accurately capture the essence of their actual personalities and behaviors" (2016, 216). All too often, animal representations, specifically when appearing as animation and with humans, can lead viewers to believe that monkeys would make great pets, they can be left alone, can learn to love the White man, and live in humanlike conditions. In reality, captive primates are the animals most often exploited, tortured, and neglected (Almiron and Cole 2016). Though these representations are harmful, some critical animal and media studies scholars indicate that animal liberation programming is possible (Loy 2016).

Not all representations of apes are necessary harmful. The media scholar and animal rights activist Loredana Loy cites *Rise of the Planet of the Apes* (Wyatt 2011) as a rare example of a media text that contains an animal liberation narrative (Loy 2016). While she notes its anthropocentric limitations, Loy cites the film as an example that leads to ape-related advocacy issues. Loy explores several animal rights projects that cite the film as a motivator towards activism. Importantly, the film is a sequel to the less progressive *Planet of the Apes* (Schafferner 1968). Another example of highly exposed ape imagery comes from Jane Goodall. Goodall has devoted her life to the study of primates, specifically chimpanzees, and her institute produces numerous nonfiction media devoted to science, conservation, peace, mentorship, and animal activism (Jane Goodall Institute n.d.).

With the rise in media programing, contemporary scientists and explorers have been using media to document their adventures with primates. Perhaps more than any other contemporary English explorer, Jane Goodall is well known for her travels to the Tanzanian jungle to explore ape habitat. As a primatologist, her mission was to save chimpanzees from extinction. There are countless images and films of Goodall and her team working to conserve the species. Globally, Goodall is the recipient of many awards, the author of several books, the recipient of several honorary degrees, the star of several films and documentaries, and a US representative for peace. While her work is to promote primates, her fame and iconic female explorer status are a product of the primates she studies.[8] Goodall demonstrates that human behavior is killing primates such as wild chimpanzees, gorillas, and bonobos. The Goodall Institute features a short film explaining their mission, titled "Make a Difference with the Jane Goodall Institute." In it Goodall names the survival of the chimpanzee species as the responsibility of humans. Humans, specifically those living near Gombe National Park, must stop over-farming and clear-cutting ape habitat. The omnipresent narrator explains that "She blazed the trail. The next steps are up to us" (Jane Goodall Institute n.d.). The overarching message of the Jane Goodall Institute is that people can make a difference. Goodall identifies her mission as teaching locals to change the world. For "unless we help the people to improve their lives, there was no way we could even try to help the precious chimpanzees." The presumption is that the local people are leading a flawed life and need the White women to help them change it. Her website features pictures of local communities empowered by Jane Goodall to become involved in the Institute's mission. The short film focuses on "helping the people improve their lives," not to mitigate human suffering, but instead so the people can "save the precious chimpanzees." The webpage also features a tribute to Goodall highlighting her communicating with chimpanzees. The typed, white-print layover reads, CURIOUS, VISIONARY, ORIGINAL, among other celebratory titles (Jane Goodall Institute n.d.). At one point, she boards a plane with a doll that resembles Curious George. The website encourages donors to get involved through monetary donations or by becoming a "Chimp Guardian." Goodall's extraordinary efforts have undoubtedly done a great deal for the preservation of chimpanzees. Yet the images on her Institute's site share a traditional colonial structure that has similarities to Curious George's origin story.

The representations of The Man in the Yellow Hat are strikingly similar to those of Jane Goodall. Though Goodall's images in the African jungle are not animated, both she and The Man in the Yellow Hat uphold a nostalgic story of US discovery. Both Western, light-skinned characters wear safari/explorer regalia and use their binoculars to get a closer look at their primates of interest. Their narratives show how to befriend wild animals, earn the trust of apes, follow curiosity, and endorse the technology that enables their missions (Jane Goodall Institute n.d.). In fact, the tablets used by Goodall's team share remarkable similarities to those the young girl's mother uses in the Nexus 7 advertisement that opens this chapter. Both White explorers venture alone into the jungle and risk their lives to learn about the science of their species' specimens. Importantly, these two characters lack faith in the local community to save African animals without their help.

The Jane Goodall Institute's web page depicts few White people, but those who do appear (who are not Goodall or her young blond son) are planting to rebuild the forest. The website puts great focus on the local people of Tanzania; they are responsible for both the over-extraction of natural resources that is destroying the chimpanzee habitat and the success or failure of the effort to save the species. Similarly, Curious George's media platforms put little faith in the African people's ability to save themselves. In the first Curious George book, The Man in the Yellow Hat has no interactions with native people in the jungle. Even in *Curious George 3: Back to the Jungle* (Weinstein 2015), when George and The Man in the Yellow Hat return to the jungle to save the helpless animals from floods, the "local" scientists lack the technology to do so for themselves. This example demonstrates how the variety and convergence of mass media circulation regarding primates provides overwhelming exposure for the narrative of exploration. The Man in the Yellow Hat and Goodall educate the deficient locals (George and the local Tanzanians) to save the jungle. Though Goodall's project is not fictional, the storyline produced by her web material alongside the journey of The Man in the Yellow Hat performs narratives of exclusion typical of science fiction. As is the case in most science fiction narratives, people of color continue to be the object of scientific inquiry (Olson 2011). The White protagonist civilizes, educates, and/or saves the Other and offers young audience members the opportunity to see a "subtext of marginalization" and "exclusion of the child of color" (Olson 2011, 66). Both narratives participate in a benevolent form of colonialism—both Goodall and George are cultural icons that stand in for curiosity and their Western explorer narratives in the name of scientific innovation.

Moreover, the inability to care for oneself or to ensure the safety of one's citizens is a central principle of imperialist attitudes that lead to colonial occupation. The failure of localities to care for their people, species, and environment features prominently in both Goodall's website and Curious George programming. These failures reinforce the colonialist narratives that only Europe and the United States have the power and technology to manage the wild jungle. As such, the colonizers possess the manifest destiny to control these lands and those who occupy them. The colonizers command the labor of the natives. A significant difference between the Curious George material and that of the Goodall foundation is that Goodall leaves the jungle to teach the locals how to live modestly and to educate the world about the extinction of chimpanzees. The chimpanzees, if healthy enough, remain in the jungle. George, on the other hand, is removed and taken to the US—a narrative that so blatantly references African enslavement that in 2006 it gets retold with a new colonial twist.

In 2006, when Universal Pictures embarked on the first major blockbuster production of Curious George, they were concerned that their depictions of a White man with a yellow hat stealing a monkey from Africa might not sit well with their audience. George's capture story clearly needed a contemporary reworking. Though traditionally accepted as innocuous, Curious George's digestible colonial narrative stills bears negative consequences. Specifically, George's origin story coupled with his ridiculous behavior positions audiences to read the enslavement of Africans as harmless and even laughable. Writing for the *Wall Street Journal*, John J. Miller argues that "the original Curious George offends so many 21st century's delicate sensibilities that if it were written today, no major publisher would accept it without demanding revisions" (2006, para. 2). Miller suggests that audiences are too fragile to acknowledge their role in colonial history and might avoid the film if confronted with that past.

While the original books continue to sell without considerable critique, in February of 2006 (Black History Month), the animated *Curious George* film premiered with huge success, grossing $58.3 million in the United States and $70 million worldwide (Box Office Mojo n.d.). The film's director, Matthew O'Callaghan, struggled to figure out how the narrative could be rewritten so that George would return with the Man in the Yellow Hat, now renamed Ted. "We couldn't have him just take George from the jungle" (Archaeological Institute of America 2006). The "21st century Man with the Big yellow Hat is no poacher," the film's director told *USA Today*. Instead, he is a "friendly museum collector (sort of a kiddie Indiana Jones)" (Munson 2006). The 2006 *Curious George* movie changes the way George journeys to the United States. Rather than being captured in a burlap sack by The Man in the Yellow Hat, George, "who is apparently orphaned, voluntarily follows The Man because he really likes him . . . and wants to return The Man's yellow hat," which George had mistaken for a banana (Cloud 2006, para. 4). This rendition erases George as a "happy little monkey" and refigures him as a hungry, lonely, orphaned monkey. Thus, George's curiosity causes him to willingly follow The Man onboard a ship as a stowaway to the United States. Once he is discovered, The Man in the Yellow Hat claims the monkey and names him George after George Washington.

The Man in the film is not the all-knowing paternalist he is in the books. Now referred to as Ted, The Man in the Yellow Hat is portrayed as a "shy, boring, bumbling museum nerd" (Cloud 2006, para. 5). As a curator for New York's "Bloomsbury Museum," run by a wealthy and very elderly man, Mr. Bloomsburg (perhaps a jab at then New York Mayor Mike Bloomberg). Ted tries to help the struggling museum by traveling to Africa (a homogenized ahistorical representation of the continent) to find the Lost Shrine of Zagawa, a forty-foot ape idol that will hopefully bring larger crowds to the museum. The film deploys the usual Curious George shenanigans, and The Man in the Yellow Hat brings back the wrong idol, loses his job at the museum, gets mad, gives George to animal control, has a change of heart, and then drives his car off a nearby pier to save George. In a relatively short snippet of the narrative, the duo sail back to Africa to steal the real forty-foot-tall Shrine of Zagawa and return to the US. The Man in the Yellow Hat gets his job back, George emerges as a hero, and the museum becomes a huge success. The 2006 film concludes with George becoming curious about a rocket ship, and him and The Man in the Yellow Hat getting shot into space and repeatedly circumnavigating the planet. Essentially, the film updates the colonial mission; rather than stealing people, the film depicts the capture of an African sacred site.

This Quest Hero (one of the oldest, hardiest, and most popular renditions of the colonial narrative) simply amends the imperial mission in the name of finding scientific collateral. The English writer W. H. Auden explains that the Quest Hero sequence includes a longing for a precious object, together with a journey to find it, a hero (the finder of the object), and a helper (in this instance George) "who has the magical powers to assist the hero" and without whom the hero would never succeed. "They may appear in human or in animal form" (Auden 1969, 44). In this narrative George possesses aspects of both forms.

The director, O'Callaghan, admits that the ethics of idol theft did come up during production, but the director and production crew ultimately decided that "the movie did not have the right audience for even a brief explanation" of the problems associated with theft of ape idols or other sacred objects, so they just went with it (Archaeological Institute of America 2006, para. 4). Sibel Kusimba, a Kenyan-based archaeology professor, raises an important objection. "If a movie is aimed at children, I don't think we should have a separate set of standards for what is acceptable. Our children are exposed and acculturated by these movies" (Archaeological Institute of America 2006, para. 6). "As good-natured as the movie is," Kusimba argues,

> The Man in the Yellow Hat is an inadvertent illustration of a very grave threat. Thefts of cultural artifacts from Africa are going on at an accelerated pace. They are being stolen from both archaeological sites and museums. And in the case of the Vigango figurines of the Kenyan coast, wooden representations of ancestors are literally being taken from people's yards while they sleep, and they end up all over the world. Trafficking in African artifacts is a serious problem. The movie doesn't help. (Archaeological Institute of America 2006, para. 7)

Ann M. Nicgorski extends Kusimba's argument. A professor of art history and archaeology, Nicgorski, expresses distaste for the main story line of the film, in which

> The Man in the Yellow Hat is an archaeologist and museum curator (as opposed to the gun-toting, pipe-smoking animal poacher of the original book series by Margret and H. A. Rey), ... the insidious underlying assumption that one simply can go to Africa and transport significant cultural artifacts to a museum in New York. Granted, this is fiction, but even so, it provides our children with a clear lesson in Western cultural hegemony, a lesson that contemporary American children definitely do not need. ... It is unfortunate that this film does not teach children more about the inherent value of cultural heritage as a receptacle of memory and an embodiment of cultural identity, which enables us to better understand ourselves and others and to appreciate human diversity. (Nicgorski 2006, para. 4)

Evidence supports Kusimba's and Nicgorski's concerns that children might learn harmful lessons from a movie in which a White man is never questioned for stealing an African treasure. In "Race-Related Content of Animated Cartoons," Klein and Shiffman explain that the race-related stereotypes infused in animated cartoons are likely to be very influential for young audiences as they begin to develop attitudes about difference and race (Klein and Shiffman 2006). Nevertheless, in the name of a scientific quest and a beloved adventurous icon, the film repeats the colonial narrative without widespread public concern.

The film's success is what prompted PBS to develop a Curious George television series. Premiering in September 2006, the shows are an adaptation of the Curious George book series. Between 2006 and 2015, PBS produced nine seasons, and it continues to air reruns. The program won two Emmys (2008 and 2010 Outstanding Children's Animated Program), was nominated fourteen times, and was PBS's most watched program (IMDB n.d.). Geared toward preschoolers, the program explicitly serves as an educational tool in STEM-based fields. The PBS program is firmly grounded in theories of curiosity and its relationship to scientific exploration. The website states that "the Curious George series takes full advantage of this natural curiosity ... children begin to observe properties, discover how things work, and, ultimately, develop scientific thought processes" (PBS Learning Media n.d.). At the nexus of media and STEM education, Curious George participates in numerous media endorsements of science as fun, adventurous, and ideologically neutral.

The episodic characterization details each show teaching STEM. For example, the first Curious George episode that aired was a version of *Curious George*

Flies a Kite (Fallon and Willard 2006) and teaches "Aeronautics"; a few days later in "Buoy Wonder" (Lamkford and Fallon 2006), George offers a lesson on buoyancy. The list of STEM lessons is extensive and includes, among other topics, volume, orienteering, animal life cycles, magnetism, dam building, planetary orbiting, temperature, weight distribution, metrics, wind instrumentation, and sound mutation. While these topics are valuable, the dangerous activities that George endures to demonstrate the STEM lessons are too hazardous to be emulated by children. Thus, children do not learn in safe responsible ways that they can practice science, but instead are expected to simply accept the dangerous experiments of their monkey "friend."

Beginning in 2016, Hulu took over Curious George production (Hulu 2016). To accompany the programs, Curious George's STEM adventure went digital. Available on an iPhone or iPad, the "George Train Adventures" is marketed as an

> educational and interactive app that brings the practice of science, technology, engineering, and math (STEM) skills directly into your child's hands.... Players will have the opportunity to incorporate their STEM skills in order to reach new levels and overcome obstacles.... (Bailey 2016, paras. 1–4)

In concert with the application, Houghton Mifflin Harcourt kicked off the "Curious World" Summer Tour, inviting all explorers to "get curious and celebrate Curious George's seventy-fifth birthday with a traveling block party" (Brill 2016). The design was a project created by both the Association of Children's Museums and The Ultimate Block Party. "Conceived as a multi-tiered social movement, the groundbreaking initiative aims to ensure that all children are provided with the competitive skills necessary to succeed in the 21st Century global economy" (Houghton Mifflin Harcourt 2015a). This announcement was important because it took Curious George rhetoric beyond STEM to positions of US economic and global leadership.

In 2018, season ten premiered in Canada on Family Jr. Then, as the coronavirus hit the US in Spring of 2020, NBC's streaming service Peacock joined a dramatically expanded streaming field. Using Curious George as one of their advertising trailers, Peacock invited viewers to meet Curious George's new friends (animals, of course), go on new adventures, and "see how far curiosity can take you" (Peacock TV 2020). Peacock offered the first nine seasons for free and launched new Curious George seasons ten through thirteen for a minimal subscription fee. Each thirty-minute mini-show is followed by a live-action short that illustrates that day's math and science lesson. In 2020, Jon Abbott, the president and CEO of WGBH (America's preeminent public media organization and the largest producer of PBS content), claimed that "More than 9 million kids start their STEM-learning trajectory by watching *Curious George* on PBS Kids, which reaches more than 7 million underserved children in low-income households." Both ABCmouse.com and Kiddie Academy funded a Curious George STEM curriculum geared toward children preK-4th grade. The lesson plans and videos are geared toward educators teaching STEM online during 2020 (PBS Learning Media n.d.).

As George moves from book pages to media screens, his iconic character-istics—his curiosity and brown monkeylike body—position him as an ideal promoter of science. Although George's narratives of slavery and colonialism are seemingly erased from his contemporary iterations on TV and elsewhere, the citations reemerge in new forms. As a primate, George is situated firmly within a colonial history grounded in a belief that the inferiority of primates is a necessary indicator of the White man's intelligence. Accordingly, primates are necessary both to motivate and to expand scientific investigation. Curious George's increasing popularity also parallels US interests in teaching STEM lessons to young people so that they can help further US leadership. The STEM methods that Curious George advances are predicated on the idea that plopping a child down in front of Curious George will "establish the science skills and 'habits of mind' that lead to academic success and lifelong learning" (DCSTEM-Network n.d.). This model of education maintains the teaching of colonial ideology, or what Paulo Freire refers to as the banking model of education.

In his germinal book, *The Pedagogy of the Oppressed*, Freire explains the banking concept of education as an instrument of oppression. In this model, the ill-equipped teacher distributes a motionless, static, compartmentalized, and predictable theory of reality that is unknown to their student. The goal is to "fill" the student with these phrases. "The student records, memorizes, and repeats these phrases without perceiving" or realizing the true significance of this capital (Freire 2014, 73). In this relationship, the teacher is the deposi-tor, and the student a container or receptacle to be "filled" by the teacher. The danger of the banking model is that it conceals "certain facts which explain the way human beings exist in the world" (2014, 83), while also negating creativ-ity, transformation, and knowledge—which emerges only through invention and reinvention—so that critical consciousness is lost. This model is central to understanding the Western push for curiosity as a motivator toward STEM as central to US global success.

When STEM is funded, pushed, and produced in the name of progress, critical awareness is sucked into a vortex of the banking model in which those historically and cotemporally oppressed by this model are further violated. For many centuries, Africans; Native Americans; Queer, Jewish, and Arab people; immigrants; and other minorities have been enslaved and killed in the name of science. Importantly, Freire admits that there are "innumerable well-intentioned bank-clerk teachers who do not realize that they are serving only to dehumanize" yet "fail to perceive that the deposits themselves contain contradictions about reality" (2014, 74). Thus, critiques like the one advanced in this book are not designed to point fingers at a single individual or author; instead, they reflect on the dangerous consequences that result from protecting cultural icons like Curious George in the name of childhood nostalgia, scientific progress, or technological destiny. It is not surprising that many postcolonial scholars turn to Freire in their understanding of education because this theory explains how well-intentioned educators aiming to "advance" societies use STEM as their mechanism. However, the critical consciousness raised in the humanities, which houses many postcolonial, women, gender, and sexuality, cultural, rhetorical, media, and race scholars (among other like-minded thinkers), are often defunded while STEM scholars and those advancing its agenda, by design or default, are protected. This protection is also extended to cultural icons such as Curious George.

Imagine a world in which critiques of curiosity at all cost could come into conversation with ideological critics who invite educators, parents, and children to become curious about the ways in which STEM has served to maintain oppression. Readers of all ages should consider why George undertakes dangerous acts, whether they want a father figure like the Man in the Yellow Hat, how George got to the US, and the dangers of Westerners taking artifacts from African countries. Answering these questions and others honestly will present reorientation in which the banking model of education seeks to maintain and engage individuals in the struggle for their own liberation (Freire 2014). Freire explains that our task as educators is to help students learn methods for evaluating "knowledge," a task only generated through "communication" (Freire 2014, 77).

In 2020, while parents struggle to find educational solutions in a world in which, because of COVID-19, most traditional schools are closed, there is an opportunity to think outside an education model that indoctrinates their children to adapt to the world of oppression. A new model would instead encourage homeschool teachers not to restrict or ban their children's favorite cartoon, but instead to invite a dialogic approach of "problem-posing" in which both parties can challenge the taken-for-granted assumptions upon which such narratives depend. For older students and educators, Curious George's popularity presents an excellent opportunity for a dialogue in which they challenge each other to question the assumptions that a curious, disobedient, childish brown monkey as science teacher might pose. These reflections will most certainly generate new challenges; but working through those, Freire explains, will enable both parties to "develop their power to perceive critically *the way they exist in the world with which* and *in which* they find themselves" (2014, 83). While educators blindly push for the prioritization of STEM education, politicians are furthering the funding that makes it lucrative.

Public Policy Citations

The 2006 emergence and continued growth of Curious George STEM education media incidentally parallels the development of the 2006 American Competitiveness Initiative—a federal assistance program designed to maintain US global leadership by funding STEM education. Curious George was not constituted by or through federal initiatives; instead, reading these discourses against one another elucidates the ways in which the promotion of STEM education continues to circulate within racist colonial legacies. Curious George and US STEM policy have come to share a common public. The increasing popularity of George as an effective and authorized ambassador of science provides an opportunity for audiences to endorse the political push for young learners to become literate in the patriotic rhetoric of the period—namely, the seeming truism that STEM education is central to the United States' global power. STEM education, funding, research, and ideological support has received exceptional acceptance in US policymaking from 2006 to 2021, becoming almost immune to widespread cuts in university, state, and federal budgets. Tragically, while STEM fields have been promoted and scholars produce business capital-informed research, the humanities and social science programs that encourage skepticism toward the scientific enterprise have faced significant funding reductions. As a STEM ambassador, Curious George has fallen in line with the ideologies maintaining that STEM education is vital to the future of US global competitiveness. In 2006, George's popularity reached an apex when he was featured in film, television, gaming platforms, and on a US postage stamp (Mystic Stamp Company 2006) as an icon specifically tasked with furthering the STEM agenda, and he continues to be an icon for STEM today. Curious George and STEM policies circulate within and among US audiences; thus, public opinion of one can logically affect the other.

In 2006, as Curious George's popularity was peaking, President George W. Bush announced the Competitiveness Initiative, which marked an important turning point for STEM policy and education. The initiative aimed "to encourage innovation throughout our economy and to give our Nation's children a firm grounding in math and science," and launched a series of resources to provide research and funding to STEM-based education (Bush 2006). Bush boasted that "if I ensure that America's children succeed, they will ensure that America succeeds in the world. Preparing our nation to compete in the world is a goal that all of us can share" (2006). The Initiative was expanded in 2007 and retitled the America Creating Opportunities to Meaningfully Promote Excellence in Technology, Education, and Science Act of 2007, or the America COMPETES Act. As Curious George made his debut on the big screen, the Competitiveness Initiative was refiguring a political scene that would push STEM education for years to come. George's films provide a means to promote public support for STEM while the US political push for global competitiveness encourages preschool STEM education practices. Together the media and policy simultaneously uphold and reinforce the myths that ground and justify contemporary scientific knowledge at all costs, specifically the dominant narrative that science equals progress.

As the STEM Education Coalition's website notes, "STEM education is closely linked with our nation's economic prosperity in the modern global economy; strong STEM skills are a central element of a well-rounded education and essential to effective citizenship" (Brown 2013). Thus, when the icon and policy are read together, George takes on a vital function—to train youth about appropriate modes of citizenship that can ensure national economic competitiveness. The US Department of Education relies on the same logic by prioritizing STEM as a means for ensuring US leadership and superiority. According to a Department of Education website:

> The United States has developed as a global leader, in large part, through the genius and hard work of its scientists, engineers, and innovators. . . . These are the types of skills that students learn by studying science, technology, engineering, and math—subjects collectively known as STEM. (The US Department of Education n.d.)

George and STEM education are anything but value neutral. Rather, they are bound up in a contemporary iteration of US American exceptionalism that enjoins young learners and their parents to take their rightful place at the head of scientific discovery and practice in order to continue the colonial enterprise that furthers US global hegemony.

Even during a Great Recession, federal funding for STEM was plentiful (America COMPETES Reauthorization Act 2011). The Obama administration contended that the 2008 recession resulted from the country's failure to provide future laborers with a rigorous STEM education (Petty 2013). Obama's 2015 budget proposed an additional $2.9 billion investment in STEM education programs (White House Office of Science and Technology Policy 2014).

When President Donald Trump took office in 2017, the future of funding and support for STEM education was unclear. Trump did not appoint a director of the Office of Science and Technology for two years (a record for a president); the executive committee for the Office of Science and Technology guides federal research spending. Some speculated that Trump's delay was motivated by his anti–global warming position and his desire to leave the international carbon-reduction pact without scientific input (Romm and Guarino 2019). However, in December 2018, the White House announced a five-year strategic plan for science, technology, engineering, and math education called North Star because it "charts a course for the nation's success" (Camera 2018). Officially titled "Charting a Course for Success: America's Strategy for STEM Education," the program adds money to the $279 million the Department of Education had already committed to STEM education (Friedman 2018). The executive summery for North Star explicitly cites the history of scientific discovery and economic leadership as justifications for Trump's program:

> Since the founding of the Nation, science, technology, engineering, and mathematics (STEM) have been a source of inspirational discoveries and transformative technological advances, helping the United States develop the world's most competitive economy and preserving peace through strength.... Now more than ever the innovation capacity of the United States—and its prosperity and security—depends on an effective and inclusive STEM education ecosystem ... to function as an informed consumer and citizen in a world [that] ... requires the ability to use ... STEM skills (Committee on STEM Education 2018)

In addition to citing the history of discovery, competitive economics, and military power, the Trump administration made competencies in STEM a prerequisite to citizenship.

Following the government's commitment, Microsoft announced a $10 million commitment to "STEM-starved communities" (Camera 2018), and the National Science Foundation gave $10 million to STEM training for existing workforces (Friedman 2018) to help colleges recruit minority students for STEM (Kelley 2018). "We need national leadership," said France Cordova, the director of the National Science Foundation (Camera 2018). The 2020 Federal Appropriation Bill for STEM Education states that despite President Trump's early flip-flop in his desire to cut STEM education, "for the third year in a row the House and Senate have advanced spending legislation" by reauthorizing the Every Student Succeeds Act of 2015. Specifically, Congress would continue to fund a minimum of $1.2 billion in grants, $200 million in STEM initiatives, and a 3 percent increase in the National Science Foundation's budget of $910 million budget. The connection between citizenship, STEM, and national leadership abounded in government materials and also reflected the message that Curious George was spreading. In 2020, when the county was facing economic cuts in almost every sector, the global race for a vaccine for the coronavirus and medical care protected STEM budgets and, in most cases, increased them (National Science Foundation 2020). In addition, Curious George was promoted to an essential worker—teaching STEM lessons on TV. Though there is no doubt that a coronavirus vaccine is worthy of federal funding, the push for STEM is not a new trend. Under the Trump administration the global race for a medical cure was being pushed on the federal level, while other protective measures such as mask wearing, social distancing, and protections for essential workers were minimal. These discrepancies are important because it has led to a push for science funding while denying funding for those hardest hit by the pandemic: Black and Brown men (Kaiser Health Network 2020).

While the election of President Joe Biden is often contrasted with that of President Trump, the two share a commitment to advancing science in the name of US leadership. In his early days in office, Biden elevated "the director of the White House office of Science and technology to a Cabinet level position" (Di Maria 2021), rejoined the World Health Organization, and announced his science and technology team, a group that will "help restore your faith in America's place in the frontier of science and discovery" (Barrow and Borenstein 2021). This message is echoed in Vice President Kamala Harris's children's book *Superheroes Are Everywhere*; like Curious George, Harris compared scientists, among others, to superheroes and told her young readers that "you can grow up to be like them" (Harris 2019).

US public policy, corporations, and cultural icons are all championing the importance of scientific education initiatives as constructive modes of citizenship and global leadership. At the same time, the rhetoric of curiosity surrounding Curious George plays an important role in providing the conditions of possibility for the public to make sense of STEM education initiatives. As US institutions pump funding into STEM education, the moral and ethical questions that technology raises remain hushed. All the while, George's material monkeyness and insatiable curiosity position him as a productive and popular servant of contemporary scientific education policy. George's curious nature has historically vindicated both the quest mentality that constitutes scientific colonialism and scientific public policy. Any ideology or area of education that touts itself as universal should not only be treated with great caution but should also be subjected to extensive intellectual analysis.

Proceed with Caution

As Curious George and STEM education policy remain popular in the throes of globalization, often at the expense of the humanities-based fields that house disciplines such as postcolonial studies, this postcolonial reading of Curious George discourses demonstrates the value of reading cultural icons in concert with public policy. Additionally, it demonstrates that postcolonial STS offers ways of reading the historical archive that document traces of the past that continue to inhabit the present. Specifically, reading cultural icons such as Curious George through a postcolonial lens explains how popular figures perform through media and government policy by illuminating the ways in which the public comes to understand science and technology as ideologically neutral. Postcolonial STS perspectives invite critical considerations of the archetypal coordinates of cultural icons, critical analyses of how these coordinates are historically situated in legacies of colonialism, and consideration of how they become refigured in present political contexts.

In addition to offering theoretical contributions to postcolonial STS studies, I call for a critical questioning of contemporary STEM education policy. Curious George has the ability to influence his audiences, defend science, and circulate scientific ideas through culture. When Curious George is taken up as an ambassador of STEM education, the public's celebratory response should include a call for scholars to consider critically the iconic nature of Curious George, his curiosity, his monkeyness, and how these properties circulate across time. What these accounts yield is often forgotten—colonial histories of the persecution of peoples and animals, justified in the name of scientific progress and confirmed through the mentalities of a positivist perception of curiosity. These are not old connections. Black persons being referred to as monkeys, apes, or gorillas and associated with primates sadly continues to be commonplace. Campbell (2019) sites several contemporary public examples such as Roseanne Barr equating Valerie Jarrett (a Black women and senior advisor to President Obama) with an ape, Prada's blackface keychain, and teachers in several states being cited for referring to their students as monkeys, apes, and gorillas. These are a few of the many times Black people are vulgarized with racist associations once supported by faulty science. In other words, while the public supports the pursuit of science, that pursuit should include understanding its complexities and its often dangerous limitations.

Curiosity, the scientific alibi of ideological neutrality, functions as a buzz word to promote a quest for what is often a vague and ill-informed journey in support of a benevolent colonization that pervades both Curious George and

STEM education policy. The mentality of curiosity for curiosity's sake is not a disinterested politics. In fact, it has great potential to legitimize a colonial past. Consequently, the public should question its use as a guiding philosophy of US global power and citizenship. As John Ball argues in "Max's Colonial Fantasy," as an engine of science, "curiosity is enlisted in the name of taming the world—it is a compulsion to understand" (1997, 3). Curiosity is a human-driven desire that necessitates caution and skepticism. Historically, it has helped to defend both the frontier mentality and the extermination of people and places. Citizens should be cautious when a popular cultural icon and the government together name curiosity as the chief characteristic guiding US global strength.

What is strikingly curious is that the material body currently used to soothe the public's anxieties about STEM competitiveness is the very same monkey body used, both historically and currently, to serve scientific discovery. Deemed subhuman, the primate has been and continues to be used as an affirmation of Western, White intelligence. George offers young people and their nostalgic parents a body they can laugh at and humiliate without consequence. As an ambassador of STEM, George's body is evidence of his qualification as the sacrificial object of scientific inquiry. George's primate body can be deployed, quite literally, as a body of sacrifice. Once stolen in literature from Africa by The Man in the Yellow Hat to entertain children, the cultural icon of Curious George has once again been stolen—this time from literature. In the name of US global leadership, George again attends to the public by selling the ideologies of scientific policy under the benevolent characteristic of curiosity.

Today, as science education is articulated as central to US freedom, no citizen, regardless of age, seems to be exempt from service to their country. Even Curious George has been drafted, to educate the youngest citizens. As the public plans for the future, I encourage a deep consideration of the cultural icons we employ. We cannot afford the privilege of inattentive blindness if we ever intend to teach children equality and social justice (Campbell 2019). The political rhetoric of economic competitiveness and global power is grounded on the foundations of US colonialism. Thus, the current circulation of Curious George and STEM education policy rely on a forgetful public who are able and willing to accept a benevolent colonial ideology in the name of US global prosperity. Writing off cultural icons such as Curious George as emblematic of a past canon of racist literature or a feel-good ambassador of science, or even a homeschool educator, is not sufficient. Instead, these texts provide salient sites of critical inquiry through which postcolonial interpretations of cultural icons, media, and policies can and should be read together, particularly as they increase in both circulation and popularity.

Chapter Four

Curious George Escapes the Holocaust: Postcolonial Nostalgia, Re-articulating World War II, and the Erasure of George's Enslavement

In 2005, Louise Borden wrote a Curious George book like no other. *The Journey that Saved Curious George: The True Wartime Escape of Margret and H. A. Rey* (Borden and Drummond 2005) chronicles the pre-George adventures of his creators, Margret and H. A. Rey.[1] The seventy-page book begins with the 1906 birth of the Jewish German-born Reys, and follows their lives through their marriage, their early careers as children's authors, and their move to Paris. However, the story focuses primarily on their 1940 escape from Nazi-occupied France to New York. Borden writes that in June 1940, the Reys grabbed minimal possessions and fled Paris by bicycle to safety at the French/Spanish border, boarded a train to Lisbon, then an ocean liner to Rio de Janeiro. A year later, they made their way to New York City, where they published the now iconic *Curious George*.

Following Borden's publication, three additional presentations emerged that centered on the Reys as Holocaust survivors. In 2009, the Nebraska-based Institute for Holocaust Education debuted their museum exhibit, *The Wartime Escape: Margret and H. A. Rey's Journey from France* (Dotan 2009). The exhibit, which included teacher education guides, traveled a national circuit of museums and Holocaust[2] centers. In 2010, the New York Museum released *Curious George Saves the Day: The Art of Margret and H. A. Rey*; their exhibition cataloged a similar narrative. Seven years later, filmmaker Ema Ryan Yamazaki released *Monkey Business: The Adventure of Curious George's Creators*, a documentary about the Reys including their escape from Nazi-occupied Paris (Yamazaki 2017). Importantly, Yamazaki's film includes historical footage of the hardships of refugees fleeing Nazi persecution during World War II.[3] In 2019, the story was developed into a theatre production with a synonymous story line and musical adaptations (Phillips and Shuber 2019).

Borden's book, the museum exhibits, and Yamazaki's documentary film, here-after referred to as the Curious George Holocaust narratives, all offer kindred accounts. Curious George accompanies his literary parents on a dangerous journey to escape Paris just prior to the Nazi invasion. They arrive in New York as model immigrants and all subsequently attain the American Dream. While the tales differ, they all position Curious George as the quintessential Holocaust hero who acts as an alibi of the Reys' innocence. The Reys were Jewish but held Brazilian passports, and like most refugees, they were often searched and questioned by German officials. In each instance, officers found drawings of George and allowed the Reys to continue their journey because they were written off as children's artists rather than Jews and/or spies. In this chapter, I explain that George's heroism began even before his literary debut. These more recent discourses retroactively position George as a Holocaust hero and elevate his cultural icon status to new heights, overshadowing his enslavement origin story and accompanying his role as STEM ambassador. I further consider how this Holocaust narrative enables George to tell a survival story that comports with traditional US values, making it appropriate or even a moral imperative to shield him from criticism.

The possibilities of these narratives are deeply foreclosed because these retellings of the Holocaust lack the horror of persecution, forcible displace-ment, pogroms, executions, ghettos, and concentration camps. Instead, George's version provides a digestible, sanitized version of the war in which George is on a new adventure and once again emerges as the hero, in the US land of universal refuge. The role of Curious George as survivor/hero fits unsettlingly into an American audience's desire to commemorate survival narratives at the expense of death, guilt, or loss. For young audiences, the popularity of these memorializations infuses Holocaust narratives with an enabling rhetoric that privileges resistance and hope. When the narratives are further permeated by the jubilant style of Curious George, the monkey becomes even more prob-lematically positioned as Holocaust hero.

While seemingly disconnected from earlier reconfigurations of George, these Holocaust narratives position the Reys as more than mere authors. They become celebrity Holocaust survivors who embody the epitome of the

American dream—with the help of their monkey companion. This recasting of Curious George as Holocaust hero and educator of US history provides an opportunity to summon World War II memories—to remember a time when America's economic and military strength was central on the global stage.

While the US government funds future STEM-skilled citizens, and George is an essential homeschool STEM teacher, Curious George Holocaust narratives provide for young audiences an introduction to the Holocaust staring George on another "adventure." For adult audiences, George stands in as the iconic reminder, evoking romantic nostalgia for a willful hero who found refuge and model immigrant status in the US, the country whose military strength was nationally credited as playing a central role in ending World War II.

As World War II survivors are aging, Curious George circulates among a resurgence of World War II commemorations. In this chapter, I consider four public narratives that recast Curious George as a Holocaust hero. I begin with a reading of postcolonial nostalgia in order to explain the popularity of Curious George Holocaust narratives as meeting a public longing for a return to a retelling of history that omits the terror of the Holocaust. To do so necessitates reading these texts as Americanized versions of history that educe imperial and postcolonial nostalgic longings for the great achievements and power of the World War II era. Second, I offer a critical consideration of the Curious George Holocaust narratives, the ways in which George plays the hero and fits into the challenges of Holocaust literature written for children. Third, by suturing theories of nostalgia together with the dynamic depictions of the Reys' departure from Paris, I explore how these texts enable US citizens to recall a day in which the country's global strength was embodied in the heroic actions of the generation now colloquially referred to as "The Greatest Generation." These Curious George stories, devoid of the horrors of the Holocaust, enable audiences to focus on an Americanized retelling of the war, in which US soldiers fought for the American dream and immigrants reaped the benefits of that victory. While these sanitized accounts of the Holocaust fail to bear witness to the horrors of Nazi persecution, they simultaneously defend the contemporary currency bestowed on Curious George and explain why audiences may have an aversion to negative critiques of him.

In addition to a tempering of the horrors of the Holocaust, I end this chapter by illuminating what is curiously absent in all four narratives—Curious George's abduction from Africa. This lack of connection between the modern-day George as a Holocaust hero and the original George as a noble slave informs the ways in which US citizens come to make sense of racial and religious violence. In spite of decades of scholarship committed to identity politics and postcolonialism, the lack of critical attention to Curious George as African captive and his creators as Holocaust survivors helps to explains the public sentiment that one cannot simultaneously escape violence (in this instance the Holocaust) and perpetuate it (in this example, producing depictions of sanitized slavery). This critical absence not only overshadows George's racist history, but also acts as an alibi to discredit any attempt to situate George in the colonial canon.

This reading contributes to scholarship that considers remembering the Holocaust as having a role in postcolonial literature. Curious George as a Holocaust survivor and hero offers US audiences comfortable narratives. One obligation of a postcolonial scholar is to recognize how the public understands their fragmented pasts and present. A desire to revisit childhood may well explain adult audiences' interest in the Curious George Holocaust narratives; such narratives offer audiences the chance to share with their children a cultural icon they remember enjoying in their own childhood.

To be clear, I am absolutely not denying the indescribable terror of the Holocaust, nor am I minimizing the courage that Margret and H. A. Rey needed to escape Nazi-controlled France. I acknowledge that the Reys' "survivor status" would be recognized under the National Holocaust Museum's definition because they were displaced due to religious persecution by the Nazis (United States Holocaust Memorial Museum n.d.).[4] Yet supporters and critics do not define many famous artists, composers, and politicians, such as Albert Einstein, Madeleine Korbel Albright, Sigmund Freud, and Henry Kissinger, primarily by their survivor status. What makes the *Curious George* Holocaust narratives so unique, and frankly so disappointing, is the *laissez-faire* descriptions of this Curious George adventure. The Curious George Holocaust narratives are not even about the violence and horror of the Holocaust or the "real" Reys. Instead, these materials retell the events of the Holocaust that represent and resurrect the Reys through nostalgia and cast George as an icon of survival and the embodiment of the American Dream. Curious George can be read as an iconic hero who not only survives, but also sanitizes the misery of World War II and supplants religious persecution with the ideology of the American Dream. This particular reading of Borden's story and subsequent Holocaust exhibits exposes the intricacies of cultural icons when entering into contemporary postcolonial conversations. I am well aware that any critique of Holocaust survivor narratives can be problematic. I clearly understand that my Jewish identity does not exempt me from critique. My hope is that it helps garner me an audience that is equally frustrated with a "light" reading of the Holocaust and the erasure of African enslavement. Such a positionality of anti-violence provides the conditions that could make possible a healing dialogue that makes sense of cultural icons like Curious George.

Postcolonial Nostalgias

The Curious George Holocaust narratives enable a trusted and recognizable icon to position audiences to accept a particular interpretation of the past. Reinterpretation of the past is not new to the fields of postcolonial studies; however, I mark a crucial distinction between postcolonial memory and nostalgia. In fact, this distinction is the foundation for my reading of Curious George Holocaust texts, because these texts provide readers with an understanding of the Holocaust that diffuses violence and celebrates US exceptionalism.

Postcolonial studies has had a profound and thoughtful relationship with memory.[5] The occupation of people, places, and knowledge by imperial powers has led postcolonial scholars to focus attention on the ways in which colonized communities remember their pasts and make sense of their present. The English scholar Sam Durant (2003) focuses on the relationship between literature, memory, race, and community. For him, postcolonial narrative is structured "by the tension between the oppressive memory of the past and the liberatory promise of the future" (2003, 1). However, the task of memory, which scholars of both collective and public memory have carefully theorized, is not to report the past accurately, but instead to refigure and select the past to serve the present and future.[6] This interpretation of memory, now recognized as its own field of inquiry, dislodges the public memory from its conventional origins and infuses it with a connotation that creates and writes a past, rather than recalling or unearthing past knowledge (Bonnett 2016, 48). Constructively conceived in this light, the task of critical memory scholars is not to challenge truth claims or to correct or revise the past; rather, their goal is to make sense of how emerging narratives of history manifest present needs and desires. Implicit in this practice, yet distinct from it, is nostalgia that basks in fragmentation without apology; scholars focused on nostalgia embrace a commitment to the incomplete, the nuanced, the nonlinear, the ambiguous, and the contradictory.

Nostalgia and memory are closely connected (Bonnett 2016); but with few salient exceptions (Bissell 2013; Hasian 2002), memory studies scholars do not always pay attention to nostalgia (Walder 2011, 4). The historian Leo Spitzer (1999) describes nostalgia as a twilight zone between history and memory, for it "fixates on fragments and moments of the past rather than total experiences, and as such, can accommodate a wide range of seemingly contradictory ideologies and purposes" (Lawrence 2011, 91). This is doubly relevant in George's story because as an icon, he has a history with both older and younger generations. Further, the heroic way in which George is positioned within the Reys' Holocaust narratives mimics a desired US story that primes audiences to read the

Holocaust as a bad event, made up of heroic survivors and brave US soldiers. Nostalgia rejects the desire for a coherent narrative and embraces how the past is implicated in the power and desire of loss. While some scholars understand nostalgia as a type of memory, others, like the social geography scholar Alastair Bonnett (2016), rejects this notion, because they fear that nostalgia might be discounted as mistaken memory, which it is not. Nostalgia's gift is that it resists the collective narratives that memory seeks. Unlike memory, which often invites audiences to recall a past, an image, a period, or an event, nostalgia asks audiences to "consider the politics of loss and, more broadly, attachments to, and uses of, the present" (Bonnett 2016, 48). For Bonnett, nostalgia is also a progressive political act—"a declaration of distance from one's object of desire" (2016, 48). For many members of Curious George's audiences, the Holocaust narratives call on both the imaginary pasts of readers and the historic pasts—the private spaces of bedtime stories as well as more public events such as walking through large museum installations.

The literary scholar Dennis Walder describes nostalgia as a sentimental return to an imaginary, idyllic past, a "fruitful dialogue between present and past, personal and public" (2011, 20). Linking the Greek terms *nostos* (returning home) and *algia* (pain or longing), nostalgia was first theorized as a medical condition, comprising numerous symptoms that spread from mind to body (Walder 2011, 8). Although no longer considered clinical, nostalgia is now read as a psychological condition (2011, 9). Walder explains that nostalgia has been viewed with suspicion and mistrust, reflecting a lack of understanding and significance of the phenomenon. Nostalgia lacks a concrete and undisputed definition, yet scholars' general understanding of the term has to do with a state of mind occupied with loss, often of one's childhood (Rosaldo 1989, 71; Spitzer 1999, 90). This reading is important to an understanding of Curious George's appeal for adults. While adult audiences understand that their childhood has passed, there is the appeal of an icon that has the potential to remind them of their former selves. For adults, looking backwards at Curious George offers opportunities to conjure up images of innocence and comfort (Jozwiak and Mermann 2006, 783). For younger audiences who have engaged Curious George at almost any level, the icon presents an opportunity to look back on that relationship and relate it to the Holocaust narratives. Thus, if audiences recall George as heroic and adventurous, then it is possible, even likely, that the Holocaust refugees might be read as heroic adventurers. Yet, postcolonial nostalgia challenges grand narratives; it denies from the onset an accurate recollection or homogenous Holocaust narrative. It involves both pain and pleasure, tapping into a reservoir of emotion that varies according to context, in order to reflect on the past and construct a present identity.

Nostalgia proves to be intellectually profitable for this project because, as the religious scholar Oren Stier argues, it is a "form engendered by the desire for memory...a style marked especially by longing for a past, one may or may not have had any knowledge of" (2009, 2). While both memory and nostalgia enlist the past in service to the present and future, constitute national identity, and anchor community, nostalgia's often-cited limitation—its abstractness—offers its greatest possibility (Jozwiak and Mermann 2006, 784). Thus, postcolonial and nostalgic studies embrace the possibilities of the incongruities and complexities of the past and present. Phillip Nel explains that for parents and educators, nostalgia in children's school literature is a crossroad with paths that lead to childhood (2017, 116). This type of restorative nostalgia does not see itself as a form of longing or remorse, but instead as the absolute truth. The Holocaust narratives that accompany Curious George take a sophisticated reading of nostalgia in which the story of the Holocaust invites readers into that classic George trope of heroism. Specifically, the abstract nature of nostalgia enables audiences of the Curious George Holocaust collection to celebrate the role the United States plays in the Reys' story without attending to the horrors of the conditions that necessitated the Reys' exodus from Europe.

The Curious George Holocaust narratives do not recall the past. Instead, they play a role in the fragmented and contradictory reconstruction of a past. In the case of adult readers of Curious George, the nostalgic loss of childhood might be tied to their relationship with Curious George books. Further, the books may also articulate with the loss of the members of the so-called Greatest Generation, who enabled their victorious nation to prevail over the horror of Nazism. In this interpretation, nostalgia offers an explanation for Curious George's colossal appeal. Read nostalgically, these Holocaust narratives create the conditions for audiences to recall the cultural icons of their childhood while also celebrating the generational value of their ancestors who made the US powerful and proud by bravely fighting for the American Dream.

According to Jozwiak and Mermann, the study of imperial postcolonial nostalgia relates to identity and can have a postive function in assisting with the difficult process of identity and community (2006, 784). Hasian explains that the project of postcolonial studies has an obligation to decode the influential nostalgic texts and to intervene in the "decolonization of the imagination" (2014, 587). Spitzer suggests that nostalgia offers the possibility of an escape from the past and the freedom to reframe the present as a justification for current policies. He goes on to explain that this "retrospective mirage sets up a positive" form of yesterday "as a model of creative inspiration and possible emulation" (Spitzer 1999, 92). Thus, Curious George narratives can appropriate and embrace the so-called Greatest Generation without having to weave through the unthinkable narratives that accompany the Holocaust (namely, execution camps).

Postcolonial nostalgia is not preoccupied with European colonialism or the period directly after decolonization. Instead, as Dennis Walder argues, it is invested in a postcolonial state of "increased globalization, ethnic tension, and national self-questioning" that has given rise to widespread redefinitions of the self (2011, 4). As evidenced by George's Holocaust narratives, the current period of globalization is far more nuanced than past postcolonial periods and thus requires new and innovative reading practices that resist compartmentalization.

A postcolonial nostalgic reading of the Curious George Holocaust narratives offers a range of positive possibilities. Walder explains:

> Like all forms of nostalgia, postcolonial nostalgias have both positives and negative aspects: usually the latter is fore grounded, as the source of an insecure idealism or sentimentality, casting a beneficent glow over past suffering and anxiety. But there is also a positive side, which admits the past into the present in a fragmentary, nuanced, and elusive way, allowing a potential for self-reflexivity or irony appropriate for former colonial or diasporic subjects trying to understand the networks or power relations within which they are caught in the modern world, and beyond which it often seems impossible to move. (2011, 16)

These fragmented, nuanced, and elusive possibilities create space for viewers to embrace George as both a hero in one time period and a noble slave in another. As such, nostalgia can be a productive way to resist colonization, because it embraces and responds to contradictions (Jozwiak and Mermann 2006, 785). Rather than discarding nostalgia as useless "yearning for a past," postcolonial nostalgia identifies potentialities inherent in those yearnings. For Walder (2011), postcolonial nostalgia is an ethical frame for modern colonialism in which fragmentation and nonlinear understandings of colonialism are the norms. The power of postcolonial nostalgia accepts that the past is unclear and that on close inspection, any linear narrative of colonialism becomes increasingly complicated.

Nostalgia's lack of clarity allows for new understandings and imagination to emerge about George, as well as new possibilities of making sense of this curious monkey. These new possibilities include George as cultural icon, diasporic slave, essential STEM educator, Holocaust hero, model immigrant, and upholder of the legacy of the American Dream. These postcolonial nostalgias are not invested in longing for a "real" past or home; instead, they represent productive uncertainty. The communication and children's literature scholar

Clare Bradford builds on Walder's theory of postcolonial nostalgia, arguing that nostalgia theory is particularly salient in children's texts. Bradford writes: "first, children's texts are always shaped by the desires and preoccupations of the adults who produce them, and frequently incorporate nostalgia for imagined childhoods" (2012, 194). The Curious George Holocaust narratives are designed to introduce young children to the Holocaust; however, Borden's book and the museum exhibits are also directed toward adolescent and adult audiences. George's Holocaust narratives exemplify Bradford's argument because adults viewing these installations may be drawn to a softer Holocaust story. This reflective aspect of positional nostalgia applies to both young and old audiences. Children can reflect on their relationship with George, and adults are offered the opportunity to reflect on their own childhood, that of their parents, and that of their children. Applying a postcolonial reading of nostalgia throws into focus several productive possibilities and compelling hazards of the Curious George Holocaust narratives. While these Holocaust presentations might invite audiences to seek deeper understandings of the Holocaust, the Curious George Holocaust discourses overwhelmingly foreclose more narrative possibilities than they offer.

The Reys' Escape

Louise Borden published *The Journey that Saved Curious George* in 2005, just a year before the release of the first Curious George film and two years prior to the award-winning television series. While audiences worldwide were familiar with Curious George, few knew the story of H. A. and Margret Rey's 1940 escape from Paris in advance of the Nazi invasion of France. Borden's account of the Reys' escape rearticulates Curious George into the matrices of history, remembrance, and nostalgia. The copy and cover for Borden's book situate the narrative less as an historical account of a treacherous journey in an era of unspeakable violence, and more as a pictorial adventure of a monkey saving his captors. The narrative clearly suggests that Curious George was the alibi that saved the Reys. The press release for Borden's book points to the nostalgic appeals used to market the Curious George series. It reads:

> You can't walk down a street or through a mall in America these days without noticing the nostalgia factor. ... Some folks may be yearning for what seemed to be a simpler time; others may simply respond to the inherent charm and quality of classic goods. Curious George, with his good-natured penchant for mischief, strikes just the right chord on both fronts. (HMH Books 2005)

Reading this book through a postcolonial nostalgic lens encourages more critical questions: Who wrote it? Where did they originate? Who read it? How did different publics interpret Borden's account? These questions prompt scholars to consider multiple perspectives including fragmented, nonlinear, but nevertheless historical interpretations of texts. Critically thinking about Curious George's escape provides opportunities to read the texts as constitutive of and constituted by politically informed memories of the Holocaust.

Borden's book, and all of the Curious George narratives that I examine, are examples of cross-writing, a term that the professor of Jewish literature Naomi Sokoloff uses to refer "to texts that address a dual audience of children and adult, or ways in which literature travels across age boundaries" (2008, 197). In this case, Curious George is likely the draw for both children and adults. This means not that audiences receive the narratives in the same way, but that the audiences range in age and that often children and adults experience the texts together.

The original large-format hard cover of Borden's book resembles a brown-paper travelogue. In the original travelogue-style design, the center of the cover is a circular, globe-like cartoon, featuring two softly brushed watercolor bicycle riders, presumably Margret and H. A. Rey. The distinguishing features of the woman's red hair and the man's hat, spectacles, and pipe (odd for a cyclist) encourage readers to presume it is a watercolor depiction of the two people portrayed on the book cover's corners. The cartoon figures pedal amidst a mob of less distinguishable figures fleeing *en masse* from Paris; the Eiffel tower looms behind them on the horizon, and fighter jets (presumably German) are visible in the background. Each corner of the book's cover interrupts the circular watercolor. In the top left is a profiled, black-and-white portrait of a young man with glasses and a pipe, his head cocked to the left. He appears to be gazing at himself in the watercolor cartoon, while also peering down at the black-and-white bust of a young woman on the bottom-right. The chest, shoulders, and bow on the female portrait reflect her classic, formal attire. She squints, as if looking into the sun, and watches the wheels of the riders in the watercolor cartoon, while in direct view of the 1940s French-styled stamp whose details remain uncertain. Like her male counterpart, she allows viewers to equate her with the female rider, who sports a similar bow holding her scarfed red hair in the pastel watercolor. The book's subtitle, *The True Wartime Escape of Margret and H. A. Rey*, identifies the photographed portraits in the upper right-hand corner. The subtitle appears on what looks to be a torn piece of pistachio-colored scrap paper, covering the top right corner of the circular drawing. Walking at the top of the torn text and off the page is the grinning, jubilant cutout of Curious George. With brown furry arms stretched wide, the cartoon monkey, lacking a tail, appears to maintain a brisk pace. To his left, the book's formal title appears in burnt red cursive: *The Journey that Saved Curious George.*

Since its inception, the travelogue cover has gone through several variations. The first edition is painted in Curious George's signature bright yellow.[7] Another, in celebration of Curious George's 75th anniversary, promises an author interview, activities for students, and a section titled "Becoming a Detective" that details Borden's research (Borden n.d., "News"). In all versions, the pages that follow adhere to a similar scrapbook-style travel journal style. Watercolor maps, letters, articles, and depictions drawn by Allen Drummond accompany early twentieth-century black-and-white historical photographs and iconography such as replicated train-ticket stubs, cards, and travel documents. Images of Curious George from the original 1941 book and other characters drawn in H. A. Rey's canonical style appear among visual portrayals of the Reys. On May 13, 1940, Borden writes, "On the northern French boarder, the Nazi tanks moved like lightning" (2005, 35), "the news from the front was grim . . . and Paris had become an open city" (2005, 42–43). On June 12, with "only a few clothes and their winter coats, some bread and cheese, a little meat, water, an umbrella, Hans' pipe, and the precious manuscript," the Reys "joined the thousands of refugees leaving Paris" (Borden and Drummond 2005, 46-47). While traveling among five million refugees, Borden details that "Margret and Hans were not afraid. They felt a sense of freedom, traveling light" (2005, 50). After a few days they pedaled into the train station in the French city of Orleans; Borden remarks that these were "difficult days for the French people" (2005, 64), though she offers no detail. The Reys, however, were safe, always finding food and shelter at each stop. They rode the train to Bayonne. There they brought clothing and warm coats and were approved to travel through Spain to Lisbon, Portugal. Borden describes their train ride to Lisbon, where officials leafed through their children's books. There they spent a few nights in a nice hotel with "A real bed . . . clean sheets. And a bathtub with hot water," depicted by a cartoon of Hans smoking his pipe and singing in the tub (Borden and Drummond 2005, 62). The Reys got money wires, shopped in Portugal, and bought first-class tickets and boarded an ocean linear to Rio de Janeiro. The story concludes in 1941 featuring the Reys' safe arrival in the "brilliant sunshine" of the land of "freedom"—America (2005, 68). The Reys had been in New York City for only a year when they succeeded in publishing their first book, the now famous *Curious George* (Rey 1941b).

While the title, *The Journey that Saved Curious George*, ironically figures George's existence as conditional on the Reys' arrival in the United States, the tale itself repeatedly positions George as the Reys' alibi for their journey and a necessary condition of their safety outside of Nazi Europe. In contrast to the book's title, Borden's monograph positions George and the Reys as Holocaust heroes. Neither the Reys nor the journey saved Curious George; rather, George himself, depicted through images and type, saved the Reys.

Borden details three specific instances in which George figures not only as a Holocaust survivor, but also as a hero. In 1939, when village police believed the couple were German spies and inspected the Reys' French countryside hotel, all they found were watercolor illustrations of George that "told the true story: Hans and Margret created books for children" (2005, 26). Borden also details the Reys' escape by train across the French border and into Spain. She depicts, in both watercolor cartoons and words, a police officer "checking identity papers with stern eyes" and looking for spies: he "asked Hans to open up his leather satchel" and asked to see papers (2005, 60). "Then the official thumbed through the pages of *The Adventures of Fifi*. . . . The Official smiled briefly . . . and moved on . . . the mischievous little monkey had rescued the Reys" (2005, 61). Their Jewish identity was concealed, and the authorities quickly dismissed Hans as an innocent children's artist. Borden concludes her account by situating the Reys safely in New York, publishing the book that "would bring all three of them enduring fame and affection through the world . . . the well-loved Curious George" (2005, 70). In all three instances, neither the Reys nor the journey saved George; rather, George saved Hans and Margret Rey. Moreover, as in all his books, George retained his iconic role as the hero.

The Horn Book, an esteemed children's literature magazine, showered the book with glowing reviews: "More than a first biography of picture book icons, this is a fine introduction to the period [the early 1940's] for young children, a model of documentation, and an exceptionally inviting and well-designed book" (Borden n.d., "About the Book"). Borden earned the Sydney Taylor Book Award, which is given annually to those outstanding works that authentically portray the Jewish experience. The United States Holocaust Memorial Museum lists Borden's book as suggested educational material for young readers. The appropriation of Curious George as a means for making sense of the Holocaust garnered widespread approval.

In an interview, Borden describes the challenge of writing about an issue as complicated as World War II in a way that young American readers can understand (Borden n.d., "News"). Many educators and librarians have adopted Borden's text as a way to teach the Holocaust. Accordingly, Houghton Mifflin designed a set of lesson plans for late-elementary and middle-school children (Houghton Mifflin n.d.). Intended as an introduction to World War II, the lesson does not begin with an overview of the historical period. Rather, it asks teachers to direct students to recall what they know about Curious George. Implying connections between the illustrations in early Curious George books and Borden's essay, the lessons instruct students to consider maps and conclude their exercise by making a timeline of the Reys' journey. Though the lesson plans encourage students to learn about writing a biography and the geography of Western Europe, they do little to challenge Borden's Americanized version of the Holocaust.

In 2009, the Nebraska-based Institute for Holocaust Education brought Borden's monograph to life through a traveling museum installation, *The Wartime Escape: Margret and H. A. Rey's Journey from France*. Based on the book, curator Beth Seldin Dotan adopted the Allen Drummond prints for her installation. It featured twenty-six of the illustrator's watercolor prints, eight archival reprints, and several interpretive panels. One hundred and twenty-five feet long, the exhibit traveled nationally to Holocaust museums, galleries, synagogues, community centers, public libraries, and memorials (Dotan 2009). Both the Mid-America Arts Alliance and the National Endowment of the Arts supported the exhibit (Vancouver Holocaust Education Centre 2011). In my informal interview, Donna Walter of the Institute for Holocaust Education said that curator Beth Dotan thought the exhibit was a "good way to involve people in a way that was not so heavy" (personal communication, February 13, 2012). Like Borden's book, the presentation avoids the traumatic, emotional experience one might expect in a Holocaust memorialization.

Educators are the intended audience of the traveling museum exhibit. It demonstrates ways to teach a "not so heavy" Holocaust by including activities for their adolescent students (sixth grade and up). For example, British Columbia's Vancouver Holocaust Education Centre compiled a twenty-seven-page teacher's guide that includes such pre- and post-visit activities as suggesting that students read the original *Curious George* (Rey 1941b) and providing future resources for study (Vancouver Holocaust Education Centre 2011). In an effort to contextualize the exhibit in classrooms, the Holocaust exhibition also includes more generic lesson plans for teachers, parents, and reading groups that are easy to download in iTunes (Taylor 2011). The Institute for Holocaust Education in Omaha provides Family Gallery Guides to accompany the exhibit. The Guide, a fourteen-page booklet, contains activities for children that include listing "mischievous" animals other than monkeys, asking children to identify which items they would take if they had just one suitcase, and providing a map that encourages children to be like H. A. Rey and keep a journal on a family vacation—a troubling comparison to the journey of Nazi refugees. Such associations underscore the educational limits of this lesson. However, the booklet devotes less than one page to a simple explanation of the Holocaust. Much like the exhibit, the booklet suggests that the Holocaust, while awful, was a minor detail in the otherwise exciting story of the Reys' trip.

What makes the Curious George Holocaust narratives unique is that people celebrate the way in which these presentations can educate audiences about the Holocaust. For example, in 2017, the Holocaust Center for Humanity in Seattle publicized their exhibit as "a fantastic way to connect a familiar and beloved literary character to lessons of history, and the dangers of religious persecution" (Richard Greene, personal communication, March 2017). While the exhibits hung on the wall, Curious George books were spread out on tables for small children to read. The celebration of George as yet another hero says little about the grotesque violence of the Holocaust. Rather, it rejoices in post–World War II American Dream narratives while ignoring the original story of George's African capture. Moreover, the Reys' Nazi escape tale is often used to dismiss the claim that Curious George has both obvious (in the original book) and obscured (in contemporary diasporic examples) racist foundations.

In some cases, the positioning of this exhibit can do a great deal for Holocaust education by default. For example, the Seattle-based Holocaust Center for Humanity situates the Curious George Nebraska installation adjacent to its core exhibit, films of local Holocaust survivors detailing their lives in concentration camps and remembering the 1.5 million children who were incinerated by the Nazis. Richard Greene, the museum's director, explained that George becomes a way to attract visitors who might not otherwise enter the Center, and he deliberately purposed the Curious George installation in order to attract families with children. He encourages audiences to educate themselves by viewing the Center's many exhibits that bear witness to racial and religious violence and include serious stories of the terror of the Holocaust. More recently, this esteemed Holocaust education center promoted a Best Practices for Teaching the Holocaust that includes in-depth activities, terminology, and videos to be used in online and remote teaching Holocaust Center for Humanity 2020). This comprehensive unit includes suggested Holocaust literature for children that appropriately excludes Curious George. In a state of heightened anti-Semitism, these Holocaust education centers are of central importance and the gift of a nostalgic reading is that it holds both the critique of George and the possibility of progressive educational methods in the same sacred space.

A year after the Institute for Holocaust Education's installation, a second museum exhibition, *Curious George Saves the Day: The Art of Margret and H. A. Rey,* traveled a more limited circuit. It premiered in 2010 at the New York Jewish Museum, considered to be "the preeminent United States institution exploring the intersection of 4,000 years of art and Jewish culture" (Johnson 2010, para. 4). It then traveled to the Contemporary Jewish Museum in San Francisco, another prominent site of Jewish art and culture. Both sites cater to a Jewish, adult-educated, and middle-class audience. It also appeared at the

Chrysler Museum of Art in Norfolk, Virginia in 2011, and the Norman Rockwell Museum in Stockbridge, Massachusetts in 2012.

The Jewish Museum's main exhibit, curated by Claudia Nahson, was a departure from Borden's book and the Nebraska installation, but adhered generally to the same narrative. The *Curious George Saves the Day* exhibit chronicled the Reys' escape from France, but also featured H. A. Rey's original illustrations with material borrowed from the de Grummond Children's Literature Collection at the University of Southern Mississippi. Designers Barbara Suhr, Kris Stone, and Katharine Staelin transformed part of the gallery space into a reading room inspired by *Curious George Flies a Kite* (Rey 1958), and created an interactive timeline on touchscreen computers where visitors, both in person and online, could explore the Reys' life, from the late 1930s through the 1940s (Art Daily 2010). A lecture series accompanied the exhibit, which featured Borden, the children's literature historian Leonard S. Marcus, and free workshops for educators hoping to link the exhibit to the study of World War II and the Holocaust (Mattoon 2010).

The Jewish Museum placed a much greater emphasis on Curious George than did Borden and the Nebraska Holocaust Institute. In the Jewish Museum's exhibit, instead of Drummond's watercolor illustrations of the Reys, curator Claudia Nahson filled the walls with eighty original H. A. Rey drawings from over thirty Curious George books, watercolors, journals, correspondences, homemade greeting cards, and even photographs Margret Rey took in Paris in the 1930s. The exhibition "is playfully anchored by two oversized structures: an arched green-shuttered, pink mockup of the Reys' residential hotel in Paris and a bright-blue version of their house in Cambridge, Mass." (Kaufman 2010).

Another important distinction between Borden's book and the Jewish Museum's exhibit is the title. Borden's title credits the Reys with saving Curious George, while in the Jewish Museum installation, it is Curious George who saves the day, and more than once. A New York journalist, Kristen Scharold (2010), reports that the exhibit "sets out to change our perceptions, earnestly presenting George as a hero." Rather than maintaining that the Reys saved George, the Jewish Museum's exhibit portrays George as crucial to the Reys' escape. Nevertheless, the book and exhibits also share a common theme. Like the book, the exhibits' narratives only peripherally attend to the history of the Holocaust; instead, they focus primarily on the Reys' escape tale. All three narratives depart from the traditional violence and seriousness of Holocaust remembrance by remaining focused on the lighthearted nature of the Reys' tale. These three Curious George Holocaust narratives—Borden's book, the Nebraska installation, and the Jewish Museum exhibit—avoid descriptions of countless refugees who lost everything in favor of a tale of Jews fleeing their vacation destination. The "whimsical," "not so heavy" account of George's tale serves as a distraction from the horrors and dark times of the war. The light-hearted affect presumes that Holocaust literature designed to include children, or literature intended exclusively for children and young adults, should not be too frightening.

While Holocaust narratives for young readers circulated in the 1960s, children's books about trauma proliferated in the 1990s (Kidd 2008). The English scholar Hamida Bosmajian explains the challenges that writers and speakers face when representing extreme situations. When writing about the Holocaust, the pressure to write a historically accurate account without scarring a child is immense. According to Bosmajian, the author may choose to conceal or limit the "site of atrocious history with reader-protective strategies that intend to spare the child but also enable the author to censor, sublimate, deny, or release personally experienced traumatic events" (2002, xv). Yet, the fear that children will internalize terror as their own has another side. Contemporary scholarly consensus suggests that it is appropriate and necessary for children to learn the actualities of history and trauma (Kidd 2008; Kokkola 2003). This dichotomy, between learning about histories and internalizing terror, is what children's literature scholars often refer to as the split agenda between telling and reassuring (Goodenough and Immel 2008). While no one story sufficiently constructs a knowledge or understanding of Nazism, few children's literature scholars favor tales such as those presented in the Curious George Holocaust narratives—glossy tales of heroism that dilute the atrocity of the event.

The Curious George Holocaust narratives tell little about why the Reys were fleeing Paris. There are no accounts of the torturous killing of millions; the narratives instead favor an adventure tale where the fear of being caught provides only momentary suspense. These accounts omit the history of Nazi mobile killing units, concentration camps, death camps, the slaughter of Jews, and the burning of babies, as well as the torture of persons with disabilities, homosexuals, political dissidents, and other non-Aryan people. Instead, they offer a relaxed introduction to an historical nightmare. This is not a typical Holocaust education. While most US middle-school students learn the magnitude of the violence from painful writings such as *The Diary of Anne Frank* (1993) and Eli Wiesel's *Night* (1956), Curious George "educational" depictions make light of the issue, presenting a happy narrative that privileges the rhetoric of adventure and heroism. No Holocaust narrative is unproblematic; even Frank's and Wiesel's canonical Holocaust narratives are complicated. For example, Anne Frank was known to have revised her diary when she became aware that others might read it as a tale of history (Bosmajian 2002). Michael Rothberg (2009), a comparative literature and Holocaust studies scholar, argues that the Holocaust transcends history. Nevertheless, both Frank and Wiesel's narratives share with the reader a horrifying story of Nazi occupation and torture—a story that the Curious George narratives gloss over. *Curious George Saves the Day* pales in comparison to most Holocaust educational events describing Nazi terror.

In addition to writing *Night*, an autobiographical account of his time in concentration camps as a teenager, Elie Wiesel won the 1986 Nobel Peace Prize for dedicating "his life's work to bear witness to the genocide committed by the Nazis during World War II" (Nobel Prize Organization 1986). According to the *OED*, to bear witness means to "to give oral or written testimony or evidence"; giving this type of testimony has been a cornerstone of Wiesel's work and of the greater Jewish community's commitment to Holocaust remembrance. Wiesel's words appear on the entrance of the United States Holocaust Memorial Museum: "For the dead and the living, we must bear witness." For Wiesel, and so many others, to bear witness to the Holocaust means to tell, teach, and speak about the devastation of the Holocaust, not in an abstract way, but in excruciating detail. People need to understand the beatings, the burnings, and the brutality, for only by hearing and learning the painful details will they be rendered unable to forget. To read his work, to visit the US Holocaust Museum, and to touch the dirt of the killing camps is to educate the soul so that no human should forget the tragedy. In his 2005 address to the United Nations, Wiesel spoke of the importance of bearing witness to the Holocaust:

> [There are] no words to describe what the victims felt when death was the norm and life a miracle. The Jewish witness speaks of his people's suffering as a warning. He sounds the alarm so as to prevent these things being done. He knows that for the dead it is too late; for them, abandoned by God and betrayed by humanity, victory came much too late. But it is not too late for today's children, ours and yours. It is for their sake alone that we bear witness. It is for their sake that we are duty-bound to denounce anti-Semitism, racism, and religious or ethnic hatred. (2005)

Wiesel's words have had an impact on the work of bearing witness to the Holocaust as a warning for future generations. For example, President Ronald Reagan, in his dedication of the United States Holocaust Memorial Museum, argued that we must "stare this evil in the face . . . and then and only then can we be sure that it will never come again" (Reagan 1988).

Each of these statements uses the Holocaust an example of moving forward having learned from terror and death. This is where the Curious George Holocaust narratives expose their true limitations. Without doubt, the accounts of the Holocaust are painful and beyond the imagination of those who did not witness the horror. By contrast, the Curious George Holocaust narratives claim to play an important role in the education of the Holocaust without being "so heavy" and in fact being "playful." The fact is that the events of the Holocaust were excruciatingly heavy; there is nothing playful about them. At this moment when the few remaining Holocaust survivors are dying and anti-Semitism and White supremacy is growing, our nation should be careful that the Holocaust and all of its devastation is understood in its true gravity. While the intent of the Curious George Holocaust narratives may be to teach about history, such lighthearted depictions dismiss the gravity of the event.

The story of Margret and H. A. Rey's escape from Nazi-controlled Europe bypasses bearing witness to horror in favor of playfulness from an iconic monkey. It evokes jubilant feelings of a past romance with George and pride in the so-called Greatest Generation. It gives audiences an opportunity to embrace a nostalgic yearning to return to narratives of childhood without apology. This wildly absurd appropriation of a deadly historical moment presents a compelling portrait to its growing and aging audiences. Borden's account and the museum exhibits present a good-natured version of the Holocaust in which innocent people escape, make it to the American promised land, live the American Dream, and enter the world of fame.

Ema Ryan Yamazaki's documentary, *Monkey Business: The Adventures of Curious George's Creators* (2017), offers a more nuanced representation of the devastation of the Holocaust than do the other narratives. This film contextualizes the Reys' escape from Paris within the larger landscape of their lives. The film sutures together the Reys' home movies as well as professional interviews of the Reys and people who knew them. It also includes Curious George–like animation graphics, photographs, and maps. Yamazaki's text is generally chronological, moving between time periods to situate the story of Margret and Hans Rey. The story begins in the early 1900s in Hamburg, Germany, and ends shortly after Margret's 1996 death in the United States. The film opens with young children sitting on the floor (presumably at story time) talking about Curious George. As the movie insightfully moves through the lives of the Reys, the film situates George as their immigrant child.

The documentary oscillates between the omnipresent narrator Sam Waterson (Academy Award nominee, Emmy and Golden Globe winner, best known for his tenure as a detective on the award-winning *Law and Order*) and interviews from the Reys and their cousins, friends, publishers, library archivists, neighbors, and scholars. Hans is positioned as the curious child-loving astronomer, Margret as the colder, more serious partner, and George, whom Margret proclaims was born in France, as their curious child. This is the first time either of the Reys publicly anthropomorphizes George. He is not a character, but a son whom all the Holocaust discourses position as a hero. George's fictional and artistic quality also positions audiences to anthropomorphically situate him to generate their human understanding of these historic events. This move is common, but also dangerous because anthropocentrism is foundational to the colonial project of domination. Though the film offers more historical context than the other Curious George Holocaust texts, the whimsical adventure of George still maintains a colonial Americanization of the past. As Yamazaki's chapters move, so do the Reys. They first meet in Brazil, though both hail from Germany. They move to Paris, travel through Spain and Portugal, then back to Brazil, and make their final home in the United States to live the American Dream.

As the narrator speaks, colorful animation of the Reys overlays historical footage and music that evokes various time periods and locations. Not until chapter three of the film is George born. Chapter four, "The Escape," tells the now familiar story of the Reys' escape from Paris. In addition to colorful renditions of the Reys bicycling out of France, the documentary shows historic black-and-white footage of the hardships that refugees faced as they fled from the Nazi invasion of France.

"The Escape" section of Yamazaki's film begins in 1939, when France and England were at war with Germany. Louise Borden and Hanna Diamond, a history professor, narrate as historical footage of German army bombings and Hitler dominate the screen. Borden explains that "the Reys had to leave Paris suddenly in June of 1940, along with five million other people." The display changes to show footage of an endless line of women with carriages, children, and multitudes of refugees. Diamond, who had no relationship with the Reys, infuses the film with a rich historical perspective, explaining the hardships these refugees faced. Compared to the previous accounts, Yamazaki does a far better job of illustrating the devastation, destruction, and death that refugees faced when fleeing. The documentary explains that the French government fled Paris on June 10, 1940, and that the German Army took over shortly thereafter. The footage of German bombings, death, sickness, and hungry children and seniors offer viewers the painful opportunity to bear witness, albeit briefly, to some of the terror that refugees faced.

When the animated George and Margret appear in "The Escape" chapter, they are in black and white, overlaid on video of horses pulling supplies with hundreds of tired and helpless refugees trudging towards the Spanish border. However, the lightness of the film and their situation quickly overcome the darkness as the Reys regain their playful color animation and retreat from the historical refugee footage back to a vibrant, cartoon world that resembles Curious George's book illustrations. As the narrator reads lines for the original *Curious George* ("George was free after escaping prison"), the documentary regains its jubilant tone. Though Yamazaki describes her new film as "trying to tell a story that is sometimes quite dark, through a whimsical positive approach" (Ainley 2016), her documentary momentarily overcomes the complete lack of seriousness about the German invasion presented in the other Curious George Holocaust narratives by situating the hardships of refugees alongside the devastation perpetrated by the Nazis. Though Yamazaki's documentary articulates some of the horrors of the Holocaust, it still falls prey to enabling rhetoric that privileges heroic gestures.

Like the first Curious George book, these Curious George narratives fall into the classic genre of the quest. As explained in the previous chapter, the hero of a quest narrative is typically accompanied by a helper whose powers enable the hero to succeed. In this story, the hero might have been Hans Rey's illustrations, which in turn position George as the helper. Another reading, suggested by the text, positions George as the hero, in that his existence enables the Reys to help him escape. Like most heroic quest narratives, the story begins with a happy "before the disaster tale," details some of the disaster, and concludes with a heroic "post-trauma" survivor story. Bosmajian explains that this predictable quest sequencing encourages a narrative mode of the quest romance in which the hero overcomes insurmountable obstacles until they are fully integrated into their new life and become living proof of their journey or become a celebrated martyr (2002). The resolved ending propels the reader into a fairy-tale mode in which all trauma is happily resolved. Bosmajian continues: "The sparing of the child about Nazism and the Holocaust contributes to the reduction of disastrous history to a set of predictable signifiers intended to facilitate collective historical memory, develop critical thought and educate in empathy" (2002, xviii). The listeners' and readers' expectations of the quest influence the storyteller to shape the narrative by using familiar conventions and language that includes heroic attitudes and gestures (Bosmajian 2002, 246). George meets these expectations by dispelling the Reys' fears, acting as their alibi, and offering the reader another adventure to share with their beloved monkey. These tales of George enable the expectations of the listener or reader to be met; the happy ending is both predictable and expected. This reading enables audiences to situate Curious George as they might remember him—as an iconic hero. His heroic nature does more than save the library cart or caged bunnies as he once did; in this tale, he is literally used to service his creators. However, taking him into the world of nonfiction, as these Holocaust narratives do, extends Curious George to an entirely new audience. Situating George and the Reys as survivors can do harm to the ways in which people are introduced to and learn about the Holocaust, because the graphic terror and murder is erased and overshadowed by the happy endings. Though educators and parents most often act with the good intention of sparing the child, they actually deny the children the possibility of processing tragedy. Bosmajian explains that "if sparing the child is part of the rhetoric of Holocaust narratives for young readers, then the belief that reading about historical trauma will prevent recurrence is illusory" (2002, xvii). In her memoir detailing her relationship with her Hungarian Jewish Mother, Adrienne Kertzer, a professor of English, explains that there are two languages for those who have experienced this persecution—the voice of Auschwitz and the voice of civilization. Children's literature about the Holocaust chooses the voice of civilization. People want to hear a heroic story (Kertzer 2002, 34). This is the story that Curious George Holocaust readers get—a civilized story of heroism. Absent from each of these texts are the stories of those victims who did not get to be positioned as heroic because they were killed. This does not mean that authors should not write to young audiences about the Holocaust—only that they should be honest about the complexities and differences between narrative truth and the truth of experience. The Curious George Holocaust narratives offer readers the opportunity to read George as hero, the Reys as survivors, and the United States as a place of refuge. The Reys' arrival in the US and their successful publication of Curious George gives readers the happy ending most quests achieve. The successful US arrival offers audiences an Americanized reading of the Holocaust—a story in which the US plays an essential role in ending the war and provides homes for immigrants who are able to enjoy the benefits of the American Dream.

An Americanized Holocaust

All of the Holocaust escape accounts give Curious George, conceived in France and figuratively taken from his home in Africa, "an all-American character complete with a paper route" (Kaufman 2010). George acts out the immigrant fantasies. He gets a job in Hollywood, travels to space, makes the front page of newspapers, "all while getting thoroughly Americanized" (Scharold 2010). Yamazaki's (2017) documentary film paints an image of the US as the land of opportunity. The trailer openly asserts that George is an American icon and immigrant. "Everybody thinks Curious George is such an American icon, and of course he is. But he was created by German Jews who lived in Paris, took him through Brazil and then brought him to the United States. So, he is as much of an immigrant as anyone" (Panoptica 2017). In the film, after leaving Paris, Hans remarks that "you never forget the day you come to America," while a cartoon of him by the Statue of Liberty fills the screen (Yamazaki 2017). A journalist with the *Seattle Post-Intelligencer*, Nancy Matoon (2010), sums it up when she writes, "The monkey from the African jungle was soon as American as banana cream pie." The Curious George Holocaust narratives provide an account of World War II from a perspective that privileges the role the US played in defeating the Nazis and the promising lives Jewish people forfeited when they immigrated to the United States. Read through an Americanized lens, George and his creators can be understood as embodying the American Dream. These narratives ignited a new element of Curious George's iconic brand—one that allegorically associates the curious monkey with American Holocaust education and the rhetoric of escape, the survivor, and heroism. Each story line echoes a familiar World War II narrative in which the war dug the US out of the Great Depression and positioned the nation as a global savior.

The rhetoric of uniqueness invoked by George's Holocaust narratives suggests that the Reys' journey falls neatly into the nostalgic reading of an Americanized understanding of the past. Power argues that "when the Holocaust is mentioned, people do appear to take notice, reacting with a range of feelings" (1999, 50). These collective understandings signal the event by focusing on a bland historical escape from the Holocaust rather than the complexities and ambiguity of the past. I am not suggesting that the Reys' journey was untrue or that the Holocaust was anything less than a series of violent and horrific events. Rather, I am underscoring the ways in which George's stories instill a desire for an Americanized version of the Holocaust that privileges a narrative in which the US eliminates rather than instigates colonial horrors. As Rothberg clarifies, the danger of Holocaust uniqueness claims is that they can create "a hierarchy of suffering (which is morally offensive) and removes suffering from the field of historical agency (which is both morally and intellectually suspect)" (2009, 9).

The Americanization of the Holocaust is predicated on a collective feeling that emerged in the 1940s and 1950s when American Jews responded to the decline of religiosity with the growth of the "victim culture" (Flanzbaum 1999). Uniting Jewish Americans around the Holocaust was a strategy to reinforce religious identity and group consciousness. Central to the American Jewish understanding of the Holocaust was the triumphant role of US troops fighting Nazism and the rhetoric of uniqueness. This rhetoric understands the Holocaust as the most horrific genocide in history. Novick explains that the contemporary American "angry insistence" is predicated on the uniqueness of the Holocaust. He writes that "insistence on its uniqueness (or denial of its uniqueness) is an intellectually empty enterprise for reasons having nothing to do with the Holocaust itself and everything to do with its 'uniqueness'" (1999, 9). For him, uniqueness as a principal lesson of American Holocaust education can effectually trivialize other atrocities. While some Jewish Americans claim that the Holocaust's uniqueness heightens individual awareness and provides a collective narrative for members of the Jewish diaspora, Novick astutely highlights how it also "promotes evasion of moral and historical responsibility. The uniqueness depends on the repeated assertion that whatever the United States has done to Blacks, Native Americans, Vietnamese, or others pales in comparison to the Holocaust" (1999, 9).

The communication scholars Barbara Biesecker and Barbie Zelizer (2001, 1998) underscore the important role that the memory of World War II has played in US public culture. Biesecker argues that resurrecting the war's memory provides a "renewed sense of national belonging [that is] persuasively packaged and delivered to U.S. audiences" (2002, 394). She suggests that this belonging is especially salient for "a generation beset by fractious disagreements about the viability of U.S. culture and identity" (2002, 394). Both Biesecker and Zelizer maintain that memorial texts do not shield audiences from the horrors of Nazi Europe. Their readings aim to explore why, how, and in what ways these memories of the war emerged when they did. Curious George Holocaust narratives ignore the many ways in which the United States rejected the plight of Jewish and other asylum seekers who tried to escape Germany before and during the height of Nazism.

For example, on the German transatlantic liner *St. Louis*, 979 passengers, mostly Jews, many of whom had applied for US visas, crossed the Atlantic seeking asylum (United States Holocaust Memorial Museum n.d., "Voyage of the *St. Louis*"). After being denied entrance to Cuba, they sailed to Miami. When they contacted President Franklin D. Roosevelt to ask for refuge and asylum, Roosevelt never responded. Instead, the US State Department sent a message to the ship's passengers that the immigration quota had been filled and no action would be taken to receive them as refugees. On June 6, 1939, the ship returned to Europe. Subsequently, only about half of the *St. Louis* passengers survived the Holocaust. This account and others like it disrupt an Americanized narrative of the Holocaust. All of the Curious George Holocaust narratives ignore events such as the refusal of the *St. Louis* passengers; even more troubling, their techniques of Holocaust education fail to sufficiently acknowledge and bear witness to the horrors of the Holocaust more broadly.

After the war, when roughly a million displaced victims of the Holocaust sought refuge, the United States under the leadership of President Truman was one of the last countries to accept refugees for resettlement. This is perhaps why the Reys went to Brazil before the United States. The Reys' US arrival was enabled by Roosevelt's Good Neighbor Policy (Marcus 2001). In 1948, David Nasaw explains, the US passed the Displaced Persons Bill granting the "vast majority of visas to those who were reliably anti-Communist, including thousands of former Nazi collaborators and war criminals, while severely limiting the entry of Jews, who were suspected of being Communist sympathizers or agents because they had been recent residents of Soviet-dominated Poland." Nationalism, Nasaw concludes, was a far great US priority than humanitarianism (2020).

American Holocaust narratives also fail to make space for the victim/oppressor problematic. For example, the Hitler Youth, a group of child soldiers who were physically and psychologically stripped of their lives and made into killing machines in the name of Nazism, has no place in an Americanized narrative of survival (Bosmajian 2002). Nazism is too often projected as a caricature or a personification of pure evil; consequently, the stories of this group of children, both perpetrators and victims of war, are often silenced. Bosmajian explains that "the often exclusive focus on the victim, who is always overwhelmed by the perpetrator and who is defenseless and mute during the disaster, actually prevents the knowledge and understanding necessary to read and resist the recurrent signs of prejudice and persecution" (2002, xxii).

The guilt involved in such stories offers no happy ending. The Hitler Youth, the Displaced Persons Bill, and the tale of the *St. Louis* are examples that demonstrate a complicity with the Holocaust—complicity for which postcolonial nostalgia is open to account. Colonialist history is filled with complicated stories of victim/oppressors and rejects grand gestures that clearly delineate between persecutors and victims. Yet the uniqueness of Holocaust survival narratives runs deep in the US collective conscious, and Curious George Holocaust narratives affirm this unique status.

The Curious George Holocaust narratives offer nostalgia for US contributions to the Nazi defeat at the expense of a more complex memory of World War II. Borden, the museums, and even the documentary ignore the horror of the war; instead, they feature heroic immigrants who achieved the American Dream after escaping the evil that American soldiers defeated. This narrative upholds two fundamental components of American popular culture stories: the happy ending and triumphant individuals. The American Dream does not come without cost. The cultural critic Ta-Nehisi Coates famously writes that American Dream narratives falsely portray the attainment of the dream as the "natural result of grit, honor, and good works" (2015, 98). The Curious George Holocaust narratives not only present the Reys and George as evidence of the American Dream, but they also depict them as evidence of a past generation of American heroes.

Rosaldo (1989) offers another theory of nostalgia that is popular in postcolonial projects. In this framework, nostalgia reflects a longing for the native culture that the empire has decimated. Through a reading of colonial films, Rosaldo aims to make sense of the empire's nostalgia for the loss of what it has intentionaly altered or completely destroyed. He explains that imperial nostalgia is paradoxical in that the empire kills, then mourns, its victims. It romanticizes not only the imperial past, but also colonial achievements, and longs for a return to a time in which there was an enemy to combat (Hasian 2014). I tread lightly here because I understand that Rosaldo is primarily concerned with the colonizer's yearning for the return of what it has destroyed. In aiming to read the resurrection of US global power through the US Jewish community, I want to be clear that I am not suggesting that viewers of the Curious George exhibit have any desire to mourn the defeat and death of the Nazi regime. Rather, I suggest that the fragmentation and abstraction of postcolonial nostalgia is a constructive framework for viewing the distortion of this historical event. Audiences desire a return to their country's identity at the point of triumph— the moment when US soldiers came home having emancipated prisoners and conquered Nazi troops. Nostalgic reading allows for US soldiers to be heroes and US politicians and policies to discriminate simultaneously. The sanitized focus on the jubilant monkey's narrative provides audiences the conditions that will elicit emotionally what Rosaldo describes as "the tender recollections of what is at once an earlier epoch and a previous phase of life" (1989, 70). Within the optimistic and patriotic exhibit, the childhood-infused icon helps audiences constitute their past selves (often embodied in their grandparents) without having to face the figures of horror that their ancestors faced. The Curious George Holocaust narratives host an Americanized and distorted recollection that refigures the possibilities of American heroism.

The fragments of Curious George stories scattered throughout the historical and manufactured imagery of the Holocaust exhibits present a narrative of George, both past and present. In addition, this yearning for the heroic US citizen gives American Jews a cultural icon with whom to associate and protect. Uniting Jewish Americans around the nostalgia of the Holocaust becomes a means of group consciousness-building. Young (1994) writes that the Holocaust is at the very center of American Jewish consciousness. In the 1980s, while the American Holocaust Museum was being built in honor of the six million Jews who died at the hands of Nazi soldiers, the claim that Jews were "America's number-one victim community was widespread" (Novick 1999, 194). This sentiment endures. In 2015, when no money was forthcoming for descendants of former US slaves, the Obama Administration earmarked $12 million in reparations for Holocaust survivors (Barnes 2015). The current US anxiety over losing Jewish culture perhaps explains the scarcity of critiques aimed at Curious George as a Holocaust hero.[8] The Jewish studies and religion scholar Jodi Eichler-Levine explains that the Holocaust "has emerged as an overwhelming force in American Jewish lives and identities" (2010, 93). As survivors such as Margret Rey die, children are obliged to maintain the national narrative of the

Holocaust (Loshitzky 2001). More than just a successor, George can be read as a survivor himself. He is encased forever in his youth, having endured Nazi France and moved on to live the American Dream. Importantly, while George may have escaped, he never bore witness. When Curious George becomes a Holocaust hero, all Curious George discourses move beyond the boundaries of criticism. As a survivor, George's immunity and protection extends to all that is associated with him.

I have endured many conversations aimed at protecting Curious George and the nostalgia that circulates around his popularity. When discussing my project with family, friends, and audiences of all ages, I have grown accustomed to hearing "oh [sigh] I love Curious George. And didn't you know the authors were Jewish and survived the Holocaust?" The assumption was that I did not know about the Reys' story, and that if I had, I was at worst a Holocaust denier, and at best smart enough to refrain from critiquing any element of Curious George. When I acknowledge that I know the history, my Jewish community offers me the dreaded look of disappointment. They claim that whatever type of Holocaust story is told, the mere fact that the Reys were Jewish and left Paris before the Nazis arrived renders them, and anything they created, unsuitable for critique. A far more nuanced response was that I did once love Curious George, and am still fascinated by the circulation of him, and I did know the Reys were Jewish and escaped the Nazi invasion of Paris. Still, I care too much about Jewish histories to accept an account that obscures the violence of Americanization and erases the record of African enslavement. This protection extends to a narrative that summons the heroic role that Americans played in World War II as historical motivation and evidence of our national capacity for success.

The Doubly Protected Curious George

Through lenses of nostalgia, readers are provided tools to understand how both the story of the Reys and the tale of Curious George are constituted through the audiences that engage them. The Reys' escape tale is no more "real" than the tale of George's capture. In fact, George's original capture makes the Reys' escape narrative particularly worthy of public consideration. The Curious George Holocaust narratives position several associations of George's creation with distorted and softened associations of the Holocaust by situating them within the Reys' escape from France. Though the Reys' journey is in part constructed from archival documentation, it is completed, sutured, and popularized by whimsical drawings that mimic those in most Curious George books. The allure of George is what draws its constituency, and this nostalgia invites audiences to read the texts as a new Curious George adventure. "Curious George, the Holocaust Hero," as I dub it, includes all of the same features as a traditional George book. It is a playful journey in which George gets into trouble, takes a wild adventure, and ends up the benevolent hero. However, the capture of Curious George by The Man in the Yellow Hat is never a point of contention in these new narratives. Instead, Yamazaki's film cites The Man in the Yellow Hat as caring and compassionate, always forgiving George for any trouble his curiosity gets him into. The serious and historical locations that display "Curious George, the Holocaust Hero"—the Holocaust Museum, the Jewish Museum of New York, and countless other Holocaust education sites such as libraries and museums—provide viewers the illusion of understanding the entirety of both Curious George and the Holocaust. The complexities of these Holocaust texts are further illuminated when attending to two significant absences: the horror of Nazis and the origins of George. Much of this chapter has focused on the former; I conclude by exploring the latter—the ways in which the George Holocaust narratives are privileged over and against capture and enslavement.

Curious George Holocaust narratives are exceptional because they embrace and even stress the story of George's extraction from the African jungle. For example, in the teacher's guide accompanying the Wartime Escape in the Vancouver Holocaust Education Centre, teachers are encouraged to ask their students to read the original 1941 *Curious George* book prior to their visit to the exhibit and to discuss not the narrative of his capture, but his popularity (Vancouver Holocaust Education Centre 2011, 6). Remarkably, the guide makes no connection between the capture and torture of Jews in the Holocaust and Africans in American slavery.

The Jewish Museum particularly emphasizes George's initial capture. The exhibit explicitly features the iconic image of George eating a banana in his jungle tree. The left third of the exhibit's invitational sign features a replica of George happily swinging from the tree, and the right two-thirds show "Curious George Saves the Day" printed in burnt red over a block-blur print of "The Art of Margret and H. A. Rey." Jaundice-yellow walls display framed images of H. A. Rey's illustrations. Amidst popular and obscure drawings are the images of the original story: The Man in the Yellow Hat in Africa spying on George with his binoculars; The Man hiding behind the tree as he tempts George with his yellow hat; George eating cereal in The Man in the Yellow Hat's house and gazing at the framed drawing of himself in the jungle; an image of H. A. Rey's drawing of his own arrival in New York harbor with the caption "Let freedom ring," and countless others. Images implicitly connect George's 1941 capture and the Reys' arrival in the US by uniting them both in bountiful Americanness. Yet creators, exhibitors, and curators fail to make the obvious connection that both the Reys and George were forced to leave their home because of oppressive forces. There is no indication that the violence George might have endured in his capture mirrors a narrative of the torture and colonization of African bodies in American slavery, and no discussion of the similarities between the torture and death of Africans during slavery and that of the murder and suffering of Jews during the Holocaust. The overjoyed Curious George exhibition provides the compelling conditions of possibility for intertwining these narratives, yet disappointingly fails to do so.

Only a handful of critics have offered any attempt at a comparison. One exception is Edward Rothstein, who skirts close to the topic by mentioning that George was "born in the jungle and lured into the strange world of humans." Rothstein tells *New York Times* readers that George's jungle origins are present mainly by their absence (2010). Other reviewers go so far as to compare the Reys' escape with George's capture by The Man in the Yellow Hat (Mattoon 2010). In particular, Wecker (2010) approaches the point, suggesting that the reference to the Reys as "refugees" reminds readers that The Man in Yellow Hat trapped George and "removes him from his home in the African Jungle." David Check, the president of the Association for Jewish Theatre, suggests that "The Man's hat could be a reference to the yellow stars Jews were forced to wear"; while the similarity is eerie, he advances the argument no farther (Wecker 2010). Nor does the reference make sense. The yellow star Jews were legally forced to sew onto their clothing in Nazi Europe were to dehumanize and identify them.[9] The gravity of the horror endured by Africans and Jews in these atrocities would indicate that the reviewers' comparisons are at best incomplete and insignificant.

While both the Reys and George landed in America, the former were free to pursue the American Dream while the latter was forcefully removed and remained under the not-so-watchful eye of his captor. I am not denying that featuring Curious George may be one way to encourage students to engage the history of the Holocaust; however, while the shadow of George's capture appears in the Holocaust narratives, the absence of Curious George's enslavement narrative privileges the horrors of the Jews over those of Africans. The traumas are not comparable, but discussing different traumatic experiences in a productive and responsible manner can offer possibilities (Craps 2012). Postcolonial nostalgia comforts fragmented and non-chronological narratives as ways of inviting conversations that respect and honor the Reys' escape from Nazi Paris while also accepting and critiquing their representation of George as a captured African slave. Though the slavery depictions in the original *Curious George* (Rey 1941b) may not have been willful or conscious, a dialogue that includes the exceptional violence that both Jews and African Americans have faced and continue to face offers a productive possibility for US citizens to understand their relationship to their communities and their nation. In this ideal discussion, George can and should be seen as a member of both Jewish and African diasporas, and the Reys can be remembered, as individuals who both escaped violence and perpetuated it.

The jockeying of first-victim status in the US is not new. Jewish and African Americans endure/d histories explicitly impacted by race; racism; religious, ethnic, and racial privilege; and oppression. Postcolonial nostalgia helps to make sense of the complex, colonizing narratives that privilege the Reys' Holocaust account over Curious George's slavery tale. The nostalgic yearning for innocent, childhood characters not only attracts audiences to the "Curious George: The Holocaust Hero," but also protects its protagonists and its narrative from public criticism, preventing a story of slavery from staining the US reputation. Postcolonial nostalgia explains these Holocaust narratives as attempts to Americanize both George and the Holocaust. These dual and contrasting Americanized narratives invite a productive nostalgia for the resurrection of the so-called Greatest Generation and provide affirmation that the present America can be as it once was—a strong global leader. The nostalgic power they wield over many US audiences can be summoned as a vision of possibility for a country whose economic recessions are blamed on its lack of global leadership. In this respect, Curious George functions as what Joseph Nye (2005) might refer to as soft power—an idea, value, attitude, or behavior that can influence public life. Finally, the obvious presence of the jungle capture, together with the blatant failure to even mention its historical antecedent, directs attention away from the enslavement inscribed onto this cultural icon, and instead privileges the Holocaust as *the only* American narrative of terror. Together, these readings explain not only why Curious George is protected from critique, but also the ways in which his story exemplifies the necessity and obligation of continued postcolonial scholarship.

A postcolonial reading of the Curious George Holocaust narratives highlights the nostalgic longing for a once vibrant Jewish community and offers an explanation for the exhibits' erasure of the terrors of World War II and George's colonial capture. The Jewish narrative focuses on the primacy and *uniqueness* of the Holocaust. Since the 1990s, the Holocaust has figured centrally in the national narrative of America (Power 1999, 5). Comparisons of the Holocaust with the slaughter of Native Americans, the disabled, Queer, Asians, Africans, the Rwandan genocide, or any other atrocity has angered many American Jews (Power 1999; Zelizer 1998). The Americanization of the Holocaust enables citizens to downplay the current high rates of racial violence. For example, Craps argues that these discourses of uniqueness explain why Black-Jewish relations in the US have become increasingly strained (2012, 136). Consequently, when American slavery is raised as a national comparison of evil, even in instances of literary fiction, the Americanization of the Holocaust provides an "alibi to devalue the notion of historical responsibility" (Novick 1999, 15). The idea that the Holocaust is a convenient distraction from other instances of historical oppression, especially the genocide of Native Americans and the history of African slavery, is well documented (Craps 2012). Young explains that while enslavement unites African and Native communities, the Holocaust is the crux of Jewish common heritage (1994, 348). Jewish and African American persecutions are entangled in directing the American imagination; they both tell stories of horror and hope. Yet their differences are equally violent and impressive. Jews and Africans often experience a new level of persecution, displacement, devaluation, and horror. In this instance, both the Reys' escape and George's capture lack a distinctively horrific element.

Ironically, perhaps the lack of horror in George's capture and the Reys' escape make these made-for-children stories enduringly popular. This uniqueness discourse of the Holocaust depicts George as a survivor, unsuitable for critique. In addition to his popularity as an essential STEM teacher, Curious George becomes doubly protected from criticism, first as a cultural icon of childhood nostalgia, and then again as a Holocaust hero.

The recasting of Curious George as a Holocaust survivor/hero defines this icon as a member of the Jewish diaspora and provides an alibi that encases and erases his slavery-based past, precluding these discourses from attending to the African diaspora. The claim that the George collection is founded under racist ideologies, even if likely unconsciously, becomes reduced to the flawed assumption that one cannot simultaneously escape colonization and perpetuate it. While historical instances of decolonization have demonstrated otherwise, this colonial artifact affirms the privileging of the Holocaust survivor/hero narrative above all other injustices. "Curious George: The Holocaust Hero" can respond to a present call for a desired past, while concurrently negating a dishonorable stain.

Rothberg explains that many people falsely assume that "collective memories are articulated as a scarce resource and that the interaction of different collective memories within that sphere takes the form of a zero-sum struggle for preeminence" (2009, 3). All too often, the State becomes the site of this struggle. In the case of Curious George, the site of struggle is the American recognition (or lack thereof) of the colonization, enslavement, and murder of Jews during the Holocaust and Africans during American slavery. Instead of "*competitive* memory—as a zero-sum struggle over scare resources," Rothberg advocates for multidirectional memory (2009, 3). His understanding of memory is distinctly different from the grand narrative linear style of memory. In fact, his understanding of memory shares with Walder's (2011) postcolonial nostalgia a complex, nonlinear, present- and past-focused labor of multidirectional interventions in which heterogeneous and changing visions of World War II can be dialogically exchanged. Curious George Holocaust narratives and George's origins reflect a debate over the ways in which the atrocities the Jewish and African people have faced and continue to face are articulated as in competition in a US context. As such, critically considering the Curious George Holocaust narratives and the images of African capture that accompany them not as competitive but as supplemental can provide an opening for optimism and understanding. Rothberg (2013) astutely argues that reading the past as multidirectional rather than competitive can produce empathy, visions of justice, and a more inclusive re-narration of the past. Doing so can offer the opportunity to decolonize narratives that dominate Holocaust memory. For example, scholars should look to dismantle the trope of the triumphant hero/ survivor over the defeated and guilty experience and the rhetoric of uniqueness over other genocides and enslavements. This should lead to discussions that do not equate atrocities, but instead become potential grounds for collectivities that embrace religious and racialized histories of difference simultaneously (Rothberg 2009). Thus, if the discussion of George's African abduction was raised in concert with the Reys' escape from Nazi occupation in lesson plans and museum exhibits, the possibilities for radical reflection might proliferate. Curious George could ascend from a diasporic slave and Holocaust hero to an icon with multiple cultural potentialities in which colonization's relationship with religion, race, nation, and identity can be rethought in terms of coalition-building rather than competition.

Chapter Five

Curious Conclusions

On occasion, we rediscover serendipitously a book we treasured as children. At such moments, Maurice Halbwachs observed, we anticipate reliving "the memory of childhood." As we leaf through the pages, we become aware that the book is quite different from our remembered childhood response. The stories seem now "less extraordinary, more formulaic, less lively." We also note gaps in the text as well as verbal and pictorial images whose significance and meaning escaped us as children. Such phenomena of the memory of reading apply both to narratives we have loved and to narratives that frightened us when we were unaware how subtly conventions and genre shape and structure our experienced and acquired memories.
—*Hamida Bosmajian*, Sparing the Child

Reading the circulation of icons through postcolonial theories illuminates the ways in which one cultural icon can simultaneously serve multiple ideologies through multiple disciplines. Most simply, nostalgia explains adults' compulsion to defend cultural icons that they remember fondly. Nel explains that "racial stereotypes safely hide in children's literature and culture because nostalgia can mystify ideology" (2017, 22). People understand themselves as "open" to all ethnicities, religions, and races, yet all too often they are unwilling to admit that the colonial narratives that wind through their childhood advocate for and extend colonial teachings and mentalities without consequence. The excuses commonly include: "It's an old story and thus should not be held to the same standards"; "the authors did not intend for it to be racist"; "why does everything have to be so politically correct?"; or, "It's complicated." In his critical readings of *Charlie and the Chocolate Factory* (Dahl 1964) and *Huckleberry Finn* (Twain 1884), Nel defends these complications as an accurate description, but is clear that "complexity shouldn't be deployed as an alibi for racism" (2017, 23). Admitting the complications of cultural icons as simultaneously racist and pleasing offer opportunities to teach young children critical sensibilities that they can use when interacting with imperialism and colonialism.

A central conclusion of this project is that Curious George should be framed as a classic example of colonial children's literature. However, the ways in which he is protected reveal a great deal not only about US history, but also about the means by which cultural icons can further reinforce the history of colonialism that coordinates US citizenship and privilege. The mining of scholarship; the occupation of planets; the advocacy for imperial ideologies; the exploitation, enslavement, and extermination of peoples; and the propaganda of popular culture all inform the ways in which cultural icons of American exceptionalism function. In this instance, George has been shielded from critique because he is a nostalgic icon of adventure and heroism that generations adore, he promotes children's STEM education, and he plays a valuable role in Holocaust hero/survivor narratives—all while demonstrating how a successful American immigrant should act. Any one of these roles might offer Curious George an alibi; together they solidify his innocence.

George's longevity, and the enduring affection previous generations have held for him, provide a sense of stability and security. Associating his story with the complacency of slavery creates a direct threat to the idyllic memories of the childhoods of the parents and grandparents who adore him. Further, positioning George as a Holocaust survivor/hero pardons him from public critique because any critique of George at best demonstrates a lack of empathy for Holocaust survivors and at worst suggests a denial of the Holocaust entirely. Criticisms of George can be read as vicious attacks on the Americanized narrative that eulogizes the end of World War II as a moment of unparalleled US global leadership—an achievement the American government is always willing to tout. As Holocaust survivors, war criminals, and World War II veterans age and pass on, disgracing or critiquing those who endured the terror of Nazi violence is increasingly offensive. The postcolonial logics introduced in this book should caution readers against immediately dismissing critiques of Curious George and encourage them to reevaluate their commitment to this cuddly monkey without critically considering the practical and theoretical limits of such naïve readings. Using George as an exemplar of the ways in which cultural icons function, this monograph is an invitation to challenge the taken-for-granted assumptions that these ciphers clandestinely convey to generations by encouraging their audiences to commit to understanding how the practice of colonization morphs swiftly from insensitivity to ideological imperialism.

I have thought a great deal about how different this project would have been had I studied empirical responses to Curious George, conducted audience research on African American and Jewish readership, critically considered the limited roles afforded to queer, disabled, or female characters, or focused on the implications of Curious George as a tourist icon for Ellis Island and other New York City destinations. However, this project not only answers why Curious George lacks critique, but also invites a host of new questions that extend beyond Curious George to other cultural icons. By reading cultural icons through postcolonial lenes, audiences can trace the mediated ways in which cultural icons service the narratives of the nation. In this reading of Curious George, I amplify broader impactions about the circulation of cultural icons within the contemporary colonial landscape. As an exemplar, Curious George offers opportunities to inform the unique and productive ways in which post-colonial studies challenge disciplinary and chronological readings of cultural icons that position audiences to service civic narratives. These icons move diachronically while circulating, refiguring, and refashioning synchronically in order to appeal to the needs and desires of the nation.

The possibilities illuminated in each chapter of *Curious about George* rely on the scholarship of postcolonial studies to provide larger recommendations for how scholars should understand the ways in which cultural icons circulate. Chapter one argues for the revitalization and renewal of the important paths of resistance that postcolonial projects encourage. As an intellectual, cultural, and textual mode of analysis, postcolonial studies remain vital to the current cultural and political moment. Unlike some of its global, decolonial, and neo-colonial dissenters, its strength is its willingness to include and extend these and other theoretical perspectives, rather than to diminish its own boundaries. This theoretical movement commits to critiquing and resisting inequities, power imbalances, Eurocentric research methods, master narratives, universal theories of culture, spatial homogenization, and temporal teleology. As a mode of resistance, postcolonialism reflects an interventionist project that actively challenges contemporary scholarship to unveil its imperialist assumptions and resistive possibilities. The freedom from disciplinary allegiance that postco-lonial studies enjoys enables the possibility of reading texts such as Curious George in motion. This type of critique enables scholars to dip into and out of literature, media, nostalgia, policy, and racial politics without apology. The initial section also illuminates the ways in which cultural icons such as Curious George function. Importantly, colonial cultural icons circulate with a currency such that they, like ciphers, service the public by deploying an archetypal rec-ognizable product through which citizens can naturalize and harmonize their past as benign missions without remorse or consequence. One of the powers that Curious George wields is that his softness and his good-natured comedic curiosity present him as palatable to the nation's youngest members as well as to older educators and parents. He is an educator not just about weather patterns and gravity, but also about a version of history which emerges anew, void of its violence and national stain.

Chapter two highlights the ways in which the histories of colonialism reemerge in contemporary colonial ideologies in multiple and often competing contexts. The Reys' first publication, *Curious George* (Rey 1941b), reflects the racism of the 1940s as well as the history of the US colonization of Africans who were stolen and forced into captivity in the United States. Postcolonial children's literary criticism provides the tools for audiences to come into contact with their own cultural ambivalences toward the US's own history of enslaving Africans. This history is evidenced in common places with such simplicity and regularity that it is often unnoticed. However, the postcolonial commitment to identity and diaspora offers critical audiences tools to read moments of resistive possibility. George's resistance to assimilation—evidenced through his obsession with the iconic jungle tree, his desire to recreate jungle imagery, his love of animals, and his troubling relationship with his captor, The Man in the Yellow Hat—enables readers to understand him through metaphors of both the noble slave and a diasporic figure.

George's situated history within the African diaspora demonstrates that the history of slavery is not merely a construction of the past. Many African Americans living in the United States are the ancestors of people forcibly abducted from various countries within Africa. They were not free in the US, and certainly were not free to return home; like George, enslaved Africans were members of the African diaspora. Whether or not African Americans chose to assimilate and adopt White Christian traditions, their histories include the terrors of slavery, as the White man's history incorporates the disgrace of slave masters. Like any stain, slavery cannot and should not be erased from US remembrance. It is equally important to remember that African Americans also resisted in powerful and progressive ways. It was not President Lincoln's pure generosity that "freed the slaves"; it was the demand of Black men and women who resisted. These colonial histories of violence and resistance are foundational to the politics of racial inequality. A postcolonial reading of Curious George not only points to the various ways that discourses of benevolent colonialism are upheld and promoted through cultural icons, but also highlights the opportunities for resistance that can emerge in these oppressive movements.

Demanding the inclusion of the US's history of colonialism in our contemporary consciousness requires that we pay attention to the devastating violence inflicted on humans in previous efforts to march toward "progress" without reflection. Chapter three exhibits the ways in which investment in postcolonial science and technology studies outlines challenges that the humanities face in examining and critiquing the curiosity-fueled history of the human limits of science, technology, engineering, and mathematics. Challenging colonialism requires naming narratives that embolden people to position themselves as charitable and productive drones marching toward an unintelligible notion of progress. The adventurous travels of Curious George through space establish how the US quest toward the new planetary frontier of Mars metaphorically rehearses how the violence of the past is destined to repeat itself. To date, there have been a significant number of undebated STEM-based investments in the new frontier. For example, in 2012 NASA landed its first jet-propelled rover on Mars, amusingly named *Curiosity*. The mission was to determine if Mars had ever supported small lifeforms. The rover is scheduled to be replaced with a bigger and stronger machine, *Perseverance* (defined as "steadfast and loyal"), which will seek out signs of ancient life; the project has few dissenters. The desire to know if Mars can sustain life appears be a logical scientific inquiry worthy of billions of dollars. Major motion pictures such as *The Martian* (Scott 2015) and *Hidden Figures* (Melfi 2016) position audiences as anti-racist supporters of this scientific agenda. In preparation for life on the newest frontier, visitors to NASA's website are encouraged to participate by virtually driving the rover, sending rovers a postcard, or reading Martian Diaries (NASA n.d.). This call to participate mimics George's journey in that it is adventurous, exciting, and innocent. This quest and historically all too many projects of this type are offered as unquestionably ideologically virtuous opportunities. As members of society, citizens have a responsibility to advocate for an educational balance that enables people to learn from colonial pasts and to demand better futures for scientific inquiries.

Challenging narratives is also an essential theme in the Curious George Holocaust narratives explored in chapter four. These readings affirm dominant narratives about what a US Holocaust survivor/hero should be and how victims, asylum seekers, refugees, and immigrants should be interpolated. These accounts rehearse a whimsical tale of an adventurous escape, while offering little that bears witness to the horror of the hideous extermination of Jews, Roma, Sinti, Polish, Russian, Serbian, queer, children, the disabled, and German dissenters. As such, these narratives articulate the Reys as model immigrants whose arrival in the US enabled them to participate almost immediately in the American Dream by becoming famous book authors whose work contributed to the neoliberal capitalist economy. Almost eighty years later, President Trump signed a policy directive to criminalize immigrants unless they followed a path similar to the one followed by the Reys—by demonstrating the ability to add to the economic output and technological productivity of the US.

A cultural icon does important work when it challenges its own identity; in this instance, George the Holocaust hero seemingly displaces George the noble and diasporic slave. The value of postcolonial nostalgia is its denial of any accurate, inaccurate, or linear interpretation of the past. Instead, postcolonial nostalgia maintains multiple and seemingly contradictory potentialities. While Curious George may invite audiences to take an interest in the Holocaust, this cultural icon also offers a dangerous foreclosure. The discourses of Curious George fail to bear witness to the terror of the Holocaust while articulating an Americanized historical version of World War II in which the US is inaccurately positioned as a safe harbor for refugees and immigrants. The contradictions of the US as both bystander and savior for European refugees can coexist within a matrix of stories. A significant benefit of postcolonial nostalgia is that it admits fragments of the past into the present, allowing for self-reflective readings of projects that seek to understand dynamic power relations. Curious George receives protection because of the character's affiliation with his creators' Holocaust survivor status. Though George's benevolent slave narrative is not completely erased, it is for many readers marginalized beyond recognition. This hierarchical structure is important because it privileges the atrocities endured by one group over those of another. The unjustifiable extension of this construct is that individuals may believe that ignoring the brutality of others is acceptable because they or their ancestors were themselves victims.

I have great empathy for the Reys' refugee status, and significantly greater disdain for the Nazi regime. This critique of Curious George as a colonial cultural icon with a racist foundation does nothing to change that. As a member of the Jewish community, I want to encourage the public to understand that some Holocaust refugees are, in fact, capable of writing racist stories; similarly, some African Americans are culpable anti-Semites. An important conclusion of this project is that a victim of oppression is not exempt from perpetuating a cycle of violence. In other words, individuals and groups can be simultaneously victims and perpetrators of violence. All too often, contending for victim status privileges one identity group over another in a game of roulette that benefits no one. Postcolonial readings can offer resistance to the zero-sum jockeying for US first-victim status. Rather than understanding cultural icons chronologically (first enslaved, then displaced, and now a model citizen), postcolonial readings instead embrace the lack of linearity, narrative fluidity, and multidirectional variability, and allow for possibilities foreclosed in an either/or reading.

Read in unison, these chapters point toward important conclusions about the relationship between colonialism, cultural icons, and US exceptionalism and the ways that they function together. Taken together, this assemblage of Curious George discourses illuminates insights about identity politics, ideological colonization of marginalized identities, the colonialization of information and knowledge production in popular culture's promotion of colonial benevolence, and possibilities for resistance.

Curious George's diasporic role and his position as Holocaust hero endow him with a splintered identity. As a member of both the African and Jewish diasporas he is, as many people are, displaced from his home of origin and forced to assimilate to his new location while also longing to return to a previous place and community. For a literary George, his longing to be with other animals and his inability to conform to the customs are evidence of his struggle. For the Reys and George as refugee/immigrant/hero, the assimilation was easier because they quickly contributed to the market economy in the US. In both instances, memories of the homeland create community for people living in new places. Histories that bond groups together provide a powerful sense of belonging and agency. Movements such as Black Lives Matter, #MeToo, Standing Rock, Mauna Kea, and MMIW & Indigenous are examples that help unite identity groups. While such groups sometimes coalesce, the histories of Curious George illustrate how often the violence inflicted on one group impairs their ability to sympathize with the plights of others.

It took thirty-five years from the end of World War II to open the United States Holocaust Memorial Museum, and it took one hundred and fifty-one years after slavery was abolished for the National Museum of African American History and Culture to open on the National Mall in Washington, DC. Notably, both museums' accounts emphasize American exceptionalism. The Holocaust Museum makes no mention of turning away Jews at the US border; yet it celebrates the US's role in ending World War II. Likewise, the African American museum ignores the US's culpability in African enslavement and instead focuses on themes of history, community, and culture (Nel 2017). Recognizing complex narratives of oppression and resistance creates the opportunity for patrons to admit that colonialism is central to narratives of American exceptionalism. Similarly, more children's books circulate in the US about the Holocaust than about slavery (Nel 2017). This comparison does not suggest that either atrocity was worse or more terrifying. In both instances, humans were painfully enslaved, abused, tortured, raped, and killed. However, this comparison does illuminate that it takes a great deal longer for US citizens to recognize the nation's stains than to publicize its perceived heroic power. In the same harbor where the *St. Louis* was denied access, boats of enslaved peoples arrived. Admittedly, Jews and African Americans have significantly different struggles; nevertheless, they often share the same enemies. The very nature of identity politics makes a plea for recognition from the hegemonically dominant center by dismissing perceived enemies claiming the same piece of the corroded pie.

A second, yet distinct conclusion is that enslaved people are not only used and abused by their captors, but are also indoctrinated to advocate for future colonization without consequence. For Curious George, this argument is manifested in the space between chapters two and three. After being captured in the African jungle, the infantile George lives as a diasporic, yet noble slave longing to be among animals and jungle trees. While his memories of his own home remain, his rearticulation as an ambassador for STEM positions him as an advocate for colonization of the universe. While George's role with STEM is extensive, his obsession with space travel plays out in books, museums, toys, advertisements, film, and television. Though there have been many real monkeys to have died in space experiments, in 2014 PBS aired "Curious George Goes to Mars" in the episode "Red Planet Monkey" (Fallon, Bennett and Romano 2014). While on Mars, George helps engineers on Earth fix the rover. The episode was promoted by Space.com, applauded by NASA astronaut Karen Nyberg, and positively reviewed by Robert Pearlman, editor of the space history news (Kramer 2014). Further, Space.com encourages young viewers to play video games that enable George to "help scientists explore planets" (such as "George's Planet Quest," "Curious George: Blast off," and "George's Paintbox"). The juxtaposition between George's slave narrative and his promotion of Mars as a future site of colonization demonstrates the ways in which colonists not only enslave people physically but also indoctrinate them as advocates for future colonization. Simply, the colonized often serve their captors by becoming promoters of future colonization. This form of ideological teaching is predicated on benevolent colonialism and promotes the exploitation of peoples and places without questions or consequences.

Support for STEM extends well beyond Curious George. A third significant conclusion of this project is that the excessive government and cooperate funding of pro-technology and anti-humanist fields of STEM simultaneously starves humanities programs that study the social, political, cultural, and economic risks that accompany a never-ending push of curiosity over caution. Historically the enslavement and extermination of people was justified and glorified in the name of science and progress. This drive for progress included, but was not limited to, Nazi medical research, eugenics, and experimentation trials forced on the poor and disabled. In the last decade, federal funding for higher education research and development in science has continued to increase at a much higher rate than funding for the humanities. Science receives the largest amount of government support ($79,285,866 in 2018). Comparatively, the government's budget for higher education in the humanities in the same year was $498,597 (Gibbons 2020). The implication of this discrepancy is that a significant proportion of resources, researchers, and administrative support is dedicated to the scholarship of STEM faculty, while departments that prioritize critical thinking are left starving for budget and backing. Even before the coronavirus financially crippled higher education, the distinguished professor of English Reshmi Dutt-Ballerstadt explained that "academic prioritization" is a buzzword "used to sacrifice the humanities and social sciences for a robust expansion of other job-oriented programs . . . that serve the market-driven, neoliberal interests and profit-driven model of education" (2019). As corporate money and government resources infiltrate higher education, the colonization of liberal arts is forced to condense and exploit the humanities. The cycle is especially dangerous, Henry A. Giroux explains, because higher education is

> under assault by a host of religious, economic, ideological, and political fundamentalists . . . the script is similar: defund higher education, impose corporate models of governance, purge the university of critical thinkers, turn faculty into a low-waged army of part-time workers, and allow corporate money and power to increasingly decide course content and determine which faculty get hired . . . public values are replaced by corporate values, students become clients . . . and working-class and poor minority students are excluded from the benefits of higher education. (2013, para. 14)

Higher education is crucial to actively teaching and debating the ideas of democracy so that its community is emboldened with agency and knowledge production. When education is paid for by science, the science it produces will be packaged as ideologically neutral. Without a vibrant humanities sector, the consequences of such science will be devastating.

An important task of humanities programs such as communication; rhetoric; media studies; women's, gender & sexuality studies; and ethnic, Holocaust, and cultural studies is to consider critically the ways in which popular cultural renders ideas as neutral. A fourth conclusion advanced by this project is that cultural icons play a powerful role in helping to assuage the public's guilt over the past by diverting their attention from painful tragedies and genocides, thereby allowing people either to forget or to ignore painful memories. Curious George, and various other cultural icons, inform the public's understanding of political issues while posing as entertainment with a sprinkle of education. That sprinkle and the innocence of the products enable them to move through both time and space so that they are both relevant and seemingly ideologically sound. Yet their role as cultural icons enables them to represent social values and to confront political issues that are often tied to the problems of the day (Arjana 2017). As popular culture, cultural icons are powerful tools that help "to form personal identity, ideals of nationhood, and beliefs about cultures and communities outside our own," and they are "one of the ways in which people come to understand their position both within a larger collective identity and within an even larger geopolitical narrative or script" (Arjana, Ali and Fox 2017, xvii). For example, as STEM becomes a priority of dominant institutions (schools, government, religion, etc.), cultural icons become a powerful way of reinforcing messages that the public is already learning or already believes to be true. In this instance, George's role as a STEM ambassador and homeschool teacher seems to be a high priority for families who need to occupy a young child in front of a screen or encourage them to read a beloved book. For children, the whimsical adventures and mistakes of the childish monkey play out as entertainment, and when engaged by adults or educators, the enslaved monkey promoting curiosity and STEM technology is rarely problematized or if even recognized. If the history of slavery is taken up, Curious George, like Pocahontas and other popular cultural icons, teaches a colonial benevolence that encourages a feel-good narrative of the past. When other historical narratives emerge, they do so in a way that soothes the public emotionally so that horrific events, such as the Holocaust, become linear chronological moments that US global power terminated. There is no mention of victims' stories that are not entitled to be shared, and no recognition of government injustices (such as those of President Roosevelt's and President Truman's administrations). With the support of popular culture, the past is presented as distinct and digestible selections that enable audiences to cope by forgetting or rewriting. The privilege not to come to terms with a troubled past is reinforced by popular cultural icons that circulate in the most innocent of spaces.

The early reading of Curious George as a popular cultural icon who, while enslaved, offers possibilities of resistance should not be lost. Though hegemonic institutions push dangerous and racist agendas supported by cultural icons, there are also cultural icons working for resistance. The Burka Avenger, Banksy's murals, Vermont's Bread and Puppet theater, *Hamilton* (Miranda 2016), *Black Panther* (Coogler 2018), and the stranded polar bear on an ice island are arguably cultural icons that have been held up as symbols of resistance to serve the interest of democratic civic society, community, diversity, and agency. Postcolonialism is committed to both critique and intervention. Critiques are especially productive when coupled with resistance afforded through alliances. While the tyranny is terrifying, the responses are encouraging; though colonialism takes many forms, so too does its resistance. When identity politics are not understood as zero-sum and the progress mentality is dislodged, amazing anti-colonial coalitions can emerge.

Historically, the frontier mentality has led to the enslavement of African Americans, the slaughter of Native Americans, the extermination of religious minorities, the imprisonment of immigrants and the disabled, and an unre-coverable loss of biodiversity. While countless examples of the unquestioned drive toward science and technology proliferate, the pressing desire to occupy land has also produced coalitions that seek to understand the intentional and unintended effects of careless technological advancement. The inspiring and powerfully resistant response to the Dakota Pipeline in 2016 is one such example. It was an unlikely alliance, but during a cold North Dakota winter, United States veterans, Black Lives Matter members, Code Pink organizers, environmentalists, and members of twenty-three Native American tribes came together to protest at the Standing Rock Sioux Reservation. United, they fought a militarized mass of US police trying to seize tribal land and water resources for a 1,179-mile oil pipeline in the name of economic infrastructure. Though this pipeline project remains tied up in court battles, this type of organizing demonstrates that conditions for resistance exist to question ideologies offered up as value neutral.

Since the 2016 election, more than two hundred totally new national resis-tance projects have emerged (Movement Voter Project n.d.). Resistance is possible but is not always pervasive. Hegemonic ideologies, whether based in literature, science, or nostalgia, are always-already informed by the colonial histories from which they emerge. A central solicitation of this book is to encourage a brand of curiosity that resists narratives promoting adventurous ideologies presented as impartial progress and instead to inspire a type of renewed curiosity, founded in the rhetorics of caution and courage.

This re-reading of Curious George is an invitation to consider cultural icons critically with attention to the metaphors included and the persons and narratives excluded from their discourses. Participating in such postcolonial re-readings enables parents and educators to introduce young audiences to the important tools of critical reading praxis. Nel articulately explains that "what we read when we are young shapes us deeply because, when we are children, we are still very much in the process of becoming" (2017, 202). *Curious about George* is an appeal not just to teach critical reading with *Curious George*, but to read/view critically when children are growing and learning about history, identity formation, and civic responsibility. Adults need not be scholars to teach elements of postcolonial thinking. They should push critical thinking with the vigor they employ when teaching the basic phonics of reading. As children learn to read, they should also read to learn, so that from an early age, they can come to understand the stories they are expected to accept as both neutral and normal.

Notes

Chapter One

1. In 2018 there was a large public outcry to save the Curious George store from real estate development that would replace it with a three-story mall or apartments. The store was sold in 2019 from Adam Hirsch (the second owner) to Astra S. Titus (who worked for the literary nonprofit REACHOUT and Read). Titus planned to move the flagship store to the nearby small business hub of Bow Market in Somerville, Massachusetts. When the coronavirus pandemic hit in early spring 2020, it halted Titus's plans to move and expand the space to function as both a bookstore and a community literacy space (Green and Rosen 2019). In March 2021, unable to keep the store afloat in the midst of COVID, Titus bid a public farewell to the "Curious Community" and "goodbye to the Curious George Store forever" (Curious George and Co. 2021). She is now auctioning off material under her new trademark, Curious George & Co.

2. US or American exceptionalism is not an agreed-upon term and is used distinctly differently in presidential rhetoric and foreign policy. In this context I am not using US or American exceptionalism to applaud the US as exceptional because of its constitution, military, diversity, etc. While presidents have historically applauded the traditions that make the United States distinct, American exceptionalism in foreign policy leads to moral judgments and the belief that "liberal values transfer readily to foreign affairs" (Koh 2003, 1481). Yet even when used to describe the United States as exceptional or an exception, the term carries both a positive and a negative interpretation. Koh argues that the term was said to have been coined in 1831 by Alexis de Tocqueville to mean that the United States differs from other developed nations because of its unique origins, national credo, historical evolution, and distinctive political and religious institutions (Ceaser 2012). While Koh does not dismiss all US American exceptionalism, he has a strong distaste for promotion of an American double standard in which the US proposes different rules for itself than it expects to impose on the rest of world. Though some scholars have understood US American exceptionalism to denote values and ideas of US Americans' unique worldly situation, other scholars (those with which I ally myself) argue that it is a cancerous ideology that justifies US colonization of people and places (Ceaser 2012).

3. In Paris, the Reys published *Zebrology* (1937), *How the Flying Fishes Came into Being* (1938c), *Le Zoo* (1938a), and *Le Cirque* (1938b; Jones 2001).

4. Forrest carries the book with him on his first visit to his childhood love (Jenny), and then the book is featured in the final scene with Forrest Jr. (Zemeckis 1994).

5. The Hollywood exhibit closed in 2013 to make room for the Wizarding World of Harry Potter, but the Orlando exhibit remained a popular attraction until COVID-19 forced the park's temporary closure.

6. The *New Yorker* writer Adrienne Raphel (2016) claims that while George's recognition was substantially higher than the national average, his familiarity fondness was at an all-time low of twenty-one percent, which likely is related to the publicity of the Reys' Holocaust escape materials (a text I take up in chapter four).

7. Readings about cultural icons can be found in the following references: Barton and Brown 2011; Edwards, Enenkel, and Graham 2012; Gilbert 2010; Goscilo 2013; Heywood and Dworkin 2003; Plumb 2004; Schwartz-DuPre 2010.

8. There is a great deal of research committed to the role of metaphor in symbols, both literary and visual. This small section is not in any way intended to be inclusive. For more on metaphor in the field of Communication Studies see Bowers and Osborn 1966; Forceville and Paling 2018; Ivie 1987; Johnson 1981; Medhurst et al. 1997; Osborn 2009 and 2018; Osborn and Ehninger 1962.

9. For a more nuanced understanding of the flawed and ahistorical relationship between childhood and innocence, see Bernstein 2011.

10. For a more developed understanding of the debate between opponents, allies, and advocates of the contemporary use of postcolonial studies in the US, see Schwartz-DuPre 2014; for a more global perspective, see Huggan 2016.

11. Throughout this book I intentionally capitalize Black and White, except in specific citations in which I defer to the original publication. I do so following Ann Thúy Nguyễn and Maya Pendleton's (2020) rationale that capitalizing Black refers not just to a color but to the history and the racial identity of Black Americans: "major news outlets that adhere to the AP Style Book, do not call for capitalizing 'B' in Black. The typographical rule by these predominantly White institutions set precedence to lowercase 'b' despite the opposing preference by many Black people . . . re-naming and reclaiming language has been an important part of the struggle for racial justice." These authors also support the capitalization of White as a race as a way to understand how Whiteness functions as an institution. Nguyễn and Pendleton argue that "the detachment of 'White' as a proper noun allows White people to sit out of conversations about race and removes accountability from White people's and White institutions' involvement in racism" (2020).

12. Coloniality scholars make an important distinction between de-colonial and decolonial. While most scholarship talks about decolonizing practices, Maldonado-Torres (2007) differentiates the traditional notion of decolonization as colonial administration occupying a nation from de-colonial, which he reads as a radical shift from the history of Western modernity.

13. A common Yiddish term denoting audacity, courage, or nerve.

Chapter 2

1. The distinction is relevant. Some scholars, such as Australian literary theorist Katharine Jones (2006), argue for a rewriting of the phrase due to its ambiguous nature. Jones concludes that referring to the work as "child literature" would reduce confusion and clarify that this literature is written almost entirely by adults with children as their target audience (2006, 305). Though Jones makes an important point, the majority of the field

uses "children's literature" to refer to literature written by adults for young children. While young-adult and adolescent literatures are important areas of study, this brief review does not attend to books written for older populations.

2. Some academic controversy engages the Reys' intentions. Greenstone (2005), for example, argues that the Reys' portrayals "were neither an accident nor a mistake," and instead reflect the pre–World War II environment of the Jewish Reys as they escaped from Europe and took refuge in the United States, a narrative I further explore in chapter four. Cummins (1997) also cites the Reys' forced exile as a likely motivation for their stories. These scholars claim that their language barriers, nostalgia for home, and cultural clashes, as well as the deaths of their pet monkeys, all inspired their collection.

3. H. A. Rey died in 1977, at which point Margret Rey gave the publisher, Houghton Mifflin, the right to write new books with her approval. It took a fifteen-person staff to accomplish this task (Blair 2016), and Margret was always listed as an author. Some post-1977 books still list H. A. Rey as an author because the illustrators after 1977 purposely emulate H. A. Rey's drawing technique and style.

4. I agree with Peter Hunt, who argues that children are people whose minds and bodies have yet to mature in various definable ways (1996, 5). In this case, I am referring to young children under the age of seven.

5. This section is not intended to be a thorough review of children's literature. Instead, it is designed to set up the value of postcolonial criticism of children literature. For a more complete history of children's literature see Hunt (1996), Marcus (2008), and Mickenberg (2005).

6. In 1972, Atkinson Films produced a limited series in Ontario, Canada. In 1982, Margret Rey rejected a television series produced for CBS. In 1996, Universal took on the trademark (Houghton Mifflin retained the copyright), producing all four *Curious George* films (Big Cartoon Database n.d.).

7. From 1941–1944, *Curious George* sold an average of just over three thousand copies annually. In 1945, sales dropped to an all-time low (possibly because of the wartime paper rationing), and then began an increasingly upward trend from 1953 to the present (Marcus 2008). Arguably, *Curious George at the Railroad Station* (Margret and H. A. Rey 1990) may be the most popular text, earning at least $4 million in sales by 1993 (Irr 1999).

8. I am excluding academics who have argued for the effectiveness of: *Curious George* in student reading (Richek and McTague 1988); the popularity of Curious George in art education classrooms (Hinshaw 2006); how the Children's Hospital of Boston asked the Reys to tour the hospital, which led to *Curious George Goes to the Hospital* (Ryan 2008); and a host of book reviews. In 2016 National Public Radio did mention in a footnote that "Aspects of Curious George's story are no doubt problematic" (Blair 2016).

9. Dr. Karen Pitcher brought this important contribution to my attention.

10. In many instances only students' first names were documented. Thus, when a surname is provided, I document it; if not, I defer to first names.

11. This number was discerned from a book list the Curious George Book Store emailed to me in 2014 listing 179 books.

Chapter 3

1. Here I am referring to monkeys and not bush babies, lemurs, or humans.

2. While the 2006 *Curious George* film was George's first successful motion picture, it was not the first time he was animated. As early as 1963, producers were working to create

animated filmstrips. Between 1971 and 1977, Teaching Research films, an educational service produced by the *New York Times*, announced School Times featuring sound Filmstrips versions of five Curious George books (letter from Miller to the Reys, para. 3, in Rey Papers, Box 93, Folder 2).

3. Science fiction has also faced great feminist criticism for depicting reproductive technology as an alternative to reproductive rights and feminist sexuality (Hayward 2012).

4. In reality, monkeys tend to overwhelmingly inhabit the jungles in tropical rainforests of Africa, Central America, South America, and Asia.

5. See Haraway 1990 for a more comprehensive reading.

6. Godzilla appears in at least thirty-two films from his debut in 1954 to 2019. The references of popular media primates extend well beyond film. While popular "news" portrayals of apes are beyond the scope of this chapter, it is worth noting a few prominent examples. Los Angeles radio referred to Rodney King as "gorillas in the mist" (Lott 1999). Professional basketball star LeBron James was the first Black man to be on the cover of *Vogue* but did so pictured as a Godzilla/King Kong figure holding the petite Brazilian supermodel Gisele Bündchen (Ono 2009). The public portrayals include Seattle Seahawks' former running back Marshawn Lynch's popular alter ego "Beast Mode" and H&M's international racist advertisement (Lubitz 2018) featuring a young black boy modeling a sweatshirt reading "the coolest monkey in the jungle." This last example circulated primarily on the internet and drew a great deal of public outrage. South African protesters destroyed several local H&M stores and H&M issued a formal apology (Lubitz 2018).

7. For a more comprehensive list, see Haraway (1988, 162–64).

8. This is a fascinating and important connection between cultural icons and primates was pointed out to me by Kent Ono.

Chapter 4

1. H. A.'s full name was Hans Augusto Reyersbach. Reyersbach was a difficult name for Brazilians to pronounce, and Hans thought it would be easier for him to make money as an artist if he shortened it to H. A. Rey (Borden and Drummond 2005, 19). Borden's book, as well and the other Curious George Holocaust-related materials discussed in this chapter, referred to him as both Hans and H. A. Margret's real name was Margarete, but she changed it shortly after her marriage in 1935.

2. In recent years the term Holocaust, which was used in a more general way prior to World War II, has been critiqued because it places greater emphasis on destruction by fire. Thus, many scholars have moved toward the common alternative *Shoah*, a Hebrew term connoting wasteland or destruction. Some also use a Yiddish variation, *Churban*, meaning destruction (often of temples). Both these alternatives reject the notion of sacrifice and emphasize Jewish victims. Yet others reject these terms because they only highlight Jewish victims and not the destruction of other non-Aryans or the role of genocide, thus they prefer the Third Reich (Kokkola 2003, 5). Through this chapter, and this book more broadly, I follow the lead of Lydia Kokkola, and will continue using the term Holocaust because it is widely understood by non-specialists and is inclusive of all people affected by the Holocaust—Jewish, Gypsies, Soviets, Poles, Slavs, Jehovah's Witnesses, Catholic priests, homosexuals, handicapped, Africans, Asians, and all non-White Aryans.

3. First-time director Ema Ryan Yamazaki funded the film through a Kickstarter campaign that has since raised $168,010 (Yamazaki 2016). After "official selection" recognition from the Nantucket, LA, and Rooftop film festivals, the mixed-media, partly animated film debuted in 2017 at select theaters.

4. The United States Holocaust Museum defines survivor as "any person who was displaced, persecuted, and/or discriminated against by the racial, religious, ethnic, social, and/or political policies of the Nazis and their allies between 1933 and 1945. In addition to former inmates of concentration camps and ghettos, this also includes refugees and people in hiding" (United States Holocaust Memorial Museum n.d.)

5. Some examples include: Bal, Crewe, and Spitzer 1998; Baxter 2011; Cordova 2008; Hasian 2006; Hasian Jr. 2002 and 2014; Nora and Kritzman 1996; Rothberg 2013; Soh 2009; Stier 2009; Walder 2011; Young and Braziel 2007; J. E. Young 1994.

6. While collective and public memories are often conflated, the philosopher Edward S. Casey does an astute job of explaining the difference. Collective memory, he argues, is the circumstance in which different people, who do not necessarily know one another, recall the same event, each in their own way (Casey 2004, 23). Public memory, in contrast, is an event that occurs in public in front of and with others (2004).

7. The color of most Curious George books is a shade of yellow called Gund 8 (some sites refer to its Hex color as #fffd54). The palette of colors designers use for Curious George motifs includes red (Hex color #eb3323); brown, often used for his body (Hex #9e4a1b); true black (Hex #000); and the shade of tan usually used for his face (Hex #f7cdaf) (ColorsWall 2019).

8. The 2013 Pew study sites a 91 percent decrease in religious American Jews (United States Holocaust Memorial Museum n.d.).

9. This practice started in the thirteenth-century Middle Ages and Renaissance but was phased out during the seventeenth and eighteenth centuries. Jewish badges were abolished in Western Europe with the French Revolution and the emancipation of Western European Jews. "The Nazis resurrected this practice as part of their persecutions during the Holocaust . . . psychological tactics aimed at isolating and dehumanizing the Jews of Europe, directly marking them as being different (i.e., inferior) to everyone else. It allowed for the easier facilitation of their separation from society and subsequent ghettoization, which ultimately led to the deportation and murder of 6 million Jews" (Arsenault n.d.).

References

Abbott, J. (n.d.). "Why STEM Education Still Matters." WGBH Educational Foundation. http://www.wgbh.org/foundation/why-stem-education-still-matters.

Achebe, C. (1977). "An Image of Africa: Racism in Conrad's 'Heart of Darkness.'" *Massachusetts Review* 18. https://polonistyka.amu.edu.pl/__data/assets/pdf_file/0007/259954/Chinua-Achebe,-An-Image-of-Africa.-Racism-in-Conrads-Heart-of-Darkness.pdf.

Adams, V. (2002). "Randomized Controlled Crime: Postcolonial Sciences in Alternative Medicine Research." *Social Studies of Science* 32 (5): 659–90. https://doi.org/10.1177%2F030631270203200503.

Ainley, N. (2016). *The Incredible True Love Story Behind Curious George.* Vice, August 13, 2016. https://www.vice.com/en_us/article/pgq9nn/curious-george-creators-documentary-interview.

Ali, W. (2017). Foreword. In *Veiled Superheroes: Islam, Feminism, and Popular Culture*, S. R. Arjana with K. Fox, ix–xiii. Lanham, MD: Lexington Books.

Alley-Young, G. (2008). "Articulating Identity: Refining Postcolonial and Whiteness Perspectives on Race within Communication Studies." *Review of Communication* 8 (3): 307–21. https://doi.org/10.1080/15358590701845311. Almiron, N., and M. Cole (2016). "Introduction: The Convergence of Two Critical Approaches. In *Critical Animal and Media Studies: Communication for Nonhuman Animal Advocacy*, edited by N. Almion, M. Cole, and C. P. Freemon, 1–7. New York: Routledge, Taylor and Francis Group.

ALSC History. (n.d.). Association for Library Service to Children. Retrieved September 16, 2015. http://www.ala.org/alsc/aboutalsc/historyofalsc.

Alter, A., and E. A. Harris (2021). "Dr. Seuss Books Are Pulled, and a 'Cancel Culture' Controversy Erupts." *The New York Times*, March 4, 2021. https://www.nytimes.com/2021/03/04/books/dr-seuss-books.html.

America COMPETES Reauthorization Act (2011). H.R. 5116, 111th Cong. http://www.govtrack.us/congress/bills/111/hr5116.

American Indians in Children's Literature (n.d.). "About AICL." Retrieved August 25, 2020. http://americanindiansinchildrensliterature.net/.

American Library Association (n.d.). "The History of the Coretta Scott King Book Awards." *Ethnic and Multicultural Information Exchange Roundtable*. Retrieved September 16, 2015. www.ala.org/emiert/cskbookawards/about.

Anderson, R. P., K. Kaufman, D. Reynolds, M. Rey and H. A. Rey (2006). *Curious George the Movie: Curious George's Big Adventures.* Boston: Houghton Mifflin Co.

Anderson, R. P., and M. O'Keefe Young, (2010). *Happy Easter, Curious George*. Boston: HMH Books for Young Readers.

Anderson, W. (2002). "Introduction Postcolonial Technoscience." *Social Studies of Science* 32.5 (6): 643–58. https://www.jstor.org/stable/3183050.

Anderson, W. (2009). "From Subjugated Knowledge to Conjugated Subjects: Science and Globalization, or Postcolonial Studies of Science?" *Postcolonial Studies* 12 (4): 389–400. https://doi.org/10.1080/13688790903350641.

Anonymous contributor (2013). "11 of The Most Racist Movies Ever Made." *Atlanta Black Star*, November 22, 2013. Retrieved December 15, 2014. http://www.atlantablackstar .com/2013/11/22/11-of-the-most-racist-movies-ever-made/3/.

Apted, M., dir. (1988). *Gorillas in the Mist*. Universal City, CA: Universal Pictures.

Archaeological Institute of America (2006). "Insider: Curious George and the Looted Idol." *Archaeology Magazine* 59 (3). Retrieved September 16, 2020. https://archive.archaeology .org/0605/news/insider.html.

Arjana, S. R., with K. Fox (2017). *Veiled Superheroes: Islam, Feminism, and Popular Culture*. Lanham, MD: Lexington Books.

Arsenault, J. (n.d.). "Jewish Stars and Other Holocaust Badges." Holocaust Memorial Center. https://www.holocaustcenter.org/visit/library-archive/holocaust-badges/.

Artazza (2012). "Thanksgiving Parade." *Artazza* (blog), December 5, 2012. Retrieved December 9, 2015. artazza.wordpress.com/tag/thanksgiving-parade/.

Art Daily (2010). "Curious George Saves the Day at the Jewish Museum." *ArtDaily*, March 23, 2010. Retrieved November 4, 2015. http://artdaily.com/news/37002/Curious-George -Saves-the-Day-at-the-Jewish-Museum#.WRvHo8IIIDVo.

Ashcroft, B., Gareth Griffiths, and H. Tiffin (2007). *Post-Colonial Studies: The Key Concepts*. 2nd ed. London and New York: Routledge.

Ashmore, A. M. (2002). "Reflection on the Black Experience in Children's Literature." *Mississippi Libraries* 66: 44–45. http://www.misslib.org/Resources/Documents/ML archive/ML2002Summer.pdf.

Ashmore, A. M. (2010). "From Elizabite to Spotty: The Reys, Race and Consciousness Raising." *Children's Literature Association Quarterly* 35 (4): 357–72. https://muse.jhu.edu/ article/404123.

Ashmore, A. M. (2012). "Elizabite: The Story of the Book—Part VI." *All Things Rey* (blog), May 31, 2012. http://allthingsrey.blogspot.com/2012/05/.

Association for Library Service to Children (n.d.). "Welcome to the Newberry Medal Home Page." Retrieved April 13, 2018. http://www.ala.org/alsc/awardsgrants/bookmedia/ newberymedal/newberymedal.

Auden, W. H. (1969). "The Quest Hero." In *Tolkien and the Critics: Essays on J. R. R. Tolkien's The Lord of the Rings*, edited by N. D. Isaacs & R. A. Zimbardo, 40–61. Notre Dame, IN: University of Notre Dame Press.

Austen, J. (2003). *Mansfield Park*. Edited by James Kinsley. New York: Oxford University Press.

Bahri, D. (1995). "Once More with Feeling: What Is Postcolonialism?" *ARIEL* 26 (1): 222–34. https://journalhosting.ucalgary.ca/index.php/ariel/article/view/33694.

Bailey, M. (2016). "New Curious George App Encourages STEM Learning." *New York Metro Parents*, June 9, 2016. http://www.nymetroparents.com/article/curious-george-train -adventure-encourages-stem-learning-in-kids20160609.

Bal, M., J. Crewe, and L. Spitzer, eds. (1998). *Acts of Memory: Cultural Recall in the Present*. Hanover, NH: Dartmouth College Press.

Ball, J. C. (1997). "Max's Colonial Fantasy: Rereading Sendak's *Where the Wild Things Are*." *ARIEL* 28 (1): 167–79. https://journalhosting.ucalgary.ca/index.php/ariel/article/view/33874.

Ball, P. (2014). *Curiosity: How Science Became Interested in Everything*. Chicago: University of Chicago Press.

Balsamo, A. (1998). "Introduction." *Cultural Studies* 12 (3): 285–99. https://doi.org/10.1080/095023898335438.

Banfield, B. (1998). "Commitment to Change: The Council on Interracial Books for Children and the World of Children's Books." *African American Review* 32 (1): 17–22. https://www.jstor.org/stable/3042264?seq=1.

Bardhan, N. (2011). "*Slumdog Millionaire* Meets 'India Shining': (Trans)national Narrations of Identity in South Asian Diaspora." *Journal of International and Intercultural Communication* 4 (1): 42–61. https://doi.org/10.1080/17513057.2010.533785.

Barnes, J. (2020). "Amazon #AtHome Is Bringing Free Content to Fire TV and Fire Tablet Devices." *CordCutters News*, April 17, 2020. https://www.cordcuttersnews.com/amazon-athome-is-bringing-free-content-to-fire-tv-and-fire-tablet-devices/.

Barnes, M. (2015). "Obama Administration Earmarks $12 Million in Reparations for Holocaust Survivors." *Rollingout*, October 7, 2015. http://rollingout.com/2015/10/07/obama-administration-earmarks-12-million-reparations-holocaust-survivors/.

Barrow, B., and S. Borsenstein (2021). "Biden Says His Advisers Will Lead with 'Science and Truth.'" AP NEWS, January 16. https://apnews.com/article/joe-biden-technology-francis-collins-022fc771e262e6f1c7e33ffe80e1d37b.

Barton, A., and A. Brown (2011). "Dartmoor: Penal and Cultural Icon." *The Howard Journal of Criminal Justice* 50 (5): 478–91. https://doi.org/10.1111/j.1468-2311.2011.00690.x.

Bates, K G. (2015). "Race and King Kong." NPR.org, December 22, 2015. http://www.npr.org/templates/story/story.php?storyId=5066156.

Baxter, K. I. (2011). "Memory and Photography: Rethinking Postcolonial Trauma Studies." *Journal of Postcolonial Writing* 47 (1): 18–29. https://doi.org/10.1080/17449855.2010.507930.

Bernstein, R. (2011). *Racial Innocence: Performing American Childhood from Slavery to Civil Rights*. New York: New York University Press.

Biederman, D. E. (2007). *Law and Business of the Entertainment Industries*. 5th ed. New York: Praeger.

Biedermann, H. (1994). *Dictionary of Symbolism: Cultural Icons and the Meanings Behind Them*. Translated by James Hulbert. 2nd ed. New York: Plume.

Biemiller, L. (1995). "Deconstructing Barbie: A Lesbian Scholar Examines a Cultural Icon." *The Chronicle of Higher Education* 41 (28).

Biesecker, B. A. (2002). "Remembering World War II: The Rhetoric and Politics of National Commemoration at the Turn of the 21st Century." *Quarterly Journal of Speech* 88 (4): 393. https://doi.org/10.1080/00335630209384386.

Big Cartoon Database (n.d.). "Curious George TV Episode Guide." *Big Cartoon Database*. Retrieved April 27, 2017. https://www.bcdb.com/cartoons/Other_Studios/A/Atkinson_Film-Arts/Curious_George/.

Bissell, W. C. (2013). "Engaging Colonial Nostalgia." *Cultural Anthropology* 20 (2): 215–48. https://doi.org/10.1525/can.2005.20.2.215.

Blair, E. (2016). "Curious George Celebrates 75 Years of Monkey Business." National Public Radio, September 28, 2016. https://www.npr.org/2016/09/28/495650014/curious-george-celebrates-75-years-of-monkey-business.

Bonnett, A. (2016). *The Geography of Nostalgia: Global and Local Perspectives on Modernity and Loss.* New York: Routledge.

Bonsu, S. K. (2009). "Colonial Images of Global Times: Consumer Interpretations of Africa and Africans in Advertising." *Consumption, Markets & Culture* 12 (1): 1–25. https://doi .org/10.1080/10253860802560789

Borden, L. (n.d.). "News." Louise Borden. http://www.louiseborden.com/news.php.

Borden, L. (n.d.). "The Journey that Saved Curious George." Louise Borden. http://www .louiseborden.com/book.php?id=journey.

Borden, L. (n.d.). "The Journey that Saved Curious George: About the Book." Houghton Mifflin Books. http://www.houghtonmifflinbooks.com/booksellers/press_release/ borden.

Borden, L., and A. Drummond (2005). *The Journey that Saved Curious George: The True Wartime Escape of Margret and H. A. Rey.* Boston: Houghton Mifflin.

Bosmajian, H. (2002). *Sparing the Child: Grief and the Unspeakable in Youth Literature about Nazism and the Holocaust.* New York: Routledge.

Boston.com (2012). "Curious George Store Returns to Harvard Square." *Boston.com*, April 27, 2012. Retrieved July 6, 2014. http://archive.boston.com/yourtown/news/cambridge/2012/ 04/curious_george_store_returns_t.html.

Botelho, M. J., and M. Kabakow Rudman (2009). *Critical Multicultural Analysis of Children's Literature: Mirrors, Windows, and Doors.* New York: Routledge.

Boulukos, G. (2008). *The Grateful Slave: The Emergence of Race in Eighteenth-Century British and American Culture.* Cambridge: Cambridge University Press.

Bowers, J. W., and M. M. Osborn (1966). "Attitudinal Effects of Selected Types of Concluding Metaphors in Persuasive Speeches." *Speech Monographs* 33 (2): 147–55. https://doi. org/10.1080/03637756609375490.

Box Office Mojo (n.d.). "Curious George." Retrieved July 6, 2014. http://www.boxofficemojo .com/movies/?id=curiousgeorge.htm.

Bradford, C. (1997). "Representing Indigeneity: Aborigines and Australian Children's Literature Then and Now." *ARIEL* 28 (1): 90–99. https://journalhosting.ucalgary.ca/index .php/ariel/article/view/33869.

Bradford, C. (2007). *Unsettling Narratives: Postcolonial Readings of Children's Literature.* Waterloo, Ont.: Wilfrid Laurier University Press.

Bradford, C. (2012). "Instilling Postcolonial Nostalgias: Ned Kelly Narratives for Children." *Journal of Australian Studies* 36 (2): 191–206. https://doi.org/10.1080/14443058.2012.6745 45.

Brantlinger, P. (1985). "Victorians and Africans: The Genealogy of the Myth of the Dark Continent." *Critical Inquiry* 12 (1): 166–203. https://www.jstor.org/stable/1343467?seq=1.

Braziel, J. E., and A. Mannur (2003). *Theorizing Diaspora: A Reader.* Oxford: Blackwell Publishers.

Breznican, A. (2014). "Animated George Takes Flight." *USA Today*, November 3, 2014. http:// usatoday30.usatoday.com/life/movies/news/2005-10-02-curious-george-inside_x.htm.

Bridenstine, J. (2019). "NASA Administrator Statement on NASA's Moon to Mars Plans, FY 2020 Budget." NASA, March 11, 2019. https://www.nasa.gov/press-release/ nasa-administrator-statement-on-nasa-s-moon-to-mars-plans-fy-2020-budget.

Brill, P. (2016). "HMH Kicks Off Curious World Tour." *Publishers Weekly*, June 30, 2016. https://www.publishersweekly.com/pw/by-topic/childrens/childrens-industry-news/ article/70792-braking-for-books-hmh-kicks-off-curious-world-tour.html.

Bronte, C. (1847). *Jane Eyre*. New York: Harper & Brothers.

Brooker, W. (2000). *Batman Unmasked: Analyzing a Cultural Icon*. New York: Continuum.

Broome, F. (2015). "Curious George and Dual Memories." *Mandela Effect*, November 4, 2015. https://www.mandelaeffect.com/curious-george-and-dual-memories/.

Brown, J. (2013). Letter to Chairman John Kline and Ranking Member George Miller, April 8, 2013. Stem Education Coalition. http://www.stemedcoalition.org/wp-content/uploads/2010/05/Letter-STEM-Ed-Coalition-to-Ed-and-WF-on-STEM-Hearing-4-8-13.pdf.

Brown, S. (2014). "She Was Fine When She Left Here: Polysemy, Patriarchy, and Personification in Brand Titanic's Birthplace." *Psychology & Marketing* 31 (1): 93–102. https://doi.org/10.1002/mar.20678.

Brubaker, R. (2005). "The 'Diaspora' Diaspora." *Ethnic and Racial Studies* 28 (1): 1–19. https://doi.org/10.1080/0141987042000289997.

Buescher, D. T., and K. A. Ono (1996). "Civilized Colonialism: Pocahontas as Neocolonial Rhetoric." *Women's Studies in Communication* 19 (2): 127–53. https://doi.org/10.1080/07491409.1996.11089810.

Burke, K. (1945). *A Grammar of Motives*. Berkeley: University of California Press.

Burke, K. (1984). *Permanence and Change: An Anatomy of Purpose*. Berkeley: University of California Press.

Burton, T., dir. (2001). *Planet of the Apes*. Los Angeles: 20th Century Fox.

Bush, G. W. (2006). "President Bush's State of the Union Address." *The Washington Post*, January 31, 2006. http://www.washingtonpost.com/wpdyn/content/article/2006/01/31/AR2006013101468.html.

Cadden, M. (1997). "Home Is a Matter of Blood, Time, and Genre: Essentialism in Burnett and McKinley." *ARIEL* 28 (1): 53–67. https://journalhosting.ucalgary.ca/index.php/ariel/article/view/33867.

Camera, L. (2018). "White House Outlines Five-Year STEM Push." *Education Reporter*, December 3, 2018. https://www.usnews.com/news/education-news/articles/2018-12-03/white-house-outlines-five-year-stem-push.

Cameron, J., dir. (2009). *Avatar*. Los Angeles: 20th Century Fox.

Campbell, E. (2019). "The Problem with Picture Book Monkeys: Racist Imagery Associating Simians with Black People Has a Long History." *School Library Journal*, December 4, 2019. https://www.schoollibraryjournal.com/?detailStory=The-problem-with-picture-book-monkeys-racist-imagery-libraries.

Carroll, L. (1865). *Alice's Adventures in Wonderland*. London: Macmillan Publishers.

Casey, E. S. (2004). "Public Memory in Place and Time." In *Framing Public Memory*, edited by K. Phillips, 17–44. Tuscaloosa: University of Alabama Press.

Cavanagh, E. (2020). "11 Books to Help Children Cope with School Closings, Not Seeing Friends, and Feeling Anxious." *Insider*, April 7, 2020. https://www.insider.com/books-to-help-children-cope-during-the-coronavirus-pandemic-2020-4.

Ceaser, J. W. (2012). "The Origins and Character of American Exceptionalism." *American Political Thought* 1 (1): 3–28. https://doi.org/10.1086/664595.

Chakravartty, P. (2004). "Telecom, National Development and the Indian State: A Postcolonial Critique." *Media, Culture & Society* 26 (2): 227–49. https://doi.org/10.1177/0163443704041174.

Chiari, E. (2016). "The Whisper with a Thousand Echoes: Tony Gentile's Photograph of Falcone and Borsellino." *Modern Italy* 21 (4): 441–52. https://doi.org/10.1017/mit.2016.48

Children's Museum of Manhattan (2011). "Children's Museum of Manhattan Kicks off Summer with Curious George: Let's Get Curious! Exhibit." News release, May 31, 2011. https://cmom.org/press/press-release-childrens-museum-of-manhattan-kicks-off -summer-with-curious-george-lets-get-curious-exhibit/.

Children's Television Act of 1990 (1990). H. R. 1677, 101st Cong. https://www.congress.gov/ bill/101st-congress/house-bill/1677#:~:text=Children's%20Television%20Act%20of%20 1990%20%2D%20Title%20I%3A%20Regulation%20of%20Children's,number%20of%20 minutes%20per%20hour.

Childs, P. (1999). *Post-Colonial Theory and English Literature: A Reader*. Edinburgh: Edinburgh University Press.

Clark, S. (2020). "NASA Astronauts Launch from US Soil for First Time in Nine Years." *Spaceflight Now*, May 30, 2020. https://spaceflightnow.com/2020/05/30/nasa-astronauts -launch-from-us-soil-for-first-time-in-nine-years/.

Cloud, M. (2006). "Curious George: The Movie versus the Books." *Yahoo Voices*, March 30, 2006. https://www.voices.yahoo.com/curious-george-movie-versus-books-40018. html?cat=38.

Coates, T. (2015). *Between the World and Me*. New York: Spiegel & Grau.

Collins, P. H. (2005). *Black Sexual Politics: African Americans, Gender, and the New Racism*. New York: Routledge.

ColorsWall (2019). "Curious George Brand Colors." Retrieved November 10, 2020. https:// colorswall.com/palette/4181/.

Committee on STEM Education of the National Science & Technology Council (2018). "Charting a Course for Success: America's Strategy for STEM Education." *Whitehouse .gov*, December 12, 2018. https://www.whitehouse.gov/wp-content/uploads/2018/12/ STEM-Education-Strategic-Plan-2018.pdf.

Concord Evaluation Group (2012). "Evaluation of Curious George." Retrieved May 14, 2015. https://www-tc.pbs.org/parents/curiousgeorge/program/pdf/Curious_George_ Evaluation.pdf.

Conrad, J. (1899). *Heart of Darkness*. Claremont, CA: Coyote Canyon Press.

Coogler, R., dir. (2018). *Black Panther*. Burbank, CA: Marvel Studios.

Cooper, M. C., and E. B. Schoedsack, dirs. (1933). *King Kong*. Los Angeles: Radio Pictures.

Cooperative Children's Book Center (n.d.). "CCBC Diversity Statistics.". Retrieved August 25, 2020. https://ccbc.education.wisc.edu/literature-resources/ccbc-diversity-statistics/.

Cooperative Children's Book Center (2020). "The Numbers Are In: 2019 CCBC Diversity Statistics." *CCBlogC* (blog), June 16, 2020. Retrieved August 26, 2020. http://ccblogc .blogspot.com/2020/06/the-numbers-are-in-2019-ccbc-diversity.html.

Cordova, N. I. (2008). "The Incomplete Subject of Colonial Memory: Puerto Rico and the Post/Colonial Biopolitics of Congressional Recollection." *Communication Review* 11 (1): 42–75. https://doi.org/10.1080/10714420801888427.

Craps, S. (2012). "Jewish/Postcolonial Diasporas in the Work of Caryl Phillips." In *Metaphor and Diaspora in Contemporary Writing*, edited by J. P. A. Sell, 135–50. Houndmills, Basingstoke, New York: Palgrave Macmillan.

Cummins, J. (1997). "The Resisting Monkey: Curious George, Slave Captivity Narratives, and the Postcolonial Condition." *ARIEL* 28 (1): 69–83. https://journalhosting.ucalgary.ca/ index.php/ariel/article/view/33868.

Curious George (n.d.). "Curious George for Parents: Activities, Curious about Space." CuriousGeorge.com. Retrieved March 22, 2015. http://www.curiousgeorge.com/parents -resources/kids-activities/space.

Curious George (2019). "Curious about George?" Retrieved May 15, 2019. http://www
.curiousgeorge.com/about%20us.

IMDB (n.d.). "Curious George: Awards." Retrieved February 15, 2019. https://www.imdb
.com/title/tt0449545/awards.

Curious George and Co. (2021). "The Curious George Store." March 30. https://curious
georgeandco.com/

Dahl, R. (1964). *Charlie and the Chocolate Factory*. London: George Allen & Unwin.

Davies, D. (2020). "Author Traces What Happened to WWII's 'Last Million' Displaced People."
National Public Radio, September 10, 2020. https://www.npr.org/2020/09/10/911111217/
author-traces-what-happened-to-wwiis-last-million-displaced-people

Davenport, C. (2021). "The Biden Administration Has Set Out to Dismantle Trump's Legacy,
Except in One Area: Space." *Washington Post*, March 2, 2021. https://www.washington
post.com/technology/2021/03/02/biden-space-artemis-moon-trump/

DCSTEMNetwork (n.d.). "Curious George STEM Interactive Lesson Plans." Retrieved
August 10, 2020. https://www.dcstemnetwork.org/resource/curious-george-stem/

de Brunhoff, J. (1934). *The Story of Babar*. New York: Random House Books for Young
Readers.

Di Maria, D. L. (n.d.). "5 Ways the Biden Administration May Help Stem the Loss of
International Students." *The Conversation*, February 3, 2021. http://theconversation
.com/5-ways-the-biden-administration-may-help-stem-the-loss-of-international
-students-153779.

Desmon, J. (2014). *Curious George: The Golden Meatball*. Palo Alto, CA: Theatre Works USA.

Dirda, M. (2016). "Curious George Turns 75: Why the Monkey and the Man in the Yellow
Hat Endure." *Washington Post*, September 6, 2016. https://www.washingtonpost.com/
entertainment/books/curious-george-turns-75-why-the-monkey-and-the-man-in-the
-yellow-hat-endure/2016/09/06/e0298f26-6f98-11e6-8365-b19e428a975e_story.html?utm
_term=.d9a80b9cbd82.

Disability Justice (n.d.). "The Right to Self-Determination: Freedom from Involuntary
Sterilization." Disability Justice website. Retrieved September 15, 2020. https://
disabilityjustice.org/right-to-self-determination-freedom-from-involuntary-steril
ization/.

Docter, P., D. Silverman, and L. Unkrich, dirs. (2001). *Monsters, Inc.* Emeryville, CA: Pixar
Animation Studios.

Dorfman, A. (1983). *The Empire's Old Clothes: What the Long Ranger, Babar, and Other
Innocent Heroes Do to Our Minds* (C. Hansen, Trans.). Pantheon.

Dotan, B. S. (2009). *Wartime Escape: Margret and H. A. Rey's Journey from France* [125 feet].
Curated by Beth Seldin Dotan, and including twenty-six framed art prints by Allan
Drummond. Houston, TX: Institute for Holocaust Education.

Duncan, R., and M. J. Smith, eds. (2013). *Icons of the American Comic Book*. Vol. 1. Santa
Barbara, CA: Greenwood.

Durant, S. (2003). *Postcolonial Narrative and the Work of Mourning: J. M. Coetzee, Wilson
Harris, and Toni Morrison*. Albany: State University of New York Press.

Dutt-Ballerstadt, R. (2019). "Shrinking Liberal Arts Programs Raise Alarm Bells
among Faculty." *Inside Higher Ed.*, March 1, 2019. https://www.insidehighered.com/
advice/2019/03/01/shrinking-liberal-arts-programs-raise-alarm-bells-among-faculty.

Edmondson, T. (2010). "The Jesus Fish: Evolution of a Cultural Icon." *Studies in Popular
Culture* 32 (2): 57–66. http://www.jstor.org/stable/23416155.

Edwards, G., dir. (2014). *Godzilla*. Burbank, CA: Warner Bros.

Edwards, P., K. A. E. Enenkel, and E. Graham (2012). *The Horse as Cultural Icon: The Real and Symbolic Horse in the Early Modern World*. Leiden: Brill.

Eichler-Levine, J. (2010). "The Curious Conflation of Hanukkah and the Holocaust in Jewish Children's Literature." *Shofar: An Interdisciplinary Journal of Jewish Studies* 28 (2): 92–115. https://www.jstor.org/stable/10.5703/shofar.28.2.92

Elder, S. L. (2020). "Junior League Releases Virtual Story Time Collection to Promote Education and Literacy during School Closures." *Yes! Weekly*, March 24, 2020. https://www.yesweekly.com/news/junior-league-releases-virtual-story-time-collection-to-promote-education/article_83120c6a-6dfe-11ea-8493-e356b07fcoda.html.

El Refaie, E. (2019). *Visual Metaphor and Embodiment in Graphic Illness Narratives*. Oxford: Oxford University Press.

Enck-Wanzer, D. (2012). "Decolonizing Imaginaries: Rethinking "the People" in the Young Lords' Church Offensive." *Quarterly Journal of Speech* 98 (1): 1–23. https://doi.org/10.1080/00335630.2011.638656.

Erekson, J. A. (2009). "Putting Humpty Dumpty Together Again: When Illustration Shuts Down Interpretation." *Journal of Visual Literacy* 28 (2): 147–62. https://doi.org/10.1080/23796529.2009.11674666.

Every Student Succeeds Act (2015). S. 1177, 114th Cong. https://www.congress.gov/bill/114th-congress/senate-bill/1177.

Eze, E. C. (1997). "Philosophy, Culture and the Technology of the Postcolonial." In *Postcolonial African Philosophy: A Critical Reader*, edited by E. C. Eze, 339–44. New York: Wiley-Blackwell.

Fallon, J., J. Bennett, and R. Romano (2007). *Curious George*. Season 2, episode 5, "Grease Monkeys in Space," dir. S. Heming. Aired October 8, 2007. Universal City, CA: Universal Animation Studios.

Fallon, J., J. Bennett, and R. Romano (2014). *Curious George*. Season 8, episode 4, "Red Planet Monkey." Aired May 19, 2014. Beverly Hills, CA: Imagine Entertainment.

Fallon, J., and S. Willard (2006). *Curious George*. Season 1, episode 1, "Curious George Flies a Kite." Aired September 4, 2006. Beverly Hills, CA: Imagine Entertainment.

Flanzbaum, H. (1999). *The Americanization of the Holocaust*. Baltimore, MD: Johns Hopkins University Press.

Florey, R., dir. (1932). *Murders in the Rue Morgue*. Universal City, CA: Universal Pictures.

Flynn, M. (2018). "Laura Ingalls Wilders Name Stripped from Children's Book Award over Little House Depictions of Native Americans." *Washington Post*, June 25, 2018. https://www.washingtonpost.com/news/morning-mix/wp/2018/06/25/laura-ingalls-wilders-name-stripped-from-childrens-book-award-over-little-house-depictions-of-native-americans/.

Forceville, C., and S. Paling (2018). "The Metaphorical Representation of Depression in Short, Wordless Animation Films." *Visual Communication* 0 (0): 1–21. https://doi.org/10.1177/1470357218797994.

Foss, S. K. (1996). *Rhetorical Criticism: Exploration and Practice*. 2nd ed. Long Grove, IL: Waveland Press, Inc.

Foster, G. A. (1999). *Captive Bodies: Postcolonial Subjectivity in Cinema*. Albany: State University of New York Press.

Frank, A. (1993). *Anne Frank: The Diary of a Young Girl*, with an Introduction by Eleanor Roosevelt. Translated by B. M. Mooyaart. New York: Bantam.

Freeman, C., and D. Merskin (2016). "Respectful Representation." In *Critical Animal and Media Studies*, edited by N. Almiron, M. Cole, and C. P. Freeman. 205–20. New York: Routledge.

Freire, P. (2014). *Pedagogy of the Oppressed*. 30th anniversary edition. London: Bloomsbury Publishing.

French, R. (2020). "With Bedtime Stories and Growing Unease, a Michigan Elementary Confronts Coronavirus." *Bridge Michigan*, April 2, 2020. https://www.bridgemi.com/talent-education/bedtime-stories-and-growing-unease-michigan-elementary-confronts-coronavirus.

Friedman, S. (2018). "Trump Administration Sets Five-Year Strategy for STEM Ed." *The Journal*, December 4, 2018. https://thejournal.com/articles/2018/12/04/trump-administration-sets-five-year-strategy-for-stem-education.aspx.

Gates, H. L., Jr. (1988). *The Signifying Monkey: A Theory of Afro-American Literary Criticism*. Oxford: Oxford University Press.

Gibbons, M. T. (2020). "Research and Development Statistics Program." National Science Foundation. https://www.nsf.gov/statistics/2020/nsf20302/overview.htm#fn1.

Gilbert, E. (2010). "The Dhow as Cultural Icon: Heritage and Regional Identity in the Western Indian Ocean." *International Journal of Heritage Studies* 17 (1): 62–80. https://doi.org/10.1080/13527258.2011.524007.

Gilbert, H., and C. Tiffin, eds. (2008). *Burden or Benefit? Imperial Benevolence and Its Legacies*. Bloomington: Indiana University Press.

Gilroy, P. (1995). *The Black Atlantic: Modernity and Double-Consciousness*. Cambridge, MA: Harvard University Press.

Giroux, H. A. (2013). "Beyond Dystopian Education in a Neoliberal Society." *Fast Capitalism* 10 (1). https://www.uta.edu/huma/agger/fastcapitalism/10_1/giroux10_1.html.

Goodenough, E., and A. Immel (2008). *Under Fire: Childhood in the Shadow of War*. Detroit, MI: Wayne State University Press.

Goncalves, W. K. (1994). "Little Black Sambo and the Legacy of Image in African American Children's Literature." Paper presented at the Annual Conference and Exhibit of the Association for Supervision and Curriculum Development, Baltimore, MD.

Google Nexus 7 (2012). "Curious George." Television commercial. iSpot.tv. https://www.ispot.tv/ad/7L1f/google-nexus-7-curious-george.

Gorsevski, E. W. (2018). "Native America Persists: Pocahontas versus Trump." *Journal of Multicultural Discourses* 13 (2): 160–75. https://doi.org/10.1080/17447143.2018.1493112.

Goscilo, H. (2013). *Putin as Celebrity and Cultural Icon*. New York: Routledge.

Graber, D. A. (1976). *Verbal Behavior and Politics*. Champaign: University of Illinois Press.

Gray, T. (1998). "A Brief History of Animals in Space." NASA. https://history.nasa.gov/animals.html.

Green, A., and G. Rosen (2019). "New Owner and Move for Curious George Store." *Publisher Weekly*, May 16, 2019. https://www.publishersweekly.com/pw/by-topic/childrens/childrens-industry-news/article/80084-new-owner-and-move-for-curious-george-store.html.

Greenstone, D. (2005). "Frightened George: How the Pediatric-Educational Complex Ruined the Curious George Series." *Journal of Social History* 39 (1): 221–28. https://www.jstor.org/stable/3790536.

Groen, J., and E. Smit (1990). *The Discipline of Curiosity: Science in the World*. Edited by J. Eijsvoogel. First paperback edition. Amsterdam: Elsevier Science Ltd.

Grosfoguel, R. (2011). "Decolonizing Post-Colonial Studies and Paradigms of Political-Economy: Transmodernity, Decolonial Thinking, and Global Coloniality." *Transmodernity: Journal of Peripheral Cultural Production of the Luso-Hispanic World* 1 (1). https://escholarship.org/uc/item/21k6t3fq.

Gurdon, M. C. (2016). "Curious George Turns 75." *Wall Street Journal*, September 30, 2016. www.wsj.com/articles/curious-george-turns-75-1475254169.

Hade, D. D. (2001). "Curious George Gets Branded: Reading as Consuming." *Theory into Practice* 40 (3): 158–65. https://doi.org/10.1207/s15430421tip4003_3.

Hall, S., and P. du Gay, eds. (1996). *Questions of Cultural Identity*. Newbury Park, CA: Sage Publications.

Hall, S., P. Gilroy, L. Grossberg, and A. McRobbie (2000). *Without Guarantees: In Honour of Stuart Hall*. London: Verso.

Hapka, C., H. A. Rey, and M. O'Keefe Young (2006). *Margret & H. A. Rey's Merry Christmas, Curious George*. Boston: Houghton Mifflin.

Haraway, D. J. (1988). "Situated Knowledges: The Science Question in Feminism and the Privilege of Partial Perspective." *Feminist Studies* 14 (3): 575–99. https://doi.org/10.2307/3178066.

Haraway, D. J. (1990). *Primate Visions: Gender, Race, and Nature in the World of Modern Science*. New York: Routledge.

Harding, S. (1998). *Is Science Multicultural? Postcolonialisms, Feminisms, and Epistemologies*. Bloomington: Indiana University Press.

Harding, S. (2009). "Postcolonial and Feminist Philosophies of Science and Technology: Convergences and Dissonances." *Postcolonial Studies* 12 (4): 401–21. https://doi.org/10.1080/13688790903350658.

Harding, S., ed. (2011). *The Postcolonial Science and Technology Studies Reader*. Durham, NC: Duke University Press.

Hariman, R., and J. L. Lucaites (2007). *No Caption Needed: Iconic Photographs, Public Culture, and Liberal Democracy*. Chicago: University of Chicago Press.

Harris, K. (2019). *Superheroes Are Everywhere*. New York: Philomel Books.

Hasian, M. (2006). *Rhetorical Vectors of Memory in National and International Holocaust Trials*. East Lansing: Michigan State University Press.

Hasian, M., Jr. (2002). "Nostalgic Longings and Imaginary Indias: Postcolonial Analysis, Collective Memories, and the Impeachment Trial of Warren Hastings." *Western Journal of Communication* 66 (2): 229–55. https://doi.org/10.1080/10570310209374734.

Hasian, M., Jr. (2014). "*Skyfall*, James Bond's Resurrection, and 21st-Century Anglo-American Imperial Nostalgia." *Communication Quarterly* 62 (5): 569–88. https://doi.org/10.1080/01463373.2014.949389.

Haskins, C. (2018). "The Racist Language of Space Exploration." *The Outline*, August 15, 2018. https://theoutline.com/post/5809/the-racist-language-of-space-exploration.

Hawley, J. C., ed. (2001). *Post-colonial, Queer: Theoretical Intersections*. 1st ed. Albany: State University of New York Press.

Hays, J., dir. (1933). *Kid "in" Africa*. Hollywood, CA: Jack Hays Productions and Educational Pictures.

Hayward, S. (2012). *Cinema Studies*. 4th ed. New York: Routledge.

Hecht, G. (2002). "Rupture-Talk in the Nuclear Age: Conjugating Colonial Power in Africa." *Social Studies of Science* 32 (5/6): 691–727. https://doi.org/10.1177/030631270203200504.

Hegde, R. (2005). "Disciplinary Spaces and Globalization: A Postcolonial Unsettling." *Global Media and Communication* 1: 59–63. https://doi.org/10.1177/17427665050100114.

Hegde, R. (2011). *Circuits of Visibility: Gender and Transnational Media Cultures*. New York: New York University Press.

Hegde, R. A. (2016). *Mediating Migration*. Cambridge: Polity.

Hergé, L. L. Cooper, and M. R. Turner (1931). *Tintin in the Congo*. Brussels: Le Petit Vingtième.

Heywood, L., and S. L. Dworkin (2003). *Built to Win: The Female Athlete as Cultural Icon*. Minneapolis: University of Minnesota Press.

Hildebrand, K. (2020). "Educators Finding New Ways to Teach." *Minden-Gardnerville (NV) Record-Courier*, March 25, 2020. https://www.recordcourier.com/news/educators -finding-new-ways-to-teach/.

Hinshaw, C. (2006). "Connecting to Curious George." *School Arts: The Art Education Magazine for Teachers* 105 (7): 37.

HMH Books. (2005). "The Journey that Saved Curious George." News release, http://www .hmhbooks.com/booksellers/press_release/borden/borden_journey.pdf.

Holocaust Center for Humanity (n.d.). "The Journey That Saved Curious George: The True Wartime Escape of Margret and H.A. Rey." Holocaust Center for Humanity website. https://www.holocaustcenterseattle.org/events/302-curious-george-exhibit.

Holocaust Center for Humanity (2020). "Best Practices." Holocaust Center for Humanity website. Retrieved November 2, 2020. https://holocaustcenterseattle.org/best-practices.

Honda, I., dir. (1954). *Godzilla*. Tokyo: Toho.

Honda, I., dir. (1962). *King Kong vs. Godzilla*. Tokyo: Toho.

Horn Book Magazine (n.d.). "Virtual History Exhibit: Bertha Mahony Miller." *The Horn Book Magazine*. https://www.hbook.com/virtual-history-exhibit/roots/bertha-mahony -miller/.

Houghton Mifflin (n.d.). "Curious George: Lesson Plans.". Retrieved May 14, 2019. http:// www.houghtonmifflinbooks.com/features/cgsite/journey_lp.shtml#during.

Houghton Mifflin Harcourt (2015a). "Houghton Mifflin Harcourt Kicks Off World Summer Tour, Inspiring Playful Learning." News release, June 15, 2015. Retrieved January 29, 2017. http://www.hmhco.com/media-center/press-releases/2016/june/curious-world-tour -launch.

Houghton Mifflin Harcourt (2015b). "It's a Curious Day: A Special Annual Celebration of Fun, Learning, and Excitement with Curious George." Retrieved May 20, 2019. http:// www.curiousgeorge.com/~/media/sites/cg/resources/cg_eventkit.pdf.

Howell, E. (2018). "Mars Curiosity: Facts and Information." *Space.com*, July 17, 2018. https:// www.space.com/17963 mars-curiosity.html.

Howington, J., and S. S. Stoner (2020). *Curious George: Go West, Go Wild*, dir. M. LaBash Internet release, September 8, 2020. Beverly Hills, CA: Imagine Entertainment.

Huffpost Education (2012). "Curious George Helping to Bridge the STEM Education Gap in Preschool: Study." *Huffington Post*, November 15, 2012. Retrieved February 15, 2015. http:// www.huffingtonpost.com/2012/11/15/curious-george-helping-to_n_2139454.html.

Huget, J. L. (2011). "No dinner for Max? Depends on What He's Had to Eat." *Washington Post*, November 8, 2011. https://www.washingtonpost.com/lifestyle/wellness/no-dinner-for -max-depends-on-what-hes-had-to eat/2011/11/02/gIQAQbsA1M_story.html?utm_term =.68de4866f74b.

Huggan, G. (2013). "General Introduction." In *The Oxford Handbook of Postcolonial Studies*, ed. G. Huggan, 1–28). Oxford: Oxford University Press.

Huggan, G., ed. (2016). *The Oxford Handbook of Postcolonial Studies*. Reprint edition. Oxford: Oxford University Press.

Hulme, P. (1995). "Including America." *ARIEL* 26 (1): 117–23. https://journalhosting.ucalgary .ca/index.php/ariel/article/view/33703.

Hulu. (2016). "Hulu and Universal Ink Groundbreaking Deal for Curious George© TV." News release, March 17, 2016. https://www.hulu.com/press/hulu-and-universal-ink -groundbreaking-deal-for-curious-george-tv/.

Hunt, P. (1996). *An Introduction to Children's Literature*. Oxford: Oxford Paperbacks.

International Entertainment News (2014, July 8). "NYC & Company Announces Curious George as New York City's Official Family Ambassador." Retrieved July 8, 2014. http:// internationalentertainmentnews.blogspot.com/2014/07/nyc-company-announces -curious-george-as.html.

Irr, C. (1999). "Curious George at the Border: American Intellectual Property and Canadian Culture." *Essays on Canadian Writing* 68: 266.

Ivie, R. L. (1987). "Metaphor and the Rhetorical Invention of Cold War 'Idealists.'" *Communication Monographs* 54 (2): 165–82. https://doi.org/10.1080/03637758709390224.

Jackson, P., dir. (2005). *King Kong*. Universal City, CA: Universal Pictures.

Jameson, F. (1982). *The Political Unconscious: Narrative as a Socially Symbolic Act*. Ithaca, NY: Cornell University Press.

Jane Goodall Institute (n.d.). "About Jane." Jane Goodall Institute website. Retrieved May 1, 2019.

Jane Goodall Institute (n.d.). "Make a Difference with the Jane Goodall Institute." Video recording. Retrieved May 1, 2019. http://www.janegoodall.org/our-story/.

Jasinski, J. (2001). *Sourcebook on Rhetoric Key Concepts in Contemporary Rhetorical Studies*. Newbury Park, CA: Sage Publications.

Jenkins, E. (2008). "My iPod, My iCon: How and Why Do Images Become Icons?" *Critical Studies in Media Communication* 25 (5): 466–89. https://doi.org/10.1080/152950308 02468057.

Jewish Musem (2010). "Curious George Saves the Day: The Art of Margret and H.A. Rey." Retrieved December 16, 2016. http://thejewishmuseum.org/exhibitions/curious-george -saves-the-day-the-art-of-margret-and-h-a-rey.

Jhally, S., dir. (1997). *bell hooks: Cultural Criticism & Transformation*. Northampton, MA: Media Educational Foundation.

Johnson, Abby (2010). "Curious George Exhibit at The Jewish Museum in NYC." *Abby the Librarian* (blog), March 19, 2010. http://www.abbythelibrarian.com/2010/03/curious -george-exhibit-at-jewish-museum.html.

Johnson, M. (1981). *Philosophical Perspectives on Metaphor*. Minneapolis: University of Minnesota Press.

Jones, D. (2001). "Retrospective Essay." In *The Complete Adventures of Curious George: 70th Anniversary Edition*, edited by M. Rey and H. A. Rey, 209–38. Boston: Houghton Mifflin Harcourt.

Jones, K. (2006). "Getting Rid of Children's Literature." *The Lion and the Unicorn* 30 (3): 287–315. https://muse.jhu.edu/article/202584.

Jozwiak, J. F., and E. Mermann (2006). "'The Wall in Our Minds?' Colonization, Integration, and Nostalgia." *The Journal of Popular Culture* 39 (5): 780–93. https://onlinelibrary.wiley .com/doi/abs/10.1111/j.0022-3840.2006.00305.x.

Kaiser Health Network (2020). "CDC Releases Demographic Data: Black Americans, Older People and Men among Hardest Hit by Pandemic." KHN Morning Briefing, April 9, 2020. https://khn.org/morning-breakout/cdc-releases-demographic-data-black-ameri cans-older-people-and-men-among-hardest-hit-by-pandemic/.

Kaufman, J. (2010). "A Monkey Born of Trials and Tribulations." *Wall Street Journal*, April 7, 2010. https://www.wsj.com/articles/SB10001424052748703312504575141603406411466.

Kavoori, A., and K. Chadha (2009). "The Cultural Turn in International Communication." *Journal of Broadcasting & Electronic Media* 53 (2): 336–46. https://doi.org/10.1080/088 38150902908353.

Kelley, S. (2018). "Feds Shell Out $10 Million for STEM Diversity." *Campus Reform*, December 17, 2018. https://www.campusreform.org/?ID=11648.

Kertzer, A. (2002). *My Mother's Voice: Children, Literature, and the Holocaust*. Peterborough, Ont.: Broadview.

Kidd, K. (2008). "A is for Auschwitz: Psychoanalysis, Trauma Theory, and the Children's Literature of Atrocity." In *Under Fire: Childhood in the Shadow of War*, edited by E. Goodenough and A. Immel, 161–84. Detroit, MI: Wayne State University Press.

Killgrove, K. (2013). "Is Curious George a Monkey or an Ape?" *Powered by Osteons* (blog), June 24, 2013. https://www.poweredbyosteons.org/2013/06/is-curious-george-monkey -or-ape.html.

King, N. B. (2002). "Security, Disease, Commerce Ideologies of Postcolonial Global Health." *Social Studies of Science* 32 (5/6): 763–89. https://doi.org/10.1177/030631270203200507.

Klein, H., and K. S. Shiffman (2006). "Race-Related Content of Animated Cartoons." *Howard Journal of Communications* 17 (3): 163–82. https://doi.org/10.1080/10646170600829493.

Knight, C. (2014). "George's Medal Haul—From Russia with Lou." *Adirondack Daily Enterprise*. www.adirondackdailyenterprise.com/page/blogs.detail/display/2102/ George's=medal-haul.html.

Koh, H. H. (2003). "Foreword: On American Exceptionalism." Symposium on Treaties, Enforcement, and US Sovereignty. *Stanford Law Review* 55 (5), 1479-.

Kohl, H. R. (1995). *Should We Burn Babar? Essays on Children's Literature and the Power of Stories*. New York: New Press.

Kokkola, L. (2003). *Representing the Holocaust in Children's Literature*. New York: Routledge.

Kraidy, M. M. (2002). "Hybridity in Cultural Globalization." *Communication Theory* 12 (3): 316–39. https://doi.org/10.1093/ct/12.3.316.

Kraidy, M. M., and P. D. Murphy (2008). "Shifting Geertz: Toward a Theory of Translocalism in Global Communication Studies." *Communication Theory* 18 (3): 335–55. https://doi .org/10.1111/j.1468–2885.2008.00325.x

Kramer, M. (2014). "Curious George Goes to Mars with PBS Kids (Video, Images)." *Space .com*, May 16, 2014. https://www.space.com/25903-curious-george-mars-pbs-show-video .html.

Krishnaswamy, R., and J. C. Hawley (2008). *The Postcolonial and the Global*. Minneapolis: University of Minnesota Press.

Laden, G, L. (2014). "Is Curious George an Ape or a Monkey?" *Greg Laden's Blog*, May 19, 2014. scienceblogs.com/gregladen/2014/05/19/is-curious-george-an-ape-or-a-monkey/.

Lamkford, R., L. Saric, and J. Fallon (2006). *Curious George*. Season 1, episode 4, "Buoy Wonder," dir. F. Marino and S. Socki. Aired September 7, 2006. Beverly Hills, CA: Imagine Entertainment.

Lang, B. (2009). *Joseph in Egypt: A Cultural Icon from Grotius to Goethe*. New Haven, CT: Yale University Press.

Lanham, R. (1991). *A Handlist of Rhetorical Terms: A Guide for Students of English Literature*. 2nd ed. Berkeley: University of California Press.

Larrick, N. (1965). "The All-White World of Children Books." *Saturday Review*, September 11, 1965. UNZ.org. www.unz.org/Pub/SaturdayRev-1965sep11-000638.

Las Vegas Weekly Staff (2017). "Try Something Spicy and Sweet at Crush." *Las Vegas Weekly*, February 2, 2017. Retrieved February 2, 2017. https://lasvegasweekly.com/nightlife/industry-weekly/2017/feb/02/first-sip-las-vegas-cocktails-crush-mgm-grand/.

Lawrence, C. (2011). "Making up for Lost Time: Yugo-Nostalgia and the Limits of Serbian Memory." In *Global Memoryscapes: Contesting Remembrance in a Transnational Age*, edited by K. R. Phillips and G. M. Reyes, 80–93. Tuscaloosa: University of Alabama Press.

Lazarus, N. (2016). "Third World and the Political Imaginary of Postcolonial Studies." In *The Oxford Handbook of Postcolonial Studies*, edited by G. Huggan, 324–39. Oxford: Oxford University Press.

Lechner, J. V. (1995). "Images of African American in Picture Books for Children." In *The All White World of Children's Books and African American Children's Literature*, edited by O. Oso, 75–83. Trenton, NJ: Africa World Press.

Le Guat, F., and S. P. Oliver (1891). *The Voyage of François Leguat of Bresse, to Rodriguez, Mauritius, Java, and the Cape of Good Hope*. London: Printed for the Hakluyt Society. https://doi.org/10.5962/bhl.title.46034.

Levy, J. (2020). "Hat Shop Madison Provides Handmade Face Masks to Grocery Workers in Madison, Chatham and Florham Park." *TapInto*, May 18, 2020. https://www.tapinto.net/towns/arvard/sections/giving-back/articles/hat-shop-madison-provides-handmade-face-masks-to-grocery-workers-in-madison-chatham-and-florham-park.

Linnaeus, C (1760). *An Introduction to Botany: Containing an Explanation of the Theory of That Science*. Appendix by J. Lee. London: J. and R. Tonson.

Loh, L., and M. Sen (2013). "Postcolonial Literature and Challenges for the New Millennium." *Textual Practice* 27 (3): 353. https://doi.org/10.1080/0950236X.2013.784015.

Loomba, A. (2015). *Colonialism/Postcolonialism*. 3rd ed. New York: Routledge.

Looney Tunes Wiki (n.d.). "Bugs Bunny." Retrieved January 27, 2016. http://looneytunes.wikia.com/wiki/Bugs_Bunny.

Loshitzky, Y. (2001). "Hybrid Victims: Second Generation Israelis Screen the Holocaust." In *Visual Culture and the Holocaust*, edited by B. Zelizer, 152–75. New Brunswick, NJ: Rutgers University Press.

Lott, T. L. (1999). *The Invention of Race: Black Culture and the Politics of Representation*. New York: Wiley-Blackwell.

Loy, L. (2016). "Media Activism and Animal Advocacy." In *Critical Animal and Media Studies*, edited by N. Almiron, M. Cole, and C. P. Freeman, 222–33. New York: Routledge.

Lubitz, R. (2018). "H & M's Hoodie Controversy: From Initial Backlash to Destroyed Stores and Everything In Between." *Mic*, January 16, 2018. https://www.mic.com/articles/187418/handms-hoodie-controversy-from-initial-backlash-to-destroyed-stores-and-everything-in-between.

Lucas, G., dir. (1977). *Star Wars*. Los Angeles: 20th Century Fox.

Lunga, V. B. (2008). "Postcolonial Theory: A Language for a Critique of Globalization?" *Perspectives on Global Development & Technology* 7 (3/4): 191–99. https://doi.org/10.1163/156914908X371349.

Mahan, S. (2016). "Curious George Birthday Bash Draws Hundreds." *Vicksburg Post*, June 25, 2016. http://www.vicksburgpost.com/2016/06/25/curious-george-birthday-bash-draws-hundreds/.

Maldonado-Torres, N. (2007). "On the Coloniality of Being: Contributions to the Development of a Concept." *Cultural Studies* 21 (2): 240–70. https://doi.org/10.1080/09502380601162548.

Marcus, L. S. (2001). "Introduction." In *The Complete Adventures of Curious George: 70th Anniversary Edition*, edited by M. Rey and H. A. Rey, 6–9. Boston: Houghton Mifflin Harcourt.

Marcus, L. S. (2008). *Minders of Make-Believe: Idealists, Entrepreneurs, and the Shaping of American Children's Literature*. Boston: Houghton Mifflin Harcourt.

Marcus, L. S. (2012). "An Interview with Walter Lorraine." *The Horn Book Magazine*, November 28, 2012. https://www.hbook.com/2012/11/choosing-books/horn-book-magazine/interview-walter-lorraine/.

Margret & H. A. Rey Center. (n.d.). "About Us" and "What's Happening?" Rey Center website. Retrieved January 14, 2016. http://thereycenter.org.

Margret & H. A. Rey Institute for Nonlinear Dynamics of Medicine (n.d.). Website. Retrieved February 15, 2015. reylab.bidmc.harvard.edu/index.shtml.

Mattoon, N. (2010). "Curious George Escapes the Nazis." *Booktryst*, March 19, 2010. www.booktryst.com/2010/03/curious-george-escapes-nazis.html.

McCallum, P. (1995). "Introductory Notes: Postcolonialism and Its Discontents." *ARIEL* 26 (3): 7–22. https://journalhosting.ucalgary.ca/index.php/ariel/article/view/33687.

McCallum, R. (1997). "Cultural Solipsism, National Identities and the Discourse of Multiculturalism in Australian Picture Books." *ARIEL* 28 (1): 101–16. https://journalhosting.ucalgary.ca/index.php/ariel/article/view/33870.

McClintock, A. (1995). *Imperial Leather: Race, Gender and Sexuality in the Colonial Context*. New York: Routledge.

McCloskey, R. (1944). *Make Way for Ducklings*. New York: Viking Press.

McGarry, M. (2020). "Cape's John Lynch Trying to Give Parents and Students a Break amid COVID-19 Crisis. *Press of Atlantic City*, March 27, 2020. https://pressofatlanticcity.com/news/cape-s-john-lynch-trying-to-give-parents-and-students/article_9dba935d-6eb5-518d-9b93-39f182a4e4d4.html.

McGills, R., and M. Khorana (1997). "Introductory Notes: Postcolonialism, Children and their Literature." *ARIEL* 28 (1): 7–20.

McNeil, M. (2005). « Introduction : Postcolonial Technoscience. » *Science as Culture* 14 (2): 105–12. https://doi.org/10.1080/09505430500110770.

Meador, M. (2020). "Efforts Help Provide Masks for Medical Staff, First Responders." *Monroe Journal*, April 2, 2020. https://www.djournal.com/monroe/news/efforts-help-provide-masks-for-medical-staff-first-responders/article_7f601f2e-7624-5e6f-9c0f-0f29e92880 01b.html.

Medhurst, M. J., R. L. Ivie, P. Wander, and R. L. Scott (1997). *Cold War Rhetoric*. East Lansing: Michigan State University Press.

Melfi, T., dir. (2016). *Hidden Figures*. Los Angeles: Fox 2000 Pictures.

Meyer, E. F., and M. O'Keefe Young (2012). *Happy Hanukkah, Curious George*. Boston: Houghton Mifflin Harcourt.

Mickenberg, J. L. (2005). *Learning from the Left: Children's Literature, the Cold War, and Radical Politics in the United States*. Oxford: Oxford University Press.

Mignolo, W. (2007). "Delinking: The Rhetoric of Modernity, the Logic of Coloniality and the Grammar of De-Coloniality." *Cultural Studies* 21 (2): 449–514. https://doi.org/10.1080/09502380601162647.

Miller, C., and J. Fallon (2006). *Curious George*. Season 1, episode 14, "Curious George's Rocket Ride," dir. D. Criswell and F. Marion. Universal City, CA: Universal Animation Studios.

Miller, J. J. (2006). "Curious George's Journey to the Big Screen." *Wall Street Journal*, February 2, 2006. https://www.wsj.com/articles/SB113883544357862588.

Minnesota Children's Museum (2015). "Curious George: Let's Get Curious!" September 21, 2015. Retrieved April 27, 2017. http://mcm.org/museum-professionals/rent-exhibits/curious-george/.

Miranda, L. (2016). *Hamilton: An American Musical*, dir. T. Kail. Richard Rodgers Theater, New York, NY.

Mishra, S. (2007). "'Liberation' vs. 'Purity': Representations of Saudi Women in the American Press and American Women in the Saudi Press." *Howard Journal of Communications* 18 (3): 259–76. https://doi.org/10.1080/10646170701490849.

Mommyofdoom (2011). "Ha! Curious George IS a Monkey!" *Babycenter* (blog). Retrieved November 3, 2014. https://community.babycenter.com/post/a28213335/ha_curious_george_is_a_monkey.

Morrison, T. (2004). *Beloved*. Reprint edition. New York: Vintage Books.

Mount, D., and S. O'Brien (2013). "Postcolonialism and the Environment." In *The Oxford Handbook of Postcolonial Studies*, edited by G. Huggan. Oxford: Oxford University Press.

Movement Voter Project. (n.d.). Retrieved May 6, 2017. https://movement.vote/about/.

Moyer, P. (2020). "Discovery Children's Museum Launches Online 'At Home Discoveries' Program." *3News Las Vegas*, April 28, 2020. https://news3lv.com/news/local/arvardp-childrens-museum-launches-online-at-home-discoveries-program.

Mubtadi, V. (2016). "This Ramadan, Curious George Helps Friend to Fast." *VOA*, July 1, 2016. http://www.voanews.com/a/ramadan-curious-george-helps-friends-to-fast/3400695.html.

Munson, K. (2006). "Munson: Does Monkey Tale Speak of Slavery?" *Des Moines Register*, February 14, 2006. https://amp.desmoinesregister.com/amp/3995653.

Murphy, D., dir. (2019). *Curious George: Royal Monkey*. Universal City, CA: Universal 1440 Entertainment.

Mystic Stamp Company (2006). "#3992—2006 39c Children's Book Animals: Curious George." https://www.mysticstamp.com/Products/United-States/3992/USA/?gclid=CJj-pd2gm9MCFQ5EfgodiJkMcw.

NASA (n.d.). "Mars Science Laboratory: Curiosity Rover." Retrieved August 25, 2020. https://mars.nasa.gov/msl/participate.

NASA (n.d.). "The Red Planet." *NASA Science: Mars Exploration Program*. Retrieved September 1, 2020. https://mars.nasa.gov/#red_planet/1.

Nasaw, D. (2020). *The Last Million: Europe's Displaced Persons from World War to Cold War*. New York: Penguin Publishing Group.

National Public Radio (2009). "Pulp and Circumstance: Tarantino Rewrites History." *Fresh Air*, August 27, 2009. Retrieved December 15, 2014. http://www.npr.org/templates/story/story.php?storyId=112286584.

National Science Foundation (2020). "RAPID Responders: How NSF Support Is Enabling the Fight against COVID-19 in Real Time." *Science Matters*, May 20, 2020. Retrieved August 19, 2020. https://beta.nsf.gov/science-matters/rapid-responders-how-nsf-support-enabling-fight-against-covid-19-real-time.

Nayar, P. K., ed. (2015). *Postcolonial Studies: An Anthology*. New York: Wiley-Blackwell.

Nel, P. (2017). *Was the Cat in the Hat Black? The Hidden Racism of Children's Literature, and the Need for Diverse Books*. Oxford: Oxford University Press.

Nguyễn, T. A., and M. Pendleton (2020). "Recognizing Race in Language: Why We Capitalize 'Black' and 'White.'" *Center for the Study of Social Policy*, March 23, 2020. https://cssp.org/2020/03/recognizing-race-in-language-why-we-capitalize-black-and-white/

Nicgorski, A. M. (2006). "Idea of Cultural Supremacy Can Mislead Viewers of Film." *Archeology*, March 9, 2020. https://archive.archaeology.org/online/reviews/curious.html.

Nobel Prize Organization. (1986). "Elie Wiesel—Facts." http://www.nobelprize.org/nobel_prizes/peace/laureates/1986/wiesel-facts.html.

Nodelman, P. (1992). "The Other: Orientalism, Colonialism, and Children's Literature." *Children's Literature Association Quarterly* 17 (1): 29–35. https://muse.jhu.edu/article/249281.

Nora, P., and L. D. Kritzman (1996). *Realms of Memory: Rethinking the French Past,*vol. 3. New York: Columbia University Press.

Norman Rockwell Museum. (2011, October). "Final Days: Through February 5, 2012." October 11, 2011. https://www.nrm.org/2011/10/curious-george-saves-the-day-the-art-of-margret-and-h-a-rey/.

Novick, P. (1999). *The Holocaust in American Life*. Boston: Houghton Mifflin.

Nussbaum, E. (2012). "It's Good Enough for Me." *The New Yorker*, February 13, 2012. http://www.newyorker.com/magazine/2012/02/13/its-good-enough-for-me.

Nye, J. (2015). *Soft Power: The Means to Success in World Politics*. New ed. New York: Public Affairs.

O'Callaghan, M., dir. (2006). *Curious George*. Universal City, CA: Universal Pictures.

Oliver, P. (2010). *The Voyage of Francois Leguat*. Charleston, SC: BiblioBazaar.

Olson, D. C. (2011). "Last in Space: The 'Black' Hole in Children's Science Fiction Film." In *The Galaxy is Rated G: Essays on Science Fiction Film & Television*, edited by R. C. Neighbors and S. Rankin, 64–82. Jefferson, NC: McFarland & Company.

OMG Facts (n.d.). "Curious George Is Not a Monkey." Retrieved November 3, 2014. https://www.omgfacts.com/lists/5007/Curious-George-is-not-a-monkey.

Ono, K. (2009). *Contemporary Media Culture and the Remnants of a Colonial Past*. Bern: Peter Lang.

Ono, K. A., and D. T. Buescher (2001). "Deciphering Pocahontas: Unpackaging the Commodification of a Native American Woman." *Critical Studies in Media Communication* 18 (1): 23. https://doi.org/10.1080/15295030109367122.

Osborn, M. (2009). "The Trajectory of My Work with Metaphor." *The Southern Communication Journal* 74 (1): 79–87. https://doi.org/10.1080/10417940802559131.

Osborn, M. (2018). *Michael Osborn on Metaphor and Style*. East Lansing: Michigan State University Press.

Osborn, M. M., and D. Ehninger (1962). "The Metaphor in Public Address." *Speech Monographs* 29 (3): 223–34. https://www.tandfonline.com/doi/abs/10.1080/03637756209375346.

Palat, L. (2020). "'Curious George': Release Date, Plot, Trailer and All You Need to Know about the Animated Series." *Meaww*, July 12, 2020. https://meaww.com/curious-george-release-date-plot-trailer-peacock-frank-welker-jeff-bennett-rino-romano.

Panoptica (2017). *"Monkey Business: The Adventures of Curious George's Creators (2017)* |Official Trailer HD" [video]. YouTube. https://www.youtube.com/watch?time_continue=67&v=Ayjx-owZxpg.

Parameswaran, R. (2002). "Local Culture in Global Media: Excavating Colonial and Material Discourses in *National Geographic.*" *Communication Theory* 12 (3): 287–315. https://doi .org/10.1111/j.1468-2885.2002.tb00271.xz.

Parameswaran, R. (2008). "The Other Sides of Globalization: Communication, Culture, and Postcolonial Critique." *Communication, Culture & Critique* 1 (1): 116–25. https://doi .org/10.1111/j.1753-9137.2007.00012.x.

Parrish, S. S. (2006). *American Curiosity: Cultures of Natural History in the Colonial British Atlantic World.* Chapel Hill: University of North Carolina Press.

Paxson, J. (1994). *The Poetic of Personification.* Cambridge: Cambridge University Press

Pazornik, A. (2010). "Curious George Goes to the Museum." *The Jewish News*, November 12, 2020. https://www.jweekly.com/2010/11/12/curious-george-goes-to-the-museum/.

PBS Kids (2012). "Educational Programming Tops September Ratings with Six Highest-Ranked Kids Shows for Ages 2–5." *PBS Kids*, October 22, 2012. Retrieved November 1, 2013. www.pbs.org/about/news/archive/2012/pbs-kids-sept-ratings/.

PBS Kids (2013). "Curious George Spring Special Brings in Top Ratings." *PBS Kids.* Retrieved July 6, 2014. http://www.pbs.org/about/news/archive/2013/curious-george-special-top -ratings/.

PBS Learning Media (n.d.). "Curious George STEM." Retrieved March 10, 2015. https:// nm.pbslearningmedia.org/collection/curiousgeorge/

PBS Parents (2016). "Curious George: Educational Philosophy." Retrieved January 18, 2016. http://www.pbs.org/parents/curiousgeorge/program/ed_phil.html.

PBS Parents (2017). "Curious George: Character Descriptions." Retrieved March 29, 2017. http://www.pbs.org/parents/curiousgeorge/program/char_desc.html.

PBS Reno (2020). "Broadcast Guide." PBS Reno TV Guide. Retrieved August 28, 2020. https:// www.pbsreno.org/campcuriosity/#page=schedule&day=20201010&provider=Broadcast

Peacock TV (2020). "Curious George | official trailer | Peacock" [video]. YouTube, June 25, 2020. https://www.youtube.com/watch?v=3XthMiZyoWQ.

People for the Ethical Treatment of Animals (n.d.). "Primates in Laboratories." PETA.org. Retrieved August 15, 2020. https://www.peta.org/issues/animals-used-for-experimen tation/primates-laboratories/.

Perrot, J. (1997). "Review Article: Children's Literature Comes of Age." *ARIEL* 28 (1): 209–20. https://journalhosting.ucalgary.ca/index.php/ariel/article/view/33877.

Petty, K. (2013). "Obama Administration Commits $3.1 Billion to STEM Education." *Independent Voter News*, April 22, 2013. http://ivn.us/2013/04/22/obama-administrat ion-commits-3-1-billion-to-stem-education/.

Pew Research Center (2013). "A Portrait of Jewish Americans." Pew Research Center Religion & Public Life, October 1, 2013. Retrieved December 19, 2016. http://www.pewforum .org/2013/10/01/jewish-american-beliefs-attitudes-culture-survey/.

Phillips, N., and J. Shuber (2019). *The Journey that Saved Curious George: The True Wartime Escape of Margret and H.A. Rey: A New Musical.* https://www.thejourneythatsaved curiousgeorge.com/

Plumb, S. (2004). "Politicians as Superheroes: The Subversion of Political Authority Using a Pop Cultural Icon in the Cartoons of Steve Bell." *Media, Culture & Society* 26 (3): 432–39. https://doi.org/10.1177/0163443704042556.

Ponzanesi, S., M. R. Waller, eds. (2012). *Postcolonial Cinema Studies.* New York: Routledge.

Post, T., dir. (1970). *Beneath the Planet of the Apes.* Los Angeles: 20th Century Fox.

Power, S. (1999). "To Suffer by Comparison?" *Daedalus* 128 (2): 31–66. http://www.jstor.org/stable/20027554.

Pratt, M. (2021). "6 Dr. Seuss Books Won't Be Published for Racist Images." *Associated Press*, March 2, 2021. https://apnews.com/article/dr-seuss-books-racist-images-d8ed18335c0331 9d72f443594c174513.

Randall, D. (2010). "Empire and Children's Literature: Changing Patterns of Cross-Cultural Perspective." *Children's Literature in Education* 41 (1): 28–39. https://link.springer.com/article/10.1007/s10583-009-9094-z.

Rankin, S., and R. C. Neighbors (2011). "Introduction: Horizons and Possibility: What We Point to When We Say Science Fiction for Children." In *The Galaxy is Rated G: Essays on Science Fiction Film & Television*, edited by R. C. Neighbors and S. Rankin, 1–14. Jefferson, NC: McFarland & Company.

Raphel, A. (2016). "Curious George Learns about Brand Recognition." *The New Yorker*, December 23, 2016. http://www.newyorker.com/business/currency/curious-george -learns-about-brand-recognition.

Ray, S., and H. Schwarz (1995). "Postcolonial Discourse: The Raw and the Cooked." *ARIEL* 26 (1): 147–66. https://cdm.ucalgary.ca/index.php/ariel/article/view/33705.

Reagan, R. (1988). "Remarks at the Site of the Future Holocaust Memorial Museum," October 5, 1988. Ronald Reagan Presidential Library and Museum. Retrieved July 16, 2019. https://www.reaganlibrary.gov/archives/speech/remarks-site-future-holocaust -memorial-museum.

Redfield, P. (2002). "The Half-Life of Empire in Outer Space." *Social Studies of Science* 32 (5/6): 791–825. https://www.jstor.org/stable/3183055.

Redlands Community News (2020). "KVCR launches partnership with local schools to help students learn at home." April 3, 2020. Retrieved August 15, 2020. https://www .redlandscommunitynews.com/news/kvcr-launches-partnership-with-local-schools -to-help-students-learn-at-home/article_1c5f9154-75d3-11ea-b195-cf9830c1820d.html.

Reeves, M., dir. (2014). *Dawn of the Planet of the Apes*. Los Angeles: 20th Century Fox.

Rey, H. A. (1937). *Zebrology*. London: Chatto & Windus.

Rey, H. A. (1938a). *Le Zoo*. Paris: Hachette.

Rey, H. A. (1938b). *Le Cirque*. Paris: Hachette.

Rey, H. A. (1938c). *How the Flying Fishes Came into Being*. London: Chatto & Windus.

Rey, H. A. (1941a). *Cecily G. and the Nine Monkeys*. London: Chatto & Windus.

Rey, H. A. (1941b). *Curious George*. Boston: Houghton Mifflin Harcourt.

Rey, H. A. (1947). *Curious George Takes a Job*. Boston: Houghton Mifflin Harcourt.

Rey, H. A. (1952). *Curious George Rides a Bike*. Boston: Houghton Mifflin Harcourt.

Rey, H. A. (1957). *Curious George Gets a Medal*. Boston: Houghton Mifflin Harcourt.

Rey, H. A. (1958). *Curious George Flies a Kite*. Boston: Houghton Mifflin Harcourt.

Rey, H. A. (1963). *Curious George Learns the Alphabet*. Boston: Houghton Mifflin Harcourt.

Rey, H. A. (1989). *Cecily G. and the 9 Monkeys*. Boston: Houghton Mifflin.

Rey, H. A. (1998). *See the Circus*. Boston: HMH Houghton Mifflin Books for Young Readers.

Rey, H. A. (2001). *Curious George Goes Fishing*. Boston: Houghton Mifflin Harcourt.

Rey, H. A. (2005). *Curious George Gets a Medal*. Boston: Houghton Mifflin Harcourt.

Rey, H. A. (2007). *Curious George: Cecily G. and the 9 Monkeys*. Boston: Houghton Mifflin Harcourt.

Rey, H. A. (2008). *Curious George Hide-and-Seek*. Boston: Houghton Mifflin Harcourt.

Rey, H. A. (2010). *Curious George a Winter's Nap (CGTV Reader)*. Boston: Houghton Mifflin Harcourt.

Rey, H. A. (2014). *Curious George Visits the Dentist*. Boston: Houghton Mifflin Harcourt.

Rey, H. A. (2015a). *Curious George Discovers Germs*. Boston: Houghton Mifflin Harcourt.

Rey, H. A. (2015b*). Curious George Discovers Space*. Boston: Houghton Mifflin Harcourt.

Rey, H. A. (2017). *Curious George Discovers Recycling*. Boston: Houghton Mifflin Harcourt.

Rey, H. A. (2020a). *Curious George and the Summer Games*. Boston: Houghton Mifflin Harcourt.

Rey, H. A. (2020b). *Curious George Votes*. Boston: Houghton Mifflin Harcourt.

Rey, H. A., & Khan, H. (2016). *It's Ramadan, Curious George*. Boston: HMH Houghton Mifflin Books for Young Readers.

Rey, H. A., and M. Rey (n.d.). H. A. & Margret Rey Papers. De Grummond Children's Literature Collection, The University of Southern Mississippi Libraries.

Rey, H. A., and M. Rey (1998a). *Curious George and the Puppies*. Boston: Houghton Mifflin Harcourt.

Rey, H. A., and M. Rey (1998b). *Curious George's Dream*. Boston: Houghton Mifflin Harcourt.

Rey, H. A., and M. Rey (2003). *Curious George and the Birthday Surprise*. Boston: HMH Houghton Mifflin Books for Young Readers.

Rey, H. A., and M. Rey (2005). *Curious George's First Day of School*. Boston: Houghton Mifflin Harcourt.

Rey, H. A., and M. Rey (2012). *Curious George Says Thank You.*_Boston: Houghton Mifflin Harcourt.

Rey, H. A., and M. Rey (2016). *Curious George and the Rocket*. Boston: Houghton Mifflin Harcourt.

Rey, M., and H. A. Rey (1990). *Curious George at the Railroad Station*. Boston: Houghton Mifflin Harcourt.

Rey, M., and H. A. Rey (1998). *Curious George Goes to a Movie*. Boston: Houghton Mifflin Harcourt.

Rey, M., and H. A. Rey (2001). *The Complete Adventures of Curious George*. Boston: Houghton Mifflin.

Rey, M., H. A. Rey, and Boston Children's Hospital Medical Center (1966). *Curious George Goes to the Hospital*. Boston: Houghton Mifflin Harcourt.

Rey, M., H. A. Rey, and M. Weston (1998). *Curious George Makes Pancakes*. Boston: Houghton Mifflin Harcourt.

Rey, M., H. A. Rey, and M. Weston (2003). *Curious George Visits the Library*. Boston: Houghton Mifflin.

Rey, M., and A. J. Shalleck (1984). *Curious George Goes to the Aquarium*. Boston: Houghton Mifflin Harcourt.

Rey, M., and A. J. Shalleck (1985). *Curious George Visits the Zoo*. Boston: Houghton Mifflin Harcourt.

Rey, M., and A. J. Shalleck (1989a). *Curious George Goes to an Ice Cream Shop*. Boston: Houghton Mifflin Harcourt.

Rey, M., and A. J. Shalleck (1989b). *Curious George Goes to School*. Boston: Houghton Mifflin Harcourt.

Rhys, J. (1992). *Wide Sargasso Sea: A Novel*. New York: W. W. Norton & Company.

Rice, K. C. (2020). "Tell Me a Story: Teachers and Students at Menlo Park Academy Stay Connected through Reading." *Freshwater*, April 29, 2020. https://www.freshwater cleveland.com/street-level/MenloReading042920.aspx.

Richek, M. A., and B. K. McTague (1988). "The 'Curious George' Strategy for Students with Reading Problems." *The Reading Teacher* 42 (3): 220–26. https://www.jstor.org/stable/20200077.

Rogers, R. A. (2007). "Deciphering Kokopelli: Masculinity in Commodified Appropriations of Native American Imagery." *Communication and Critical/Cultural Studies* 4 (3): 233–55. https://doi.org/10.1080/14791420701459715.

Romm, T., and B. Guarino (2019). "Senate Confirms Trump's Science and Tech Adviser after Lengthy Vacancy." *Washington Post: The Switch*, January 3, 2019. https://www.washingtonpost.com/technology/2019/01/03/senate-confirms-trumps-science-tech-adviser-after-lengthy-vacancy/?noredirect=on&utm_term=.ee73e965dd1e.

Rosaldo, R. (1989). *Culture & Truth: The Remaking of Social Analysis*. Boston: Beacon Press.

Rosen, D. N. (1975). "King Kong: Race, Sex, and Rebellion." *Jump Cut: A Review of Contemporary Media* 6: 7–10.

Rosen, J. (2016). "Curious George Turns 75." *Publishers Weekly*, August 12, 2016. https://www.publishersweekly.com/pw/by-topic/childrens/childrens-book-news/article/71175-curious-george-turns-75.html.

Rothberg, M. (2009). *Multidirectional Memory: Remembering the Holocaust in the Age of Decolonization*. Stanford, CA: Stanford University Press.

Rothberg, M. (2013). "Remembering Back: Cultural Memory, Colonial Legacies, and Postcolonial Studies." In *The Oxford Handbook of Postcolonial Studies*, edited by G. Huggan, 359–79). Oxford: Oxford University Press.

Rothstein, E. (2010). "Monkey Business in a World of Evil." *New York Times*, March 26, 2010. https://www.nytimes.com/2010/03/26/arts/design/26curious.html.

Rottenburg, R. (2009). "Social and Public Experiments and New Figurations of Science and Politics in Postcolonial Africa." *Postcolonial Studies* 12 (4): 423–40. https://doi.org/10.1080/13688790903350666.

Ryan, J. (2008). "The Play's the Thing at CHB: The Life and Times of Curious George's Play Lady." *Contemporary Pediatrics* 25 (10): 112–12.

Said, E. W. (1978). *Orientalism*. New York: Pantheon Books.

Said, E. W. (1993). *Culture and Imperialism*. New York: Alfred A. Knopf.

Samuels, K. (2020). "10 Incredibly Fun and Educative Netflix Shows for Toddlers." *Babygaga*, May 26, 2020. https://www.babygaga.com/fun-educational-netflix-shows/.

Sayers, F. C. (1965). "Walt Disney Accused." *The Horn Book Magazine*, December 7, 1965. https://www.hbook.com/?detailStory=walt-disney-accused-vhe.

Schafferner, F. J., dir. (1968). *Planet of the Apes*. Los Angeles: 20th Century Fox.

Scharold, K. (2010). "Curious George at the Jewish Museum." *First Things*, April 23, 2010. https://www.firstthings.com/web-exclusives/2010/04/curious-george-at-the-jewish-museum.

Schwartz, R. (2020). "Peacock: Guide to Upcoming Shows." *TV Line*, January 16, 2020. https://tvline.com/gallery/peacock-streaming-service-tv-shows/.Schwartz-DuPre, R. L. (2007). "Rhetorically Representing Public Policy." *Feminist Media Studies* 7 (4): 433-53. https://doi-org./10.1080/14680770701631620

Schwartz-DuPre, R. L. (2010). "Portraying the Political: *National Geographic*'s 1985 Afghan Girl and a US Alibi for Aid." *Critical Studies in Media Communication* 27 (4): 336–56. https://doi.org/10.1080/15295030903583614.

Schwartz-DuPre, R. L. (2014). *Communicating Colonialism: Readings on Postcolonial Theory(s) and Communication*. New York: Peter Lang.

Schwartz-DuPre, R. L., and R. Hegde (2016). "A Conversation with Radha S. Hegde: Globalization: It's Everywhere; It's Nowhere." In *Talking Back to Globalization: Texts and*

Practices, edited by B. M. Goss, M. R. Gould, and J. P. Caranana, 21–35). New York: Peter Lang.

Schwartz-DuPre, R. L., and H. M. Parmett (2017). "Curious about George: Postcolonial Science and Technology Studies, STEM Education Policy, and Colonial Iconicity." *Textual Practice* 4, 707–25. https://doi.org/10.1080/0950236X.2016.1267038.

Scott, R., dir. (2015). *The Martian*. Los Angeles: 20th Century Fox.

Sell, J. P. A. (2012). *Metaphor and Diaspora in Contemporary Writing*. London: Palgrave Macmillan.

Sendak, M. (1963). *Where the Wild Things Are*. New York: Harper & Row.

Seth, S. (2009). "Putting Knowledge in Its Place: Science, Colonialism, and the Postcolonial." *Postcolonial Studies* 12 (4): 373–88. https://doi.org/10.1080/13688790903350633.

Seuss, Dr. (1937). *And to Think that I Saw It on Mulberry Street*. New York: Vanguard Press.

Seuss, Dr. (1957). *Cat in the Hat*. Boston: Houghton Mifflin.

Shaddock, J. (1997). "*Where the Wild Things Are*: Sendak's Journey into the Heart of Darkness." *Children's Literature Association Quarterly* 22 (2): 155–59. https://muse.jhu .edu/article/249657/.

Sharpe, J. (1995). "Is the United States Postcolonial? Transnationalism, Immigration and Race." *Diaspora* 4 (2): 181–99. https://muse.jhu.edu/article/443862.

Shome, R. (1996). "Postcolonial Interventions in the Rhetorical Canon: An 'Other' View." *Communication Theory* 6 (1): 40–59.

Shome, R. (2014). *Diana and Beyond: White Femininity, National Identity, and Contemporary Media Culture*. Champaign: University of Illinois Press.

Shome, R., and R. Hegde (2002). "Postcolonial Approaches to Communication: Charting the Terrain, Engaging the Intersections." *Communication Theory* 12 (3): 249–70. https://doi .org/10.1093/ct/12.3.249.

Silvey, A. (2001). "Curious George: A Publisher's Perspective." In *The Complete Adventures of Curious George: 70th Anniversary Edition*, edited by H. A. Rey, 1–3. Boston: HMH Houghton Mifflin Books for Young Readers.

Sloop, J. M. (2004). *Disciplining Gender: Rhetorics of Sex Identity in Contemporary U.S. Culture*. Amherst: University of Massachusetts Press.

Smith, A. (2020). "Keep Your Child Learning at Home with Free Access to ABC Mouse." *Android Central*, April 1, 2020. https://www.androidcentral.com/keep-your-child -learning-home-free-access-abc-mouse-limited-time-updated.

Smith, D. (2016). "Walking Competition Celebrating Curious George's 75th Birthday Begins Sept. 15." *University of Southern Mississippi News*, September 9, 2016. http://news.usm .edu/article/walking-competition-celebrating-curious-george-s-75th-birthday-begins -sept-15.

Social Justice Books (n.d.). "Council on Interracial Books for Children (CIBC)." Retrieved May 20, 2019. https://socialjusticebooks.org/council-on-interracial-books-for-children-cibc/.

Soh, C. S. (2009). *The Comfort Women: Sexual Violence and Postcolonial Memory in Korea and Japan*. Chicago: University of Chicago Press.

Sokoloff, N. (2008). "Gila Almagor's Ayiyah: Remembering the Holocaust." In *Under Fire: Childhood in the Shadow of War*, edited by E. Goodenough and A. Immel, 161–84. Detroit, MI: Wayne State University Press.

Spangler, T. (2016). "'Curious George' All Seasons Coming to Hulu in Exclusive Streaming Deal." *Variety*, March 17, 2016. http://variety.com/2016/digital/news/curious-george-hulu -exclusive-streaming-1201733036/.

Spitzer, L. (1999). "Back through the Future: Nostalgic Memory and Critical Memory in a Refuge from Nazism." In *Acts of Memory: Cultural Recall in the Present*, edited by M. Bal, J. Crewe, and L. Spitzer, 75–86. Hanover, NH: Dartmouth College Press.

Spivak, G. C. (1988). "Can the Subaltern Speak?" In *Marxism and the Interpretation of Culture*, ed. C. Nelson, 271–313. Champaign: University of Illinois Press.

Spivak, G. C. (1999). *A Critique of Postcolonial Reason: Toward a History of the Vanishing Present*. Cambridge, MA: Harvard University Press.

Stabile, C. A., and D. Kumar (2005). "Unveiling Imperialism: Media, Gender and the War on Afghanistan." *Media, Culture & Society* 27 (5): 765–82. https://doi.org/10.1177/0163443705 055734.

Stam, R., and E. Shohat (2012). "Whence and Whither Postcolonial Theory?" *New Literary History: A Journal of Theory and Interpretation* 43 (2): 371–90. https://muse.jhu.edu/ article/483026.

Steinberg, B. (2014). "Curious George: Endangered Species?" *Variety*, March 25, 2014. http:// variety.com/2014/tv/news/curious-george-endangered-species-1201146284/.

Stier, O. B. (2009). *Committed to Memory: Cultural Mediations of the Holocaust*. Amherst: University of Massachusetts Press.

Stowe, H. Beecher (1852). *Uncle Tom's Cabin: or, Life among the Lowly*. Boston: John P. Jewett.

Straight Dope (2011). "Is Curious George a Monkey or a Chimpanzee?" *The Straight Dope Message Board*, April 24, 2011. boards.straightdope.com/sdmb/showthread.php?t=605959.

Stuff (2016). "Kiwi Director Andrew Adamson Is Making a Curious George Movie." Stuff, August 10, 2016. Retrieved December 16, 2016. http://www.stuff.co.nz/entertainment/ film/83014651/kiwi-director-andrew-adamson-is-making-a-curious-george-movie.

Sturken, M., and L. Cartwright (2009). *Practices of Looking: An Introduction to Visual Culture*. 2nd ed. Oxford: Oxford University Press.

Swann Auction Galleries (2018). "2018: Year in Review." *Swann Galleries News*, December. https://www.swanngalleries.com/news/2018/12/2018-year-in-review/.

Tarán, L., and D. Gutas (2012). *Aristotle Poetics: Editio Maior of the Greek Text with Historical Introductions and Philological Commentaries*. Leiden: Brill.

Taylor, D., dir. (1971). *Escape from the Planet of the Apes*. Los Angeles: 20th Century Fox.

Taylor, S. (2011). "The Great Escape." *Humanities: The Magazine of the National Endowment for the Humanities* 31 (2). https://www.neh.gov/humanities/2011/marchapril/statement/ the-great-escape.

TeacherVision (2008). "Curious George Takes a Job: Jungle Mural Printable." *TeacherVision*, February 14, 2008. Retrieved November 17, 2015. www.teachervision.com/painting/ printable/56763.html.

TeddyTurkey. (2012). "2011 McDonald's Thanksgiving Parade—Curious George Balloon" [video]. YouTube. www.youtube.com/watch?v=-ulbkjs69OI.

Terhune, M. (2015). "A Good Little Monkey: Curious George's Undercurrent of White Dominance and the Series' Continued Popularity." *Journal of the CAS Writing Program* 7 (2014–2015): 106–21. https://www.bu.edu/writingprogram/journal/past-issues/issue-7/.

Thackeray, W. M. (1999). *Vanity Fair: A Novel without a Hero*. New York: Modern Library.

Theaterworks USA (2018). "Curious George: The Golden Meatball." Retrieved May 18, 2019. https://twusa.org/shows-artists/past-shows/curious-george-the-golden-meatball/.

Thompson, J. L., dir. (1972). *Battle for the Planet of the Apes*. Los Angeles: 20th Century Fox.

Thompson, J. L., dir. (1972). *Conquest of the Planet of the Apes*. Los Angeles: 20th Century Fox.

Tomaszewski, J. (2012). "'Curious George' Sparks Math, Science Achievement." *Education World*. http://www.educationworld.com/a_curr/curious-george-sparks-math-science-achievement .shtml.

Toussaint, K. (2016). "Curious George Store Starts Petition to Keep Shop in Harvard Square." *Metro*, September 19, 2016. http://www.metro.us/boston/curious-george-store-starts -petition-to-keep-shop-in-harvard-square/zsJpis---3BoZaVlIyZEY.

Twain, M. (1884). *The Adventures of Huckleberry Finn*. London: Chatto & Windus.

Tyson, E. (2014 [1699]). *Orang-Outang, Sive Homo Sylvestris: Or, the Anatomy of A Pygmie Compared With That of A Monkey, An Ape, and A Man. to Which Is Added, A Philological Essay Concerning the Pygmies, the Cynocephali, the Satyrs, and Sphinges of the Ancients. Wherein It Will Appear That They Are All Either Apes Or Monkeys, and Not Men, As Formerly Pretended*. Reprint edition. Provo, UT: Repressed Publishing.

United States Holocaust Memorial Museum (n.d.). "Children's Books." Retrieved July 6, 2014. https://www.ushmm.org/collections/bibliography/childrens-books.

United States Holocaust Memorial Museum (n.d.). "Office of Survivor Affairs." Retrieved January 16, 2017. www.ushmm.org/remember/office-of-survivor-affairs.

United States Holocaust Memorial Museum (n.d.). "Voyage of the St. Louis." *Holocaust Encyclopedia*. https://www.ushmm.org/wlc/en/article.php?ModuleId=10005267.

University of Minnesota Libraries (n.d.). "What is Preseparated Art?" Online Exhibits, University of Minnesota Libraries. Retrieved September 20, 2019.http://gallery.lib.umn .edu/exhibits/show/pre-separated-art/presep.

U.S. Department of Education (n.d.). "Science, Technology, Engineering and Math: Education for Global Leadership." Retrieved March 11, 2021. https://www.ed.gov/sites/ default/files/stem-overview.pdf.

Vancouver Holocaust Education Centre (2011). *Teacher's Guide: The Wartime Escape Margret and H.A. Rey's Journey from France*. Retrieved May 14, 2019. https://www.vhec.org/ images/pdfs/CG%20Teachers%20Guide%20FINAL.pdf.

Van Dyke, W. S., dir. (1932). *Tarzan the Ape Man*. Beverly Hills, CA: MGM Studios.

Vats, A. (2016). "(Dis)owning Bikram: Decolonizing vernacular and dewesternizing restructuring in the yoga wars." *Communication and Critical/Cultural Studies* 13 (4): 325–45. https://doi.org/10.1080/14791420.2016.1151536.

Virgien, N., dir. (2009). *Curious George 2: Follow That Monkey!* Universal City, CA: Universal Studios Home Entertainment.

Visit Philadelphia (2019, November 28). "Philadelphia Thanksgiving Day Parade." *visitphilly .com*, November 28, 2019. Retrieved April 9, 2021. http://www.visitphilly.com/events/ philadelphia/philadelphia-thanksgiving-day-parade/.

Wachowski Brothers, dirs. (1999). *The Matrix*. Burbank, CA: Warner Brothers.

Walder, D. (2011). *Postcolonial Nostalgias: Writing, Representation and Memory*. New York: Routledge.

Wander, P. C. (1976). "The Rhetoric of Science." *Western Speech Communication* 40 (4): 226–35. https://doi.org/10.1080/10570317609373907.

Wanzer-Serrano, D. (2015). *The New York Young Lords and the Struggle for Liberation*. 1st ed. Philadelphia, PA: Temple University Press.

Warren, J. (2019). "25 Things You Don't Know about the Amazing (Real) Adventures of Curious George." *CBC Books*, September 25, 2019. http://www.cbc.ca/books/2016/09/25 -curious-george-facts.html.

We Need Diverse Books (n.d.). "Imagine a World in which All Children can See Themselves in the Pages of a Book." Retrieved August 11, 2020. https://diversebooks.org/.

Weaver-Hightower, R. (2014). "Introduction: New Perspectives on Postcolonial Film." In *Postcolonial Film: History, Empire,* Resistance, edited by R. Weaver-Hightower and P. Hulme, 1–22. New York: Routledge.

Wecker, M. (2010). "Monkey Business: Is Curious George Jewish?!" *Chron* (blog), July 28, 2010. blog.chron.com/iconia/2010/07/monkey-business-is-curious-george-jewish/.

Weinstein, P., dir. (2015). *Curious George 3: Back to the Jungle.* Universal City, CA: Universal Pictures.

Weisman, S., dir. (1997). *George of the Jungle.* Burbank, CA: Buena Vista Pictures.

Wonderopolis (n.d.). "What's the Difference between Apes and Monkeys?" *Wonderopolis* website. Retrieved May 12, 2019. https://www.wonderopolis.org/wonder/ whats-the-difference-between-apes-and-monkeys.

White House Office of Science and Technology Policy (2014). "The 2015 Budget: Science, Technology, and Innovation for Opportunity and Growth." WhiteHouse.gov. Retrieved May 14, 2014. https://obamawhitehouse.archives.gov/sites/default/files/microsites/ostp/ Fy%202015%20R&D.pdf.

Wiesel, E. (2005). "Bearing Witness, 60 Years On." Speech delivered to the General Assembly of the United Nations, January 24, 2005. Transcript retrieved from Beliefnet. http://www .beliefnet.com/faiths/judaism/2005/02/bearing-witness-60-years-on.aspx.

Wiesel, E., and F. Mauriac (1956). *Night.* Translated by S. Rodway. New York: Bantam Books.

Wilder, L. I. (1932). *Little House in the Big Woods.* New York: Harper & Brothers.

Wilder, L. I. (1935). *Little House on the Prairie.* New York: Harper & Brothers.

Wilder, L. I. (1940). *The Long Winter.* New York: Harper & Brothers.

Williams, L. (2010). "Irrational Dreams of Space Colonization." *Peace Review* 22 (1): 4–8. https://doi.org/10.1080/10402650903539828

Williams, M. T., and H. B. Carver (1995). "African-Americans in Children's Literature— From Stereotype to Positive Representation." In *The All White World of Children's Books and African American Children's Literature,* edited by O. Oso, 13–31. Trenton, NJ: Africa World Press.

Williams, S. (2021). "News Corp to Buy Houghton Mifflin Consumer Books for $349M." *Talesbuzz,* April 5. https://talesbuzz.com/news-corp-to-buy-houghton-mifflin-consumer -books-for-349m/

Wojik-Andrews, I. (2002). *Children's Films: History, Ideology, Pedagogy, Theory.* New York: Garland Publishing.

Wyatt, R., dir. (2011). *Rise of the Planet of the Apes.* Los Angeles: 20th Century Fox.

Yamazaki, E. R. (2016). "Curious George Documentary." Kickstarter campaign. https://www .kickstarter.com/projects/1344946756/curious-george-documentary.

Yamazaki, E. R., dir. (2017). *Monkey Business: The Adventures of Curious George's Creators.* New York: Panoptica.

Yang, K. W., and E. Tuck (2012). "Decolonization Is Not a Metaphor." *Decolonization: Indigeneity, Education & Society* 1 (1). https://jps.library.utoronto.ca/index.php/des/ issue/view/1234.

Yano, C. R. (2013). *Pink Globalization: Hello Kitty's Trek across the Pacific.* Durham, NC: Duke University Press.

Young, J. A., and J. A. Braziel (2007). *Erasing Public Memory: Race, Aesthetics, and Cultural Amnesia in the Americas.* Macon, GA: Mercer University Press.

Young, J. E. (1994). *The Texture of Memory: Holocaust Memorials and Meaning.* New Haven, CT: Yale University Press.

Young, R. (2003). *Postcolonialism.* Oxford: Oxford University Press.

Young, R. (2012). "Postcolonial Remains." *New Literary History: A Journal of Theory and Interpretation* 43 (1): 19–42. https://muse.jhu.edu/article/477476.

Zabus, C., ed. (2015). *The Future of Postcolonial Studies.* 1st ed. New York: Routledge.

Zelizer, B. (1998). *Remembering to Forget: Holocaust Memory through the Camera's Eye.* Chicago: University of Chicago Press.

Zelizer, B., ed. (2001). *Visual Culture and the Holocaust.* New Brunswick, NJ: Rutgers University Press.

Zemeckis, R., dir. (1994). *Forrest Gump.* Los Angeles, CA: Paramount Pictures.

Zielinski, S. (n.d.). "*Most Valuable First Edition Children's Books.*" *Children's Picture Book Collecting.* Retrieved July 5, 2014. http://1stedition.net/mostvaluable.html.

Zornado, J. L. (2001). *Inventing the Child: Culture, Ideology, and the Story of Childhood.* New York: Garland.

Index

About the Author

Rae Lynn Schwartz-DuPre (PhD, University of Iowa) is professor of Communication Studies and Women, Gender & Sexuality Studies at Western Washington University in Bellingham, WA. Her research and teaching centers on postcolonialism, rhetoric, identity, and popular culture in primary US contexts and critically considers the circulation of cultural icons and the ways in which their linguistic and visual representations constitute knowledge. She is the editor and a contributor to *Communicating Colonialism: Readings on Postcolonial Theory(s) and Communication* (Peter Lang, 2014), and her scholarship has appeared in such journals as *Feminist Media Studies, Critical Studies in Media Communication, Textual Practice, Communication, Culture & Critique,* and *The Journal of Contemporary Argumentation and Debate.* Her commitment to children's icons is inspired by her two beloved daughters.